LEARN LIBRARY SKILLS SERIES

Learn CATALOGING THE RDA WAY

INTERNATIONAL EDITION

Lynn Farkas
Helen Rowe

TotalRecall Publications, Inc..
1103 Middlecreek
Friendswood, Texas 77546
281-992-3131   281-482-5390 Fax
www.totalrecallpress.com

All rights reserved. Except as permitted under the United States Copyright Act of 1976, No part of this publication may be reproduced, stored in a retrieval system, or transmitted in any form or by any means electronic or mechanical or by photocopying, recording, or otherwise without prior permission of the publisher. Exclusive worldwide content publication / distribution by TotalRecall Publications, Inc.

Copyright © 2015 Lynn Farkas and Helen Rowe

ISBN: 978-1-59095-436-2
UPC: 6-43977-44360-1

Printed in the United States of America with simultaneous printing in Australia, Canada, and United Kingdom.

INTERNATIONAL EDITION
1 2 3 4 5 6 7 8 9 10

Library of Congress Control Number: 2015936639

Judgments as to the suitability of the information herein is the purchaser's responsibility. TotalRecall Publications, Inc. extends no warranties, makes no representations, and assumes no responsibility as to the accuracy or suitability of such information for application to the purchaser's intended purposes or for consequences of its use except as described herein.

The scanning, uploading and distribution of this book via the Internet or via any other means without the permission of the publisher is illegal and punishable by law. Please purchase only authorized electronic editions and do not participate in or encourage electronic piracy of copyrighted materials. Your support of the author's rights is appreciated.

Logos and images from the RDA Toolkit (www.rdatoolkit.org) used by permission of the Co-Publishers for RDA (American Library Association, Canadian Library Association, and CILIP: Chartered Institute of Library and Information Professionals).

TABLE OF CONTENTS

Preface		v
1.	What is Cataloging?	1
2.	Descriptive Cataloging	7
3.	RDA (Resource Description and Access) Basics	15
4.	FRBR (Functional Requirements for Bibliographic Records)	19
5.	ISBD (International Standard Bibliographic Description)	29
6.	MARC (Machine Readable Cataloging)	37
7.	Introduction to the RDA Toolkit	53
8.	Using the RDA Instruction Set	63
9.	Attributes of Manifestations and Items	71
10.	Further Attributes of Manifestations and Items	87
11.	Attributes of Works and Expressions	99
12.	Access Points	107
13.	Attributes of Persons, Families and Corporate Bodies	113
14.	Attributes of Concepts, Objects, Events and Places	137
15.	Recording Relationships	141
16.	Entities Related to Resources	147
17.	Entities Related to Each Other	151
18.	Putting it All Together	159
19.	Copy Cataloging	167
20.	More Practice	185
Answers		211
Glossary		269
Bibliography		279
Index		281

ACKNOWLEDGEMENTS

This book is an extension of the manual we developed for the intensive training course, *'Cataloging the RDA Way'*, that we have presented to library staff in cities and rural centers around Australia since 2013. Our thanks to the hundreds of students who attended *'Cataloging the RDA Way'* courses. Your questions and feedback were invaluable in developing this workbook. Our thanks also to our patient husbands and families, who accepted our absences as we traversed the country delivering courses, and supported us as we labored over preparing this publication.

PREFACE

Learn Cataloging the RDA Way covers the skills needed to catalog in a library or other information agency, at a professional or a paraprofessional level. Since the bibliographic record is the foundation of all the tools used in a library, from catalog to bibliography to online database, it is important for all library staff to be familiar with at least basic principles.

This book can be used by those who are new to cataloging, by copy catalogers, and also by experienced catalogers who are transitioning to the new RDA cataloging standard.

- New catalogers will find it useful to work through the entire book, including the early chapters that explain the basics of descriptive cataloging.
- Those involved primarily in copy cataloging will still need to understand RDA cataloging (Chapters Seven onwards). In addition, Chapter Nineteen is devoted to copy cataloging and cloning issues, with an extensive checklist that highlights the main areas to be checked when accepting a record for copy cataloging, and indicates changes to be made.
- Experienced catalogers wishing to upgrade their skills to create RDA–compliant records should read Chapters Three and Four as background, and begin their study with Chapters Seven and Eight onwards. This part of the book introduces the RDA Toolkit and takes readers through all aspects of the RDA Instruction Set, culminating in the creation of full RDA catalog records in Chapters Eighteen and Twenty.

Learn Cataloging the RDA Way is a combination text and workbook, designed for use on its own or in a formal course of study. It is suitable for use in a classroom, and by those who are studying cataloging by themselves, either with a specific goal or as part of their continuing professional development. Throughout the book there are exercises to practice and test skills, and quizzes to test understanding. There are answers for self-checking at the back of the book. Users may not always agree completely with the answers given, and it will be useful to check them with a teacher or experienced cataloger. This is especially important in RDA cataloging, since the flexibility of the scheme means there is often room for more than one approach or application of the guidelines.

Note on Spelling and Capitalization

This workbook is used in North America, Europe and Australasia, across countries that employ different spelling conventions for English words. For consistency, American spelling has been adopted for the text. However, English spelling has been kept in some examples and exercises, where it would normally be used.

Titles included in the text are capitalized according to standard library cataloging practice—that is, apart from names, only the first word of the title has a capital letter. This is intended to accustom library students and staff to this style.

CHAPTER ONE
What is Cataloging?

Introduction
The word catalog is used in many ways, sometimes with different meanings. Libraries define catalogs as:
> A list of library materials contained in a collection, a library, or a group of libraries, arranged according to some definite plan.

Objectives of the Catalog
Charles A. Cutter defined the objectives of the library catalog in his *Rules for a printed dictionary catalogue (1876)*:

1. To enable a person to find a book of which either
   - (a) the author
   - (b) the title } is known;
   - (c) the subject

2. To show what the library has
   - (a) by a given author
   - (b) on a given subject
   - (c) in a given kind of literature

3. To assist in the choice of a book
   - (a) as to its edition (bibliographically)
   - (b) as to its character (literary or topical).

More recently, the International Federation of Library Associations and Institutions (IFLA) identified four 'user tasks' as functions of the catalog in their *Functional requirements for bibliographic records (1998)*. These 'user tasks' are key functions users expect a catalog to help them with:

1. **Find**—locate a resource in a database or catalog as the result of a user's search on one or more of its characteristics, e.g., title

2. **Identify**—use the descriptive data to confirm that the resource found is what was sought, or to distinguish between resources with similar characteristics (e.g., two works with the same title)

3. **Select**—choose the resource that meets the user's needs regarding format and content (e.g., a DVD rather than a videocassette, or a text in a specific language)

4. **Obtain**—acquire or access the resource through loan, purchase, electronic connection etc.

ACTIVITY 1.1
Has the purpose of the catalog changed very much? Which objectives or functions are the most important? Discuss this in a group, or think about these questions yourself.

Cataloging

Cataloging is the preparation of bibliographic information for catalog records. Catalogers use a set of cataloging 'tools' to create catalog records. These tools are agreed international rules and standards.

Cataloging consists of:
- descriptive cataloging
- subject cataloging
- classification.

Descriptive cataloging describes a resource, identifies access points and indicates relationships using the cataloging tool *Resource description and access (RDA)*.

Subject cataloging determines subject headings for a resource, using *Library of Congress subject headings (LCSH)* or a similar authoritative subject headings list.

Classification determines a classification number for a resource, using *Library of Congress classification (LCC)*, *Dewey decimal classification (DDC)* or a similar authoritative classification scheme. The classification number also provides a shelving location for a resource in a physical collection.

A Catalog Record

 *Here is a catalog record, also called a **bibliographic record**, from an online catalog. Note how the catalog record incorporates the three aspects of cataloging described above.*

CALL NUMBER	Reference collection REF 572.80285 KAL	} classification
TITLE	Principles of biomedical informatics	
EDITION	Second edition	
PUBLISHER	Amsterdam : Elsevier, [2013]	} descriptive cataloging
DESCRIPT'N	xxxvii, 668 pages : illustrations ; 25 cm. text, unmediated, volume	
CREATOR(S)	Kalet, Ira, author	
SUBJECT	1. Medical informatics 2. Computational biology 3. Bioinformatics 4. Molecular biology	} subject cataloging

Purpose of Cataloging Standards

1. To provide consistency within a single library
   That is, a description and headings created by one cataloger need to be consistent with a description and headings created at a different time or by another cataloger.

2. To provide consistency between libraries
   In order to share catalog records and thus reduce costs in a centralized or cooperative library system, libraries use an agreed set of cataloging standards.

3. To reduce time involved in cataloging
   If cataloging standards did not exist, catalogers would have to start from scratch with every resource they cataloged.

4. To provide ease of access for patrons who use more than one library
   Cutter states: 'The convenience of the public is always to be set before that of the cataloger'.

5. To ensure that the purposes of the catalog are achieved
   That is, the catalog must enable users to find what they need efficiently and reliably.

The Catalog is for Users
The purpose of creating and maintaining a catalog is that library users can find, identify, select and obtain what they need. Each library must therefore consider its particular users when it constructs its bibliographic records.

4 LEARN CATALOGING THE RDA WAY

 EXERCISE 1.2

Here are two very different types of library. Consider the differences between their users, and indicate the implications for creating suitable bibliographic records.

	Southside Elementary School Library	Institute of Criminology Library
Describe a typical user		
What information do they need in the description of the item?		
What kinds of access points do they need— i.e., what do they want to be able to look up in the catalog?		
List other types of libraries with the same or similar kinds of users		

Cataloging Networks

Catalogers use agreed standards in order to share their records with other libraries, thus minimizing the time and costs involved in creating catalog records. Libraries share their records by submitting them to centralized databases, where they can be viewed and downloaded into the catalogs of member libraries that hold the same resource. These cooperative data-sharing arrangements are known as cataloging networks.

The world's largest cataloging network, OCLC (Online Computer Library Center Inc.), has over 325 million items cataloged, and libraries all over the world share its records. But libraries can also be members of smaller cataloging networks within their sector (e.g., university library networks), their region (e.g., state-based networks), their country (e.g., the national Libraries Australia network) or their specialization (e.g., health library networks).

If your library belongs to a cataloging network, the network may have additional cataloging standards and guidelines that members are expected to follow.

 **ACTIVITY 1.3**
Does your library belong to a cataloging network? If so, what is it called and what libraries are included? If not, find out the names of some cataloging networks in your region or country. Which libraries or types of libraries are members of the network?

CHAPTER TWO
Descriptive Cataloging

Introduction
This workbook focuses on identifying and recording the physical or electronic details of a resource. This is known as describing bibliographic information, or descriptive cataloging. Subject cataloging and classification are not covered here; however, students can gain a good understanding of these aspects from the publications *Learn Library of Congress Subject Access* and *Learn Dewey Decimal Classification* in the 'Learn Library Skills' series.

Describing Bibliographic Information
To describe a resource bibliographically, catalogers gather information from the resource itself and sometimes from accompanying material or reference works. The data found is recorded in a standardized format to create the bibliographic record.

Data collected from a book or journal, for example, could include:
- title and one or more authors or editors
- publisher, place and date of publication (or that information might be found in a publisher's catalog or on a bookstore website)
- size (either physical e.g., centimeters; or electronic e.g., bytes) and number of pages
- whether it contains illustrations, a summary, references or a bibliography
- whether it is a second or third etc. edition, or a revised edition
- whether it is part of a series, and its number in that series.

Other types of material have different data to record, for example playing times of films or DVDs. The cataloging guidelines in *Resource description and access (RDA)* indicate all the possible data, called cataloging elements, to record.

Catalogers then identify those aspects of the resource that would be useful as search terms for finding it. These **access points** are recorded in the descriptive catalog record. They can include:
- titles
- variations of the title, by which the resource may be known
- authors or creators
- additional people or organizations associated with the resource (e.g., editors, illustrators, etc.)
- series titles

Other information is added to the catalog record: a **classification number** that brings similar material together on the shelves, and **subject headings** that indicate the topic or topics of the resource. These components are part of the subject cataloging process.

The Process of Descriptive Cataloging

In general, catalogers follow this process when they catalog a resource:

1. *Examine the resource in hand.* If it is a print item, start with the title page. If it is an electronic item, look for the equivalent area, for example a movie title screen or screen credits, or the label or container of a music DVD. RDA will guide you on other places you should check to find out about the resource. These are called **preferred sources of information**.

2. *Identify key elements of the resource, using the appropriate chapter of RDA.* For example, RDA Chapter 2 indicates the elements at the Manifestation and Item levels, and provides instructions on how to record them for cataloging purposes. RDA Chapter 6 does the same for the Work and Expression levels.

3. *Record the information into your library's preferred cataloging format.* RDA tells you what information to gather from a resource, but it does not specify what order to display it in, or what format to use for coding the data. RDA is a *content standard* not an *encoding standard*, and the content it talks about can be encoded in many different ways.

The MARC format is one of the ways in which data is most commonly encoded in libraries. Most libraries use cataloging software or cataloging databases for presentation purposes. Catalogers enter the information they have gathered using RDA's guidelines into their software or database, using the formats provided. This data can be displayed in various ways for the library catalog user.

MARC is covered in detail in Chapter Six of this workbook.

REVISION QUIZ 2.1

Use the following questions to revise your understanding of library cataloging. You do not need to write down the answers.

1. Define: descriptive cataloging, subject cataloging, classification.

2. What are the advantages of adopting cataloging standards?

3. Name three cataloging standards.

4. What type of data would be useful to include in a catalog record for a book? What different data would be useful for a television series on DVD?

5. Name two access points that can be recorded in a descriptive catalog record.

6. What three steps do catalogers follow when creating a catalog record?

CHAPTER TWO   Descriptive Cataloging   9

The Catalog Record

Library catalogs consist of bibliographic records for the resources that make up a collection. These are the records you consult when using the public catalog. Catalogers also create another type of catalog record, called an **authority record**, containing details about the access points needed in the bibliographic records. Authority records are often maintained as separate files and not shown in the public catalog. They are dealt with later in this chapter.

Bibliographic Records

The bibliographic record includes a description of the resource, containing standardized information such as author(s) and title, publication and distribution details and the physical characteristics of the resource. The description contains information taken from various parts of the resource itself.

   Here is a bibliographic record, with the description highlighted:

TITLE	The cutting garden : growing & arranging garden flowers / Sarah Raven ; photographs by Pia Tryde ; [foreword by Penelope Hobhouse].
AUTHOR	Raven, Sarah, (author)
OTHER AUTHORS	Tryde, Pia, (illustrator)
EDITION	1st paperback edition
PUBLISHED	London : Frances Lincoln, 2013.
PHYSICAL DESCRIPTION	168 pages : colored illustration ; 26 cm.
SUBJECTS	Flower gardening.
	Flower arrangement.
	Cut flowers.
NOTES	Originally published: 1996.
	Includes index.
LANGUAGE	English
ISBN	9780711234659 (pbk.)
	0711234655 (pbk.)
DEWEY NUMBER	635.9

Access Points

The bibliographic record also includes access points that tell us the name of the author, title or other information by which the resource can be identified. Each record in the catalog has a number of access points. We use the access points to find a record when searching the catalog—whether we are looking for the author, title, series, organization or subject.

Subject access points are created during subject cataloging, rather than descriptive cataloging, but they form part of the bibliographic record. A bibliographic record also contains a classification number, so the user can locate the item on the library's shelves. Subject headings and classification numbers are not dealt with in this workbook, but they are important access points in a catalog record.

 EXERCISE 2.2

Here are three catalog records. Highlight all the access points.

a.

CALL NUMBER	JQ 24 C48 2015
TITLE	Comparing Asian politics : India, China, and Japan / Sue Ellen M. Charlton.
EDITION	Fourth edition
PUBLISHER	Boulder, Colo. : Westview Press, 2014.
PHYSICAL DESCRIPT'N	xv, 380 pages ; 23 cm.
CREATOR	Charlton, Sue Ellen M.
SUBJECTS	1. Asia – Politics and government – Case studies.
	2. India – Politics and government.
	3. China – Politics and government.
	4. Japan – Politics and government.

b.

CALL NUMBER	709.04
TITLE	History of modern art : painting, sculpture, architecture, photography / H.H. Arnason, Elizabeth C. Mansfield, National Humanities Center.
EDITION	Seventh Edition
PUBLISHER	Boston : Pearson, [2013]
ISBN/ISSN	9780205259472 (paperback)
PHYSICAL DESCRIPT'N	xvi, 816 pages : illustrations ; 30 cm.
CREATOR(S)	Arnason, H. Harvard, author.
	Mansfield, Elizabeth, 1965– , author.
SUBJECTS	Art, Modern – 20th century.
	Art, Modern.
NOTES	Includes bibliographical references (pages 763–789) and index.

c.

CALL NUMBER	ND 497.Y46 M66 2013
TITLE	The many faces of Jonathan Yeo / texts by Martin Gayford, Giles Coren, Tim Marlow and Sarah Howgate.
PUBLISHER	London : Art Books Publishing Ltd, [2013?]
COPYRIGHT DATE	©2013
ISBN/ISSN	9781908970091
PHYSICAL DESCRIPT'N	240 pages : illustrations (some colour) ; 27 cm.
CREATOR(S)	Yeo, Jonathan, 1970– , artist
	Gayford, Martin, 1952– , author
	Coren, Giles, author
	Marlow, Tim, 1963– , author
	Howgate, Sarah, author
	National Portrait Gallery (Great Britain), sponsoring body
SUBJECTS	Yeo, Jonathan – Exhibitions.
	Yeo, Jonathan, 1970–
	Portrait painters – Great Britain.
	Celebrities – Portraits.
	Portrait painters – England – Exhibitions.
	Painters – Great Britain – Exhibitions.
	Portrait painting – Great Britain – Exhibitions.
NOTES	Published to coincide with the exhibition "Jonathan Yeo portraits" at the National Portrait Gallery, London, 11 September 2013 – 4 January 2014.
	Includes bibliographical references and index.

Access points are covered in more detail in Chapter Twelve of this workbook.

Authority Records

In addition to the bibliographic record created for the library catalog, catalogers also create authority records. These are records that give details of the preferred name for a person or corporate body, or for a title of a resource when there might be a number of variations in use. These records are not visible to the library catalog users, as a rule. They are tools for the cataloger, to link different records (such as 'all those by a particular author'). They are usually maintained in a separate database or card catalog called an authority file.

Authority records in authority files are consulted by other catalogers in the organization to ensure that the same form of a person's name or a resource's title is used throughout the library's catalog. Authority records are often uploaded to national databases or cataloging networks so that other catalogers can use them to maintain consistency across catalogs.

Authority records indicate:

- the preferred title or name to be used as an access point in a descriptive catalog record, called an **authorized access point**
- the non-preferred variations of a title or name, called **variant access points**
- some information about the title or person that helps identify them uniquely, for example a person's gender, occupation, dates of birth and death, etc.
- details about how the cataloger came to the decision to use a particular form of title or name.

 For example, think about Australia's former Prime Minister Bob Hawke. His given name is Robert James Lee Hawke, but he is generally known as Bob Hawke. Catalogers must decide what form of name to use in the catalog for any resources he has authored, so that all his publications can be viewed together. Once that decision is made (and in this case it was decided to use Bob Hawke as his preferred name), it is recorded in an authority record.

Here is the authority record that the Library of Congress created for Bob Hawke:

LC control no.: n 81019695
Personal name heading: Hawke, Bob, 1929—
Variant(s): Hawke, Robert J.L. (Robert James Lee), 1929—
Hawke, R.J.
Hawke, R.J. (Robert James), 1929—
Found in: His The Role of arbitration in preserving industrial ... 1970.
Pullan, R. Bob Hawke, 1980: t.p. (Bob Hawke)
Anson, S. Hawke, 1992: p. 4 of cover (Australia's longest serving Labor Prime Minister)
National Library of Australia online catalog, Nov. 18, 2008 (hdg.: Hawke, Bob, 1929—)
Wikipedia WWW site, Nov. 18, 2008 (under Bob Hawke: Robert James Lee (Bob) Hawke, AC; b. Dec. 9, 1929, Bordertown, S. Aust.; Prime Minister of Australia, Mar. 11, 1983–Dec. 20, 1991)
LC database, Nov. 18, 2008 (hdg.: Hawke, Robert J. L. (Robert James Lee), 1929— ; usage: Bob Hawke [predominant form], R.J.L. Hawke, R.J. Hawke, Robert J.L. Hawke, Hawke; usage in works about him: Hawke [predominant form], Bob Hawke, Robert J. Hawke)

This record shows:

- the preferred name (authorized access point), including Hawke's date of birth (Hawke, Bob, 1929);
- all the variant access points that will refer users of the library catalog to Hawke's preferred name; and
- details of where the cataloger found the information that led to the decision to choose 'Bob Hawke' as the preferred form of his name.

Authority records can be created for people, organizations, series and subject headings. They cover different types of information than you see in a bibliographic catalog record. Note that this authority record doesn't give you any details about specific publications or resources Bob Hawke created. It just focuses on the 'authority', or correct form, for his name.

Authority records are covered in detail in Chapter Thirteen of this workbook.

 EXERCISE 2.3
Here are the preferred names for a number of people, organizations and topics. Write down as many non-preferred versions as you can think of for each. These preferred and non-preferred terms become the building blocks for authority records.

1. Joseph Smith, middle name Edward

2. International Business Machines

3. Books

4. Charles Wentworth Jones

5. Alicia Mary Peyton

6. Sadness

7. Organisation for Economic Co-Operation and Development, formerly called Organisation for European Economic Cooperation

8. Dogs

9. Samuel Clements, also known as Mark Twain

10. James Robert Ewing

11. Elton John, who changed his name from Reginald Kenneth Dwight

12. Elizabeth K. Inchley

CHAPTER THREE
RDA (Resource Description and Access) Basics

Introduction
RDA: Resource description and access is a cataloging standard designed for the digital world. Built on the foundations established by the *Anglo-American cataloguing rules* (AACR2), RDA provides a comprehensive set of cataloging guidelines and instructions covering all types of content and media.

Benefits of RDA include:
- A structure based on the conceptual models of FRBR (*Functional Requirements for Bibliographic Records*) and FRAD (*Functional Requirements for Authority Data*) to help catalog users find the information they need more easily
- A flexible framework for content description of digital resources that also serves the needs of libraries organizing traditional resources
- A better fit with emerging database technologies, enabling institutions to introduce efficiencies in data capture and storage retrievals.

Source: 'RDA Background' http://www.rdatoolkit.org/background

Background to RDA
The *Anglo-American cataloguing rules* were used in libraries for over 50 years, and were designed primarily to deal with print material (books and journals). As libraries expanded their range of resources to include more non-book material, it became obvious that significant adjustments would be needed in cataloging rules. A new version of AACR was considered, but a decision was made to step back and review the entire cataloging process.

In the 1990s, the International Federation of Library Associations and Institutions (IFLA) established a Study Group to examine what the library and information community wanted from its cataloging activities and how to achieve this—in other words, what functions should bibliographic records have? Their findings, the *Functional Requirements for Bibliographic Records* (FRBR), form the conceptual basis behind RDA. A Joint Steering Committee of major libraries and library associations then developed RDA between 2004 and 2009.

RDA represents a change in direction for cataloging. It was designed for a digital world, and for digital catalogs. Its structure uses key bibliographic elements of interest to users (e.g., title, statement of responsibility, physical details) and emphasizes their relationships. RDA deals with *what* to record, not *how* to record it. Content, not format, is its focus.

RDA as a Content Standard
RDA is described as a 'content standard'. This means it provides instructions on recording the *content* of resources, not on how the information can be displayed or encoded. MARC and ISBD are still used in most libraries for *presentation* of their content and these are dealt with later in this workbook. However, because RDA is a 'format neutral' content standard—not

tied to any particular encoding scheme—it can be used by a range of cultural collecting agencies like museums and archives, as well as libraries. This provides both flexibility and greater interoperability for the exchange of catalog records.

RDA and AACR2

RDA is relatively new. Although early drafts were first published in 2009, it wasn't until 2013 that RDA began being implemented by major library collections around the world. Many library catalog records have been created using the former standard, AACR2 (*Anglo-American Cataloguing Rules*, 2nd edition). In fact, most libraries currently have the majority of their catalog records in AACR2 format, and some libraries will still be using AACR2 to catalog new material for some time to come.

The massive number of resources cataloged using AACR2 means there is a lot of **legacy data** in catalogs. So it is important to be aware of AACR2 and be able to recognize differences between AACR2 and RDA cataloging.

 Here is a resource cataloged under the two standards: RDA and AACR2. The differences between them are highlighted in bold in the RDA record, and explained below. Note the additional information provided in the RDA record, and the efforts made to use 'plain English' terms rather than abbreviations.

RDA		AACR2	
Creator	Olney, Martha L., 1956— , **author.**	*Creator*	Olney, Martha L., 1956— .
Title	Macroeconomics as a second language / by Martha Olney.	*Title*	Macroeconomics as a second language / by Martha Olney.
Published	Hoboken, **New Jersey** : Wiley, **[2011].**	*Published*	Hoboken, N.J. : Wiley, c2011.
Copyright	**©2011.**	*Edition*	3rd ed.
Edition	**Third edition.**	*Description*	xvi, 334 p. : ill. ; 24 cm.
Description	xvi, 334 **pages : illustrations**; 24 cm.		
Content	**text**		
Media	**unmediated**		
Carrier	**volume**		

1. **Creator field**—RDA includes more information about what type of relationship the person has to the resource: she is the author (as opposed to editor, composer, etc.).
2. **Publication field**—RDA avoids abbreviations where possible, so the place 'New Jersey' is spelled in full.
3. **Copyright field**—Copyright statements are given more prominence in RDA.

4. **Edition field**—RDA transcribes information as it appears on the resource and doesn't use abbreviations for the sake of convention.
5. **Description field**—RDA avoids abbreviations for 'pages' and 'illustrations' (unlike AACR2, that has a great many abbreviations).
6. **Content, Media, Carrier fields**—these are new RDA elements that indicate what type of item the resource is (text); what type of media is needed to view it (none, it is unmediated); and how it is packaged (in a physical volume).

RDA Terminology

Below are some of the main differences in terminology between RDA and AACR2. For explanations of these terms, refer to the glossaries in this workbook or in the RDA Toolkit.

RDA	AACR2
creator	author, composer, artist, etc.
access point	added entry
authorized access point	heading / main entry / added entry
variant access point	see reference
authorized access point for related entity	see also reference
access point control	authority control
preferred sources of information	chief source of information
preferred title and the **authorized access point for the creator**	main entry
authorized access point for the creator	name main entry
preferred name	name added entry
preferred title	title added entry / title main entry
preferred title plus differentiating information to make it unique, e.g., language, date, etc.; or: a collective title such as 'Works'	uniform title
carrier description extent	physical description
content	physical characteristics (color, illustrations, scale, sound, etc.)
content type media type carrier type	general material designator *(Note: this AACR2 term is now broken into the three RDA attributes listed to the left)*

Formats for RDA

The RDA guidelines are available in two formats:
- as the RDA Instruction Set, a part of the online RDA Toolkit
- as a loose-leaf print copy, updated at intervals.

Chapter Seven of this workbook describes the structure of the Instruction Set and of the RDA Toolkit. The remaining chapters of this workbook deal with the content of the RDA Instruction Set in detail.

REVISION QUIZ 3.1
Use the following questions to revise your understanding of what RDA is. You do not need to write down the answers.

1. What does RDA stand for?

2. Why was a new cataloging scheme needed?

3. What is RDA based on?

4. What is meant when we say that RDA is a content standard?

5. Name three new terms that RDA uses, and their AACR2 equivalents.

CHAPTER FOUR
FRBR (Functional Requirements for Bibliographic Records)

Introduction
FRBR was developed by the International Federation of Library Associations and Institutions (IFLA). It is the conceptual framework that underlies the cataloging guidelines used in RDA.

FRBR focuses the catalog on its functional tasks, as it:
- confirms the traditional functions of a catalog, as originally expressed by Cutter: to find, identify, select, and obtain information
- provides a framework for what a bibliographic record gives information *about*
- outlines how bibliographic records answer users' needs
- recommends basic data requirements for the creation of bibliographic records.

FRBR is concerned with the user's tasks of retrieving and accessing resources from library catalogs and bibliographic databases. It uses an 'entity-relationship' model that identifies key elements (entities) and how they interact. FRBR is not itself a cataloging code. Instead, it provides a generalized way of looking at the bibliographic information that libraries, museums, archives and other cultural collecting agencies gather for their users.

FRBR:
- isolates the entities that are the key objects of interest to users of bibliographic records
- identifies characteristics (attributes) associated with each entity
- identifies relationships between entities that are most important to users.

How does FRBR Work?
In order to gather characteristics together more easily, FRBR is divided into three groups of entities:
- Group One consists of the products of intellectual or artistic endeavor (Work, Expression, Manifestation, Item)
- Group Two covers those entities responsible for that intellectual or artistic content (a Person, Family, or Corporate Body)
- Group Three includes the entities that serve as subjects of intellectual or artistic endeavor (Concept, Object, Event, Place, and Groups One & Two as subjects).

As well as the creation of the entities themselves, a key aspect of FRBR is that it shows the relationships that exist between and among entities. These relationships are usually recorded using access points controlled by authority records.

 Relationships give users pathways to other relevant material.

FRBR identifies three types of relationships:
- Primary relationships—indicating what the resource *is*
- Relationships *to*—Persons, Families and Corporate Bodies associated with a resource; indicating who is involved
- Relationships *between*—Works, Expressions, Manifestations and Items; indicating related resources.

Or in other words, these relationships are shown:
- to Works (i.e., 'created by ...')
- between Works (i.e., 'based on ...')
- between Expressions of the same Work (i.e., 'translation of ...')
- between whole and parts of Works, Expressions, or Manifestations (i.e., versions, revisions, adaptations, arrangements, etc.)
- beyond physical: ownership, production, creation, subjects.

Group Entities
We will now look at the entities for each of these three groups in greater detail.

Group One Entities
Group One contains four hierarchical levels that represent resources:
- the **Work**, a distinct intellectual or artistic creation
- the **Expression**, the intellectual or artistic realization of a Work
- the **Manifestation**, the physical embodiment of an Expression
- the **Item**, a single exemplar (example or instance) of a Manifestation.

This group is also known by the term WEMI (made up of the first letter of each of the terms—Work, Expression, Manifestation, Item).

Group One entities consist of the things that we catalog. The hierarchical relationships between these entities are:
- a Work is *realized through* one or more Expression
    - each of which *is embodied in* one or more Manifestation
        - each of which *is exemplified by* one or more Item.

The Work is an abstract concept representing the initial intellectual creation. It is best described as the ideas that someone has in their head.

A Work is realized through one or more Expression in some form of notation—like text, music, sound, an image, etc., or a combination of any of these. An Expression might be a performance or a translation or a version of a particular Work, and it is described by the way that it is expressed.

Both the Work and the Expression are abstract concepts that are not presented in a physical form. Once a resource takes on a physical form it becomes a Manifestation. In FRBR terms, a Manifestation is the physical embodiment of an Expression of a Work. In a Manifestation, all the physical objects bear the same characteristics or are produced together at the same time.

One example or copy of a Manifestation is called an Item. This is a single object with particular characteristics that differentiate it from the rest of the collection in that Manifestation.

This hierarchical relationship can be seen in the diagram below:

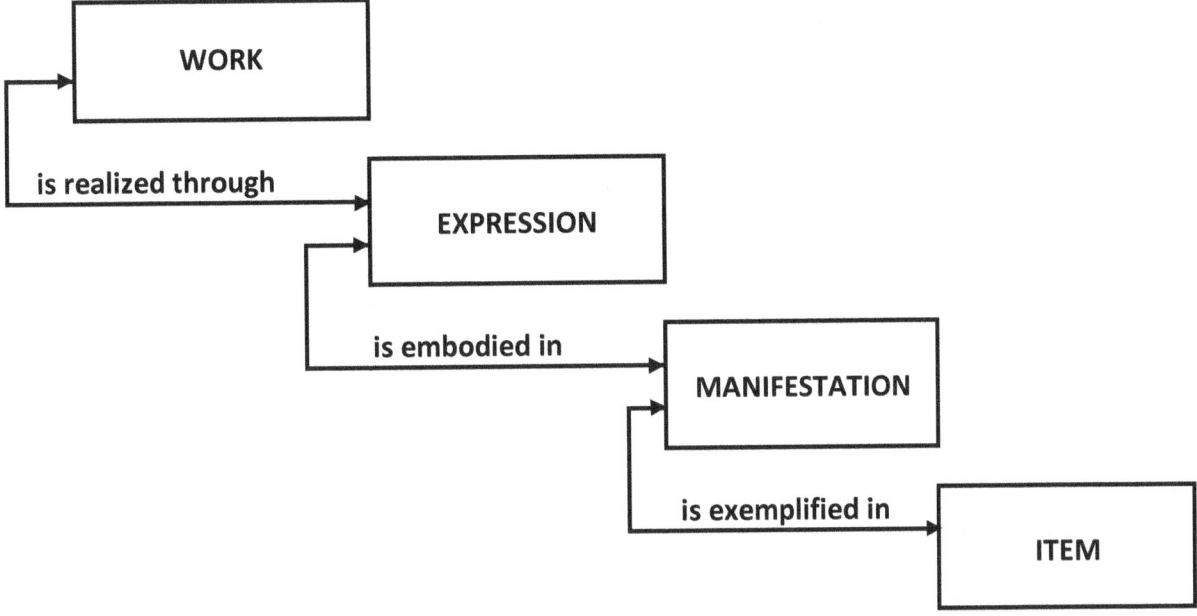

Group 1 entities and primary relationships (IFLA Study Group on the Functional Requirements for Bibliographic Records, 1998/2009, page 14, Figure 3.1)

 For example:

Work	Harry Potter and the philosopher's stone, by J.K. Rowling
Expression	Text material, English
Manifestation	(1) Harry Potter and the sorcerer's stone by J.K. Rowling. New York : Arthur A. Levine Books, 1988 (*American version, note title change*) (2) Harry Potter and the philosopher's stone by J.K. Rowling. London : Bloomsbury, 2001 (*British version, different publisher but same content*)
Item	Copy 1 held in Southside Library, with torn cover

EXERCISE 4.1

Fill in the blanks with the correct answers from the list provided. Answers can be used more than once:

Answers: Entity/ies   Work/s   Expression/s
                 Manifestation/s   Item/s

1. The FRBR term for the various elements that are the basis for bibliographic description is _____. FRBR identifies three Groups of these.

2. A _____ is the physical embodiment of a resource. In a _____, all the physical objects bear the same characteristics or are produced together at the same time.

3. Two of the Group One entities are conceptual rather than physical. These are the _____ and _____ entities.

4. The initial intellectual creation of a resource is known in FRBR as the _____.

5. A single object with particular characteristics that differentiate it from the rest of the collection is called the _____.

6. The realization of a Work is referred to as the _____. The textual play 'Romeo and Juliet' written in English is one _____ of Shakespeare's work.

EXERCISE 4.2

Draw a line from each description on the left to the appropriate Group One entity (Work, Expression, Manifestation, Item) on the right. More than one description may be associated with any Group One entity.

German translation   **Work**

ISBN

Electronic version of *Cloudstreet*   **Expression**

Resource to be read in library only

Movie of C.S. Lewis' *The lion, the witch and the wardrobe*   **Manifestation**

Library barcode

Shakespeare's *Romeo & Juliet*   **Item**

Fifth edition

Group Two Entities
Group Two contains three entities:
- Persons
- Families
- Corporate Bodies

Group Two entities 'do' something to Group One entities. Group Two entities are responsible for:
- the intellectual or artistic creation of a Work or Expression
- the physical production, manufacture, and dissemination of Manifestations
- the ownership or custodianship of Items.

Group Two entities are often part of the statement of responsibility (i.e., information after the title in a bibliographic record, showing who created the resource), or they are included as access points in the record.

This diagram represents how Group One and Group Two entities relate to each other:

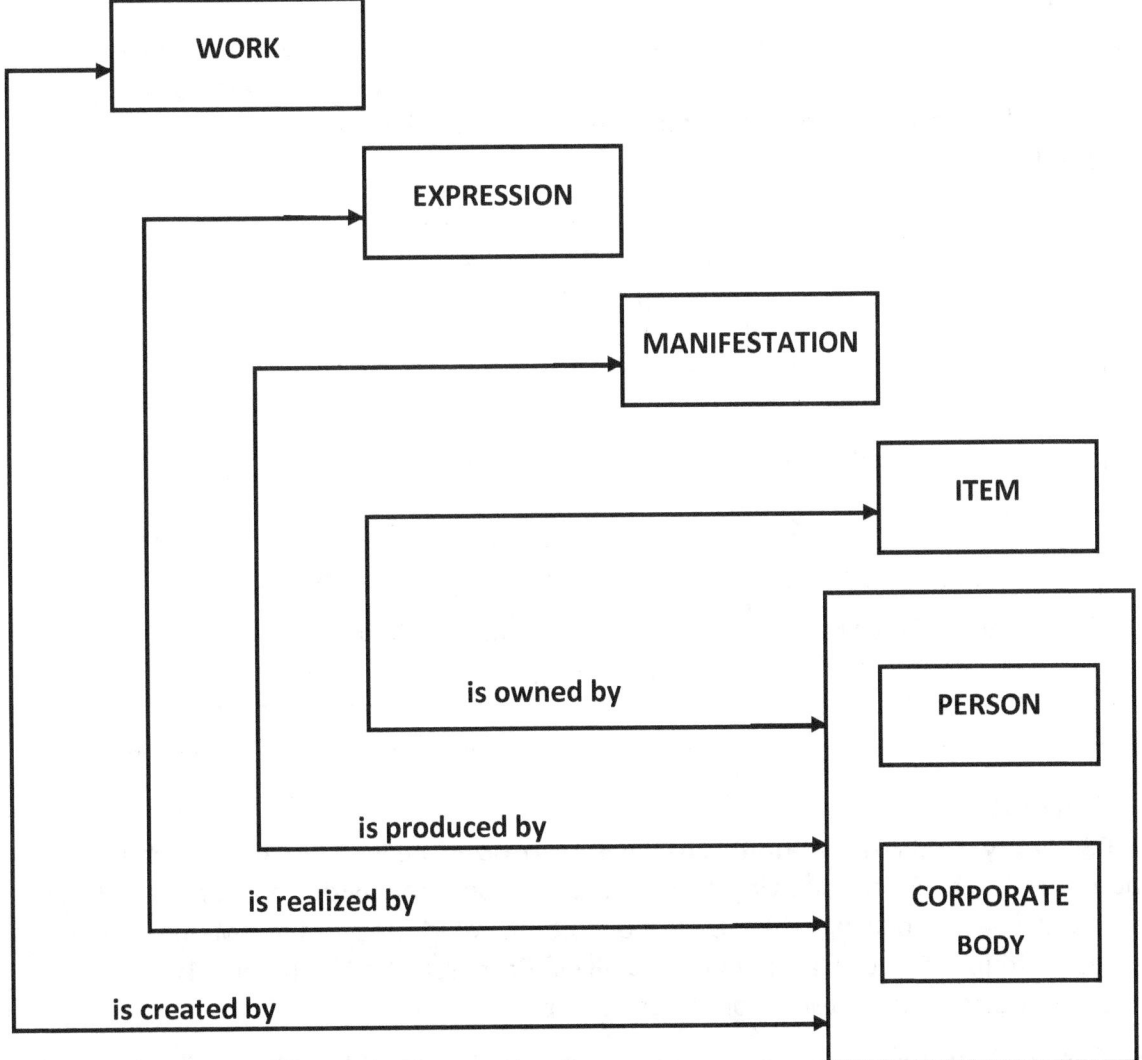

Group 2 entities and "responsibility" relationships (IFLA Study Group on the Functional Requirements for Bibliographic Records, 1998/2009, page 15, Figure 3.2)

Group Three Entities

Group Three deals with subject analysis and subject cataloging. Not only can each of the entities in Group Three be the subject of a Work, but also Group One (the works themselves) and Group Two (people and organizations) can be subjects of Works. Group Three is not yet fully developed in the RDA guidelines, but covers:

- **Concepts**—as subjects, e.g., 'ethics', 'nuclear fission'
- **Objects**—as subjects, e.g., 'snakes', 'candlesticks'
- **Events**—as subjects, e.g., 'Winter Olympics', 'Battle of Hastings'
- **Places**—as subjects, e.g., 'Paris', 'Antarctica'
- **Group One entities as subjects**—other Works as the subject of a Work (e.g., a film about the Dead Sea Scrolls). These have traditionally been cataloged as Name-Title added entries.
- **Group Two entities as subjects**—people, families or corporate bodies that are the subject of a Work (e.g., a biography). These have traditionally been cataloged as personal or corporate body subject added entries.

Entities, Attributes and Relationships

The key to effectively using the RDA Instruction Set is to understand and use all three aspects of the FRBR entity-relationship model (i.e., entities, attributes and relationships). This integrates bibliographic, access point and authority data. This workbook will cover each of these aspects in turn.

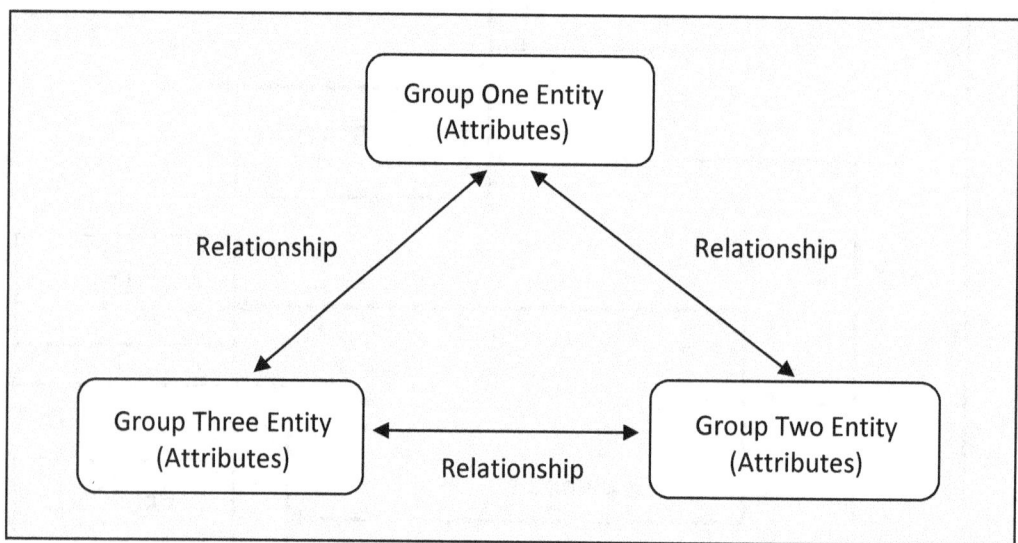

FRBR Attributes

Each FRBR entity has its own **attributes** (or characteristics). The RDA Instruction Set gives the attributes for each entity. Knowing the attributes associated with each entity will help determine if you are dealing with descriptions at the Work, Expression, Manifestation or Item level (Group One), or with Persons, Families, Corporate Bodies (Group Two), or with Subjects, Concepts, Objects, Events or Places (Group Three).

 The RDA Instruction Set is laid out according to the FRBR entities. Knowing the attribute associated with each entity will help you find relevant instructions in RDA.

The most commonly used attributes for each entity in Group One and Group Two are noted in the tables below, and the full list of all the attributes is in the RDA Instruction Set. Some of the attributes are designated as 'core' elements in RDA. This means they must be recorded in a bibliographic record if they can be ascertained from the resource.

Group One Attributes

Here is a table of attributes for Group One entities. Note how each attribute is unique for its entity. For example, even though it looks like there are two 'title' attributes, the *Preferred title for the Work* is a different element to the *Title of the Manifestation*, and different instructions are given in RDA for how to determine and record them.

Group One Attributes	
Attributes of a Work	**Attributes of a Manifestation**
Preferred title for the Work	Title of the manifestation
Form of the Work	Statement of responsibility
Date of the Work	Edition / issue designation
Place of origin of the Work	Production / Publication / Distribution / Manufacture statements
History of the Work	Numbering of serials
Cartographic coordinates and scales	Series statement
Intended audience	Type of carrier (volume, microfiche, etc.)
	Type of media (audio, video, computer, etc.)
Attributes of an Expression	Extent (number of pages, units, etc.)
Form (i.e., content type) of Expression	Dimensions
Date of Expression	Identifier for the manifestation
Illustrative content (i.e., color and illustrations)	
Language of expression	**Attributes of an Item**
Medium of performance for musical content	Item identifier
	Provenance / Custodial history
Summarization of content	Marks or inscriptions
	Exhibition history
	Condition of the item
	Treatment history
	Access restrictions on the item

EXERCISE 4.3

The **bolded portion** of each of the following resources relates to an attribute of a Group One entity. Using the table provided above, name the attribute, and match it to its appropriate WEMI Entity (WEMI = Work, Expression, Manifestation, Item). The first two have been done for you.

	Resource	Attribute	WEMI Entity
1.	**Author's inscription** on title page	Marks or inscriptions	Item
2.	Version of Harry Potter **with colored illustrations**	Illustrative content	Expression
3.	**Italian translation** of *Going solo* by Roald Dahl		
4.	**Parliamentary Papers series; no. 16 of 2014**		
5.	Tolkien's **The Hobbit**		
6.	Shakespeare's First Folio, **owned by the British Museum**		
7.	**Spoken version** of *Wild Swans: three daughters of China* by Jung Chang		
8.	Sculpture **manufactured by** Morris and Company **in 1975**		
9.	A library copy of a DVD with **barcode number 23456**		
10.	**Random House publication** of *The narrow road to the deep north*		
11.	**Braille version** of David Attenborough's book, *Life on earth*		
12.	Map **80 x 40 cm**		
13.	*New York Times* on **microfiche**		
14.	Sketchbook with original drawings **not available for loan**		
15.	**TV series**, *60 minutes*		

Group Two Attributes

Here is a table of attributes for Group Two entities. These are quite different because they record the characteristics of people and organizations, not resources. In RDA, *every* entity has attributes, no matter whether they are inanimate objects or living beings.

Group Two Attributes	
Attributes of a Person	**Attributes of a Family**
Preferred name of the person	Name of the family
Title of the person	Type of family
Fuller form of name	Dates associated with the family
Dates associated with the person (birth/death/period of activity)	Places associated with the family
	History of the family
Occupation	Prominent members of the family
Gender	
Country /Place of residence	
Affiliation	**Attributes of a Corporate Body**
Address	Name of the corporate body
Language of the person	Dates associated with the body
Biography / history	Place associated with the body
	Language of the corporate body
	Address
	Field of activity
	Location and number of conference
	History of the corporate body

EXERCISE 4.4

Refer to the table of Group Two attributes above to complete the following:

1. *What Group Two attributes of a corporate body can you identify in this history?*

   The UK Film Council (UKFC) was set up in London in 2000 by the Labour Government to develop and promote the film industry in the UK. John Woodward was the Chief Executive Officer of the UKFC. As at 30 June 2008, the company had 90 full-time members of staff. UKFC closed on 31 March 2011, with many of its functions passing to the British Film Institute.

2. *Here is an access point for a family. In each case identify the underlined attribute.*

    Austen (Family : <u>Austen, Jane</u>, 1775 – 1817)   _____

    <u>Austen</u> (Family : Austen, Jane, 1775 – 1817)   _____

    Austen (<u>Family</u> : Austen, Jane, 1775 – 1817)   _____

3. *Fill in this table with as many of the attributes of a person as apply to you.*

Preferred name of person	
Title of person	
Fuller form of name	
Dates associated with the person (birth/death/period of activity)	
Occupation	
Gender	
Country/Place of residence	
Affiliation	
Address	
Language of person	
Biography / history	

CHAPTER FIVE
ISBD (International Standard Bibliographic Description)

Introduction
RDA is a 'format neutral' content standard—not tied to any particular encoding scheme. It focuses on describing the content of resources, rather than on how to code that description or present it to the user. This allows RDA to be used by a range of cultural collecting agencies like museums and archives, as well as libraries.

But using different encoding schemes makes it harder to share data. In order to make it easier to globally share catalog records, many libraries will continue their current practice of using ISBD (International Standard Bibliographic Description) punctuation and MARC (MAchine Readable Cataloging) coding to present their data. The AACR2 legacy data still in most library collections relied heavily on coding; so it is important to understand how these encoding formats have been, and continue to be, used in catalog records.

What is ISBD?
International Standard Bibliographic Description (ISBD) is a format for recording cataloging information in a standard way, in order to be able to exchange catalog records internationally. It was developed between 1969 and 1971 by IFLA, the International Federation of Library Associations and Institutions, and has been upgraded regularly since then.

The ISBD's purpose is to:
- standardize bibliographic descriptions
- provide a cataloging structure that is not dependent on language or culture
- create a system that can be adapted to the electronic environment.

ISBD identifies a standard set of descriptive elements in a specific order (called **areas of description**), and uses special punctuation to separate components of the elements. There are nine areas of description:

    Area 0: Content form and media type
    Area 1: Title and statement of responsibility
    Area 2: Edition
    Area 3: Material or type of resource specific
    Area 4: Publication, production, distribution, etc.
    Area 5: Material description
    Area 6: Series and multipart monographic resource
    Area 7: Notes
    Area 8: Resource identifier (e.g., ISBN, ISSN, etc.) and terms of availability

Each area of description, and some sub-elements within each, is preceded by nominated punctuation. AACR2 records the ISBD areas in the following order, and with the punctuation shown:

> Author main entry.
> Title proper = Parallel title : other title information / first statement of responsibility ; each subsequent statement of responsibility. - Edition statement / first statement of responsibility relating to the edition. - Material (or type of publication) specific details. - First place of publication, etc. : first publisher, etc., date of publication, etc. - Extent of item : other physical details ; dimensions. - (Title proper of series / statement of responsibility relating to series, ISSN of series ; numbering within the series. Title of subseries, ISSN of subseries ; numbering within subseries)
>
> Note/s.
> Standard number : price.
> Added entries for authors, titles, series and subjects

The current RDA guidelines still use ISBD's descriptive elements, although not necessarily in ISBD's specific order given above.

 EXERCISE 5.1
Write out each of the following bibliographical records using the ISBD arrangement noted above. Begin each note and the ISBN on a new line. Retain the punctuation supplied. Remember that punctuation precedes each element and area.

a.

First statement of responsibility	/ Paul Little with Carolyne Meng-Yee
Place of publication, publisher, date	. – Auckland [N.Z.] : Allen & Unwin, 2012.
Title proper	After Everest
Extent of item, other physical details, dimensions	. – xiii, 250 pages : illustrations (some color) ; 24 cm.
Standard number	ISBN 9781877505201.
Other title information	: inside the private world of Edmund Hillary

b.

Date of publication	, 2011
Standard number	ISBN 9 78098 079 159 4.
Extent of item	. – 458 pages
Title proper	Guardianship
Publisher	: Victorian Law Reform Commission
Statement of responsibility	/ Victorian Law Reform Commission
Dimensions	; 30 cm.
Other title information	: consultation paper
Series	– (Consultation paper / Victorian Law Reform Commission ; number 10)
Place of publication	. – Melbourne, Vic.

c.

Title proper	Fishing tips & tricks
Extent of item	. – 175 pages, 16 unnumbered leaves of colored plates
Date	, 2008.
Dimensions	; 28 cm.
Place of publication	. – Minneapolis, Minn.
Series	– (Freshwater angler series)
Other physical details	: illustrations
First statement of responsibility	/ by C. Boyd Pfieffer
Standard number	ISBN 9781589234086.
Publisher	: Creative Publishers
Edition statement	. – Abridged edition
Note	Includes index.

d.

Note	Maps on lining papers.
Note	Includes bibliographical references (pages 269–272) and index.
Series	– (The Southwest Center series)
Other physical details	: illustrations (some color), maps
Statements of responsibility	/ Cathy Moser Marlett ; foreword by Richard S. Felger
Standard number and price	ISBN 9780816530687.
Title	Shells on a desert shore
Publisher	: The University of Arizona Press
Dimensions	; 29 cm.
Place of publication	. –Tucson, Ariz.
Other title information	: mollusks in the Seri world
Extent of item	. – xx, 281 pages
Date of publication	, 2014

ISBD Punctuation

All ISBD spacing and all its punctuation is very carefully determined and has quite specific meaning:

- Punctuation separates areas of description, and elements within each area of description, in the catalog record.
- In cataloging, ISBD punctuation always precedes an area or element rather than following it. Thus if an element is missing, the rest of the record still has the correct punctuation attached.
- Areas of description and various sub-elements can be identified by the punctuation that precedes them. For example, a period <space> dash <space> (. –) indicates the start of a new area of description, whereas a <space> forward slash <space> (/) always precedes a statement of responsibility.
- Square brackets [ ] are used to indicate data supplied by the cataloger, or information that has been taken from sources other than the resource itself or its preferred sources of information.

RDA does not include specific instructions for punctuation in the main Instruction Set. However, two Appendices deal with punctuation:
- *Appendix D: Record syntaxes for descriptive data* covers ISBD punctuation for descriptive cataloging.
- *Appendix E: Record syntaxes for access point control data* indicates other punctuation that can be used when creating access points.

 The catalog record below uses ISBD punctuation. You can check the AACR2 outline in the section above to identify the various areas and elements in this record:

Wong, Yoon-wah.
Durians are not the only fruit : notes from the tropics / Wong Yoon-wah, translated from the Chinese by Jeremy Tiang. – First edition. – Singapore : Epigram Books, 2013. – xxxi, 175 pages : illustrations ; 23 cm. – (Cultural medallion series)
In English, translated from Chinese.
ISBN : 9789810766702 (paperback)

Punctuation Marks
ISBD punctuation is still used in RDA records, particularly those records that code their data using the MARC format. Although many library cataloging software systems now automatically insert ISBD punctuation, it is useful to be aware of the correct punctuation to expect in a catalog record.

These are common punctuation marks used in ISBD:

. period / full stop	– dash
, comma	/ diagonal slash
: colon	[ ] square brackets
; semicolon	( ) parentheses
- hyphen	+ plus sign

Appendix D of the RDA Instruction Set gives the full list of ISBD punctuation.

 Remember, punctuation always precedes (or comes before) each area or element within an area. Thus, size is always preceded by a semicolon (;), whatever else is in the physical description.

 *xi, 309 pages : illustrations **; 23 cm**.*
*665 pages **; 21 cm**.*

34 LEARN CATALOGING THE RDA WAY

 EXERCISE 5.2
Insert the correct punctuation in the following entries. Use the model above to identify the punctuation needed to precede each element.

a.
   BALZER, Julie Fei-Fan
   Carve, stamp, play   designing and creating custom stamps   Julie Fei-Fan Balzer. – Loveland, Colorado   Interweave   2013. – 143 pages   color illustrations   26 cm.
   Includes index.
   ISBN 9781596688865 (paperback)

b.
   NEW ZEALAND. Office of the Auditor-General
   Earthquake Commission   managing the Canterbury Home Repair Programme   Controller and Auditor General   Wellington   Office of the Auditor-General   2013   94 pages   colour illustrations   30 cm.   Parliamentary paper   B.29
   Includes bibliographical references
   Title from cover
   Online version available
   ISBN 9780478410372

Look at the following descriptions. Based on their position, and on the ISBD punctuation used, identify the particular pieces of information listed:

c.
   Floortje Bellefleur vindt een poes / Cok Grashoff ; ill. door Lies Veenhoven. – 9e dr. - Alkmaar : Kluitman, 2011. – 92 pages : illustrations ; 20 cm. – (Ons genoegen)
   Leeftijd tot 9 jaar.
   ISBN 90-206-7061-1   geb : f.4.40.

   Floortje Bellefleur vindt een poes
   Cok Grashoff
   ill. door Lies Veenhoven
   9e dr.
   Alkmaar
   Kluitman
   2011
   92 pages
   illustrations
   20 cm.
   Ons genoegen
   Leeftijd tot 9 jaar
   ISBN 90-206-7061-1
   geb : f.4.40

d.
Pjesme kroz zivot i bajke za djecu /autor svih stihova u ovoj knjizi, pjesama, crteza i fotografija je isto umjetnica Depcinski Veronika. – Prvo izdanje. – Sydney : Depcinski, 2013. – 15 pages : illustrations ; 25 cm.
Cover title.
ISBN 0 9588754 0 5 : $6.50 Aust.

illustrations
Cover title
autor svih stihova u ovoj knjizi, pjesama, crteza i fotografija je isto umjetnica Depcinski Veronika
Prvo izdanje
Sydney
2013
Pjesme kroz zivot i bajke za djecu
15 pages
Depcinski
25 cm.
ISBN 0 9588754 0 5
$6.50 Aust.

CHAPTER SIX
MARC (Machine Readable Cataloging)

Introduction
Most libraries still use ISBD punctuation and MARC coding to present their bibliographic data. This chapter introduces the MARC encoding format. There are many other encoding schemes, like Dublin Core metadata and MODS (Metadata Object Description Schema), that can be used with RDA; however, MARC is the most widely used scheme for library catalogs.

What is MARC?
MARC stands for MAchine Readable Cataloging. It is a format for coding bibliographic information so that it can be stored and retrieved by automated systems. MARC was developed and is maintained by the Library of Congress through the Network Development and MARC Standards Office. It has enabled libraries around the world to exchange cataloging data since the early 1970s. The current version of MARC is MARC 21.

MARC 21 is an encoding format. It does not tell catalogers what information to gather for a catalog record, or what terminology to use when recording that information. It simply provides codes that match the various cataloging elements, so catalogers can transfer their information into a form that computer systems can read and manipulate. If the data is not put correctly into MARC, the computer cannot interpret it correctly.

MARC 21 has a special format, or set of codes, for bibliographic data. There is also a separate format for authority data, as well as a number of other specialist formats. MARC bibliographic and authority data formats are the two that are most often used by catalogers. MARC formats can be found at http://www.loc.gov/marc, or via the RDA Toolkit.

MARC Terminology
The MARC format uses some standard database terminology like 'fields', 'subfields' and 'delimiters', as well as some terms like 'main entry fields' and 'indicators' that have specialized meanings. The table below defines the most commonly used MARC terms. It is important to recognize and understand these terms in order to correctly interpret the MARC format.

Field	A unit of information in a MARC record. Different fields contain either coded information or text.
Tag	A label that identifies each field of a MARC record, e.g., a 245 tag identifies the Title field. Tags consist of three digits.
Indicator	A character that gives additional information about a field, e.g., the first indicator 1 added to the tag 245 shows that a title added entry is to be made. All MARC fields have provision for two indicators, but only some fields use them. You will often see # or _ (hash or underscore) used when there is no indicator.
Subfield	A part of the MARC record that contains an element of description or other piece of small information, e.g., the date of publication within the 260 'Publication Details' field.
Subfield code	The two-character code that precedes a subfield data element in a MARC record, consisting of a delimiter (usually a $ or | symbol) and a letter (or sometimes a number) code.
Delimiter	A symbol used to introduce a new subfield. The symbol used can vary according to the user's system, but the convention is to use a $ or | symbol.
Variable fields	Fields in a MARC record that contain data content. **Variable control fields** contain coded information that is used in processing machine-readable records. They have MARC tags numbered 00X, e.g., 006, 007, 008. They are fixed in length and use letter and number codes to record data. **Variable data fields** contain the textual bibliographic information created by the cataloger—what we think of as the traditional catalog record, covering the physical description of the resource, access points, subject headings and a classification number. They use MARC tags numbered 01X–9XX and each field is unlimited in length.
Main entry fields	Variable data fields with MARC tags 100, 110, 111, 130, that nominate one of the resource's authorized access points as the most important for the purposes of filing items in catalogs and bibliographies. The main entry is usually the first-named author of a resource. This concept is not supported in RDA cataloging but remains an essential component of MARC coding.
Added entry fields	Variable data fields that represent all the resource's authorized access points other than the main entry. These can include additional authors, editors, illustrators, translators, titles, series and organizations by which a user may wish to find the record. This concept is not supported in RDA cataloging but remains an essential component of MARC coding.

MARC Record Structure

The MARC record structure consists of three parts:
1. **Leader** (000 field), that tells the computer information about the data that follows (for example, the length of the record).
2. **Directory,** a computer-generated index to the MARC record. It allows machines to 'read' the data and thus display, retrieve and exchange MARC records.
3. **Variable fields**, that form the bulk of the MARC record. They are identified by MARC tags.

MARC variable fields are each identified by a three-digit MARC tag. The fields are grouped into blocks of tags from 0 to 9. Each block covers various aspects of that component of cataloging data. For example, block 2 covers titles, editions and the imprint. There are a number of tags within block 2, so, when referring to the block as a whole, 'X' is used to represent any other characters in the tag.

In bibliographic records, the variable fields are:

0XX	Variable control fields, identification and classification numbers etc.
1XX	Main entry
2XX	Titles, edition, imprint
3XX	Physical description
4XX	Series statements
5XX	Notes
6XX	Subject access
7XX	Added entries (other than subjects or series)
8XX	Series added entries
9XX	Local fields, e.g., accession numbers

On the following page is a record from a library's public access catalog (OPAC), and the same record in MARC format. Note the MARC tags that are used for the fields.

It is standard practice (although not mandatory) to list the MARC tags in numerical order, so the order in which information is presented in a MARC record may be different from the way it appears in a library's public catalog.

Library catalog		MARC format		
Record ID:	17449703	000		01609cam a22004457i 4500
Creator:	Browne, Michael E., author.	001		17449703
		005		20130909142154.0
Title:	Physics for engineering and science / Michael E. Browne, PhD, Professor of Physics, University of Idaho.	008		120831t20132013nyua 001 0 eng d
		020	__	$a 9780071810906 (paperback)
		035	__	$a (OCoLC)ocn845013268
Also Titled:	Schaum's outlines physics for engineering and science.	040	__	$a CCE $b eng $c CCE $e rda $d YDXCP $d ZQP $d BWX $d DLC
		042	__	$a lccopycat
Edition:	Third edition.	050	00	$a QC31 $b .B76 2013
Published (Imprint):	New York : McGraw-Hill Education, [2013]	082	04	$a 530 $2 23
		100	1_	$a Browne, Michael E. $e author.
Copyright Date:	©2013	245	00	$a Physics for engineering and science / $c Michael E. Browne, PhD, Professor of Physics, University of Idaho.
Description:	xiii, 427 pages : illustrations ; 28 cm.			
Content Type:	text			
Media Type:	unmediated	246	1_	$a Schaum's outlines physics for engineering and science
Carrier Type:	volume			
		250	__	$a Third edition.
ISBN:	9780071810906 (paperback)	264	_1	$a New York :$b McGraw-Hill Education, $c [2013]
LC Number	QC31 .B76 2013	264	_4	$c ©2013
Dewey Number:	530	300	__	$a xiii, 427 pages :$b illustrations ; $c 28 cm.
Notes:	Includes index.	336	__	$a text $2 rdacontent
Subjects:	Physics – Outlines, syllabi, etc. Physics – Problems, exercises, etc.	337	__	$a unmediated $2 rdamedia
		338	__	$a volume $2 rdacarrier
		490	1_	$a Schaum's outlines.
		500	__	$a Includes index.
Series:	Schaum's outlines	650	_0	$a Physics $v Outlines, syllabi, etc.
		650	_0	$a Physics $v Problems, exercises, etc.

CHAPTER SIX   MARC   41

The MARC21 Bibliographic Format

Library management systems deal with MARC coding in different ways. Some systems expect catalogers to know the MARC codes while others supply labels that link to the codes in the background. Even if your library's cataloging module automatically inputs MARC codes, you should be able to recognize the MARC format and understand how it is applied.

To successfully apply MARC coding, it is important to correctly interpret what you see in the MARC *Format for Bibliographic Data,* located at http://www.loc.gov/marc. This format provides details for all the MARC tags. Each 'data element' entry is listed numerically by its tag number. The layout of the information is the same for each data element entry.

Here is the data element entry for the 245 'Title Statement' field, with an explanation of what you see on the right:

MARC Data Element	Explanation
245 — TITLE STATEMENT (NR)	• *3 digit tag and field name.* • *Indication of whether the field is repeatable (R) or non-repeatable (NR). NR means you can have only one occurrence of this tag in a catalog record.*
FIELD DEFINITION AND SCOPE The title and statement of responsibility area of the bibliographic description of a Work.	• *a short explanation of what the field does.*

INDICATORS
 	
First Indicator – Title added entry
Whether a title added entry is to be made.
 	
    0 – No added entry
    No title added entry is made either because no title added entry is desired or because the title added entry is not traced the same as the title in field 245.
 	
    1 – Added entry
    The desired title added entry is the same as the title in field 245.
 	
Second Indicator – Nonfiling characters
Number of character positions associated with a definite or indefinite article (e.g. Le, A, An) at the beginning of the title that are disregarded in sorting and filing processes.
 	
    0 – No nonfiling characters
    1-9 – Number of nonfiling characters
	• *two extra digits used to include additional coded information in some MARC fields.*
	• *The name of the first indicator*
	• *a short explanation of what the indicator indicates.*
	
	• *The first option for the first indicator (which is '0')*
	• *a short explanation of the option.*
	
	• *The next option for the first indicator (which is '1')*
	• *a short explanation of the option.*
	
	• *The name of the second indicator, known as the 'filing indicator'.*
	• *a short explanation of what the indicator indicates.*
	
	• *the options for the indicator to be used in this position.*

SUBFIELD CODES $a - Title (NR) $b - Remainder of title (NR) $c - Statement of responsibility, etc. (NR) $f - Inclusive dates (NR) $g - Bulk dates (NR) $h - Medium (NR) $k - Form (R) $n - Number of part/section of a Work (R) $p - Name of part/section of a Work (R) $s - Version (NR) $6 - Linkage (NR) *See* Control Subfields $8 - Field link and sequence number (R) *See* Control Subfields	• *a 1-character letter or number, preceded by a delimiter ($ or |), that sets apart each subsection of a field.* • *all the options available for use as subfield codes with this 245 field. The full MARC format explains what each one means. Subfield codes, and what they mean, change for each field.* *(Note: RDA no longer uses the $h subfield, but it is still included in the MARC format for those libraries that have not changed to RDA).*
EXAMPLES 245 04$aThe Year book of medicine. 245 18$aThe ... annual report to the Governor. 245 00$aMap of Nelson, Richmond, Motueka :$bscale 1:20000. 245 15$aThe "winter mind" :$bWilliam Bonk and American letters /$cBurt Kimmelman. 245 15$aTōn meionotētōn eunoia :$bmythistorēma /$cSpyrou Gkrintzou. 245 00$aPortals to the world.$pSelected Internet resources.$pMaldives $h[electronic resource] /$ccreated and maintained by the Asian Division, Area Studies Directorate.	• *a range of examples illustrating how the coding is applied to this field.*

Reading a MARC Record

When 'reading' a MARC field, each component tells you something. Look at this example:

 245 14 $aThe complete Asian cookbook /$cby Charmaine Solomon.

245 tells you that this area is recording the title and statement of responsibility.

1 tells the computer to make an added entry for the title. Note that there is no special added entry field for a title in a MARC record; the indicator is the only way the computer knows that an added entry should be created.

4 shows that the first four characters—'t', 'h', 'e', and the space—need to be ignored when the title is filed in alphabetical order. So the item will be filed under **c** for **complete**, not **T** for **The**.

$a introduces the title proper part of the 'title and statement of responsibility' field.

$c introduces the author (statement of responsibility) part of the 'title and statement of responsibility' field.

However, in a different MARC record:

245 10 $aLearn library management /$cby Jacinta Ganendran.

the second indicator is **0**, since the computer does not need to ignore any characters, and it will file this title under **L** for **Learn**.

 Here is another extract from the MARC 21 bibliographic format, for a different MARC field. The subfields in the examples have been bolded for ease of reading.

> **300 – Physical Description (R)**
> **Indicators**
>   Both undefined; each contains a blank (#)
> **Subfield Codes**
> $a Extent of item (R)
> $b Other physical details (NR)
> $c Dimensions (R)
> $e Accompanying material (NR)
> **Examples**
>   300 ## **$a**149 pages ;**$c**23 cm
>
>   300 ## **$a**1 score (16 pages) ;**$c**29 cm
>
>   300 ## **$a**11 volumes :**$b**illustrated ;**$c**24 cm
>
>   300 ## **$a**1 map :**$b**colored ;**$c**30 x 55 cm
>
>   300 ## **$a**1 sound disc (20 minutes) :**$b**analog, 33 1/3 rpm, stereo. ;**$c**30 cm
>
>   300 ## **$a**14 film reels (157 min.) :**$b**Panavision ;**$c**16 mm
>
>   300 ## **$a**160 slides :**$b** colored ;**$c**5 x 5 cm
>
>   300 ## **$a**1 computer disk ;**$c**3 1/2 inches +**$e**reference manual, teacher's manual, answer book.

The **tag** is 300, and the name of the field is Physical Description. The next symbol is (R). This stands for Repeatable, and means that the field can appear more than once in the bibliographic record.

The **indicators** are undefined. This means that we enter two blanks following the tag and the blanks are shown as ##.

The subfield for the extent of item—i.e., how many pages in a book, how many slides in a slide set—is denoted by the **subfield code $a**, and is shown as (R). That is, this subfield can be repeated.

The second subfield, identified by the **subfield code $b**, is 'Other physical details'— i.e., whether the picture is colored, whether the videorecording has sound. It is shown as (NR), which means that these details can only be given once in a record.

The subfield for dimensions, **subfield code $c**—i.e., the size of the item—is repeatable (R). The subfield for accompanying material cannot be repeated (NR), so two or more pieces of accompanying material are contained in the same subfield, introduced by a single **$e**. This is shown in the last example.

EXERCISE 6.1

Use the MARC Format for Bibliographic Data located at http://www.loc.gov/marc to answer the following questions.

1. In the example: **700 1# $aSawer, Marian,$d1946–**

    a. What MARC field is used and what does that field represent?

    b. What does (R) in the heading for the MARC field mean?

    c. What does the first indicator '1' mean?

    d. What does the subfield code '$d' indicate?

2. In the example: **110 2# $aBritish Library. $bLending Division. $bResearch Section**

    a. What MARC field is used and what does that field represent?

    b. What does the subfield code '$b' mean? Can you have two subfield 'b' codes in this example? Why or why not?

c. What does the first indicator '2' mean?

3. In the example: **082 04 $a388.0919$223**
   a. What MARC field is used and what does that field represent?

   b. What information is provided in the indicators and subfields?

MARC Variable Length Fields (Data Fields)

Variable data fields contain bibliographic information. Fields with tags that do not begin with 00 are variable data fields. They contain the content of the traditional catalog record, as well as some additional information in the 0XX fields. They are sometimes called variable length fields because the size of the field can vary, unlike 00X fields that are fixed in length.

In a MARC record, the most commonly used variable data fields are:

010	Library of Congress control number
020	ISBN number
040	Cataloging source
050	Library of Congress classification number
083	Dewey Decimal Classification number
1XX	Main entry
2XX	Titles, edition, imprint
3XX	Physical description
4XX	Series statements
5XX	Notes
6XX	Subject added entries
7XX	Added entries other than subject or series
8XX	Series added entries

Coding Tags and Conventions

MARC uses three means to indicate the types of information that make up a record: tags, indicators, and subfield codes. These are called **content designators**.
- Tags are the three-character labels used to identify the field.
- Indicators provide additional information about how to process the data in a field.
- Subfield codes identify individual components of a field and precede each of these components (called data elements).

Indicators

Sometimes we want to tell the computer to do more than just store the information. For example:

- In the title field (245), we want to indicate whether or not the title should be an access point in the catalog, and where it should be filed in the index.
- In the Dewey Decimal classification field (082) we want to indicate the type of edition used (full or abridged) and which agency has assigned the class number.
- In the author field (100, 110) we want to indicate what type of name is in use (forename, surname, family name, name in direct or inverted order for corporate entities, jurisdiction name for government agencies, etc.)

We want to indicate different things in different MARC fields. The computer can then use this information to enhance the catalog record, by indexing it in a special way or by storing and filing it in a separate index.

To note this additional information we code it using two extra characters, inserted just after the field tag and before the body of the field data. These characters are called **indicators**. In fields where indicators are not needed, they are left blank.

Note that the number zero (0) is often used as an indicator and has a value or code. To show that there is no value for a particular indicator, catalogers use the hash/hatch sign (#) or leave the space blank.

 Indicators have completely different functions in different MARC fields. You must check each field to see if it uses indicators, and what it uses them for.

Subfields and Subfield Codes

The data elements within a field are called **subfields**.

Each subfield is introduced by a **subfield code**. These codes enable the computer to identify all the pieces of information that make up the record. Thus the system can retrieve any information it needs. The subfield code consists of two characters—the delimiter and the data element identifier.

Delimiters are the symbols that separate subfields. In this workbook, we use the symbol $. Other symbols are also used as delimiters, including | and ‡.

The **data element identifier** is the letter or number that identifies the particular data element or subfield. For example, in the 'Production, Publication, Distribution, Manufacture and Copyright Notice' field (264) field, the place of publication is stored in subfield **a**, the publisher in subfield **b** and the date of publication in subfield **c**. 'a', 'b' and 'c' are the **data element identifiers**. They are the codes that introduce a subfield.

Data element identifier codes are usually single letters, but occasionally they can be single numbers. For example, in the DDC field 082 the subfield code for the classification number is $a, but for the edition of DDC used it is $2. So it is perfectly correct for a 082 field to look like this:

082 04 $a025.3076**$2**23

(i.e., a DDC number, using the full edition of DDC and assigned by an agency other than the Library of Congress that is performing original cataloging. The DDC number is 025.3076, created from DDC edition 23)

In this 'Production, Publication, Distribution, Manufacture and Copyright Notice' field, the subfield codes are bolded:

264 #1 **$a**Canberra :**$b**DocMatrix,**$c**2014.

Note that the subfield code takes the place of a space. In this workbook we often insert a space after the subfield code for ease of reading; however in MARC coding there is no space between the punctuation mark and the subfield, or the subfield code and the data.

EXERCISE 6.2

Look at this sample line from a MARC 21 record (# indicates a blank space). Then fill in the blanks with the correct answers from the list provided. Answers can be used more than once:

651 #0 $aRussia $xHistory $y18th century $vMaps

Answers:	field/s	subfield/s	tag/s
	indicator/s	subfield code/s	delimiter/s

a. The sample line represents one _____.

b. The number 651 is its _____.

c. There is one blank in the _____ position.

d. What we see on the sample line is a _____ that is made up of four _____.

e. The characters $a, $x, $y and $v are four examples of _____.

f. The symbols $ are examples of _____.

g. In this sample line, the first _____ has no assigned meaning. In other words, the first _____ is undefined.

h. In MARC 21 records, there are 3 types of content designators: _____, _____, and _____.

i. The 651 _____ identifies this as the 'Subject Added Entry—Geographic Name' _____.

j. There are four _____: Geographic name, General subdivision, Chronological subdivision, and Form subdivision.

MARC Leader and Control Fields

MARC records contain two types of fields: variable length fields that record textual data, and fixed-length fields that record coded data. The fixed length fields all occur in the 00X range:

000 – Leader and Directory
001 – Control Number
003 – Control Number Identifier
005 – Date and Time of Last Transaction
006 – Fixed-Length Data Elements—Additional Material Characteristics
007 – Physical Description Fixed Field
008 – Fixed-Length Data Elements

We will focus on the 000 (Leader), 006, 007 and 008 fields.

The Leader in a Nutshell

- The leader 'drives' the choice of information in other fixed-length fields.
- Each character position (or block of positions) represents a different characteristic of the resource being cataloged.
- Most of the leader is generated by the computer system; but some positions (especially 06, 07) are crucial for catalogers to enter. Other data entered by catalogers appear at positions 05, 17, and 18.
- The most important characteristics in the leader are the codes given in character position 06 (Type of record) and character position 07 (bibliographic level). These codes affect the information gathered in part of the 008 field, and this information is the basis for advanced search options in library catalogs.

eg *This is what a Leader field looks like:*
00718nam//2200217/a/4500

The 008 Field (Fixed-Length Data Elements) in a Nutshell

- 008 provides coded information about the record as a whole and about special bibliographic aspects of the resource.
- There are 40 character positions in field 008, numbered from 00–39.
- Positions 00–17 and 35–39 are the same for all forms of material.
- Codes and data for positions 18–34 change, depending on the type of material.
- Separate lists of codes are provided for the 18–34 positions for the following types of material: books, computer files, maps, music, continuing resources (serials), visual materials, mixed materials.
- The cataloger chooses which code list to use in the 18–34 positions, based on the 'type of record' code used in the 000 leader field, character position 06.
- The Leader 06 and 07 positions determine which aspect of the 008 field is used.

CHAPTER SIX   MARC   49

- The 008 field is not repeatable, so it only captures details of the major aspect of a resource (e.g., a serial).
- For additional aspects of a resource (e.g., a serial in electronic format), use the 006 field in addition to the 008 field. Repeat 006 fields for additional aspects as required.

 This is what a 008 field looks like:
140922s2014####si#acfo#s#####000#0#eng#d

 EXERCISE 6.3
Code the following parts of a 008 field. The character position numbers are given under each position to be coded.

1. A record entered on March 4, 2000

   |____|____|____|____|____|____|
    00   01   02   03   04   05

2. A work with the single publication date of 2014

   |____|____|____|____|____|
    06   07   08   09   10

3. A serial that began in 1990 and ceased in 2005

   |____|____|____|____|____|____|____|____|____|
    06   07   08   09   10   11   12   13   14

4. A serial that began in 1972 and is still being published

   |____|____|____|____|____|____|____|____|____|
    06   07   08   09   10   11   12   13   14

5. Published in the Czech Republic

   |____|____|____|
    15   16   17

6. Book illustrations including genealogical tables and plans

   |____|____|____|____|
    18   19   20   21

7. A publication intended for preschool children

   |____|
    22

8. A bibliography published by a state government

   |____|____|____|____|____|
    24   25   26   27   28

9. A book of plays in Hindi with an index

   |____|____|____|____|____|____|____|
    31   32   33   34   35   36   37

The 006 Field (Fixed-Length Data Elements—Additional Material Characteristics) in a Nutshell

- 006 is used in conjunction with the 008 field, never used alone.
- It provides additional coded information about bibliographic aspects of resources with multiple characteristics (e.g., maps in electronic format; multi-part kits whose contents contain multiple formats like slides, posters and music CDs).
- It is only used when a resource has the characteristics of more than one form of material. In such cases, the primary characteristics are coded in the 008 field, and the secondary characteristic or characteristics are coded in the 006 field.
- 006 can be repeated many times, to cover all aspects of a resource (unlike 008, that is non-repeatable and therefore only describes the primary bibliographic aspects).
- There are seven separate 006 field configurations: one each for books, electronic resources (computer files), maps, music, continuing resources (serials), visual materials (films, videos, etc.), and mixed materials. The entire 006 field is repeated under each of these headings. For each material type, the data collected is different.
- In general, the 008 and 006 fields contain 'bibliographic' information about a resource, while the 007 field carries information about its physical characteristics.

eg *This is what a 006 field looks like:*
m####d###g#s######

The 007 Field (Physical Description Fixed Field) in a Nutshell

- 007 provides description of the physical formats of different types of resources and their accompanying material.
- It can be used for all resources; however, because the information collected for 'texts' (i.e., books and serials) in the 007 field is fairly limited, many catalogers ignore this field for books and serials.
- It is essential, however, to include the 007 field for audiovisual and electronic resources, because this is where searchable data on sizes, formats, system requirements, file formats, etc. are kept. Although some of this information is repeated in other parts of the record (for example in some 34X or notes fields), computer systems collect it for search retrieval from the 007 field.
- 007 can be repeated many times, to cover all aspects of a resource, its parts and its accompanying material.
- There are fifteen separate 007 field configurations: one each for maps, electronic resources, globes, tactile material, projected graphics, microform, nonprojected graphics, motion pictures, kits, notated music, remote-sensing images, sound recording, text (books, serials, print material), videorecordings and unspecified material. The entire 007 field is repeated under each of these headings. For each material type, the data collected is different.
- The number of character positions for this field varies depending on the format of the material. The field size ranges from 2 character positions for kits, notated music and text to 23 positions for motion pictures.

eg *This is what a 007 field looks like for an electronic resource:*
co#ag|---uuuuu

MARC and RDA

Many libraries will continue to use MARC as their encoding format. While MARC has made some adjustments to accommodate RDA, it is still not fully 'FRBR-ized'.

Below is a quick guide to where the Group 1 entities fit into MARC. For further details about MARC coding under RDA, use the 'RDA to MARC' and 'MARC to RDA' mappings in the 'Tools' section of the RDA Toolkit.

Marc Field	Work	Expression	Manifestation	Item
1XX/240	✓	✓	x	x
245-260, 490	x	x	✓	x
300	x	✓	✓	x
other 3XX	✓	✓	✓	x
5XX	✓	✓	✓	✓
700-730	✓	✓	x	x
760-787	✓	✓	✓	x
8XX	✓	✓	✓	x

Source: *Teaching RDA: Train-the-trainer course RDA: Resource description and access* presented by the National Library of Australia in 2012 and made available under a Creative Commons Attribution 3.0 Australia License.

Basic changes to MARC encoding, for RDA–compliant records
- Leader/18 contains the value 'i' for an RDA–compliant record
- 040 $e contains the code '**rda**'
    - Note the order of this field is now 040 $a $b **$e** $c $d
- 100 $e is used to indicate creator relationships
- New fields 336 (content type), 337 (media type), 338 (carrier type)
- New 264 field providing more detail than 260
- New MARC Authority fields for name attributes: 046, 368, 370–378
- New MARC Authority and Bibliographic fields for Work and Expression attributes: 336, 377, 380, 381–384
- Fuller details are given in the MARC standards 'RDA in MARC Summary of Additions' http://www.loc.gov/marc/RDAinMARC.html.

To keep up to date with all MARC changes (not simply the new RDA provisions), use the 'MARC Format Overview' page at http://www.loc.gov/marc/status.html. Here you will find lists of the changes that are made in each half-yearly update to MARC bibliographic and authority data.

EXERCISE 6.4

Here is a catalog record with the coded MARC record below. Some of the MARC tags, indicators and subfield codes have been omitted. Supply the missing items in the underlined spaces. For help, refer to the MARC Bibliographic Standards http://www.loc.gov/marc/bibliographic/.

PERSONAL NAME	Murawski, Darlyne, author.
MAIN TITLE	Ultimate bug-opedia : the most complete bug reference ever / by Darlyne Murawski & Nancy Honovich.
PUBLISHED	Washington, D.C. : National Geographic, [2013]
DESCRIPTION	271 pages : color illustrations ; 28 cm
ISBN	9781426313769 (hardcover)
LC CLASSIFICATION	QL462.3 .M87 2013
VARIANT TITLE	National Geographic kids ultimate bug-opedia
RELATED NAMES	Honovich, Nancy, author.
SUBJECTS	Insects – Encyclopedias, Juvenile.
NOTES	At head of title: National Geographic kids.
	Includes bibliographical references (pages 264–265) and index.
DEWEY CLASS NO.	595.703
CONTENT TYPE	text
	still image
MEDIA TYPE	unmediated
CARRIER TYPE	volume

000 02525cam a22004337i 4500

001 18082551

___ 140326s2013 dcua j be 001 0 eng d

020 ## $a 9781426313769 (hardcover)

040 ## $a UKMGB $b eng $c UKMGB $__ rda $d OCLCO $d DLC

050 00 $a QL462.3 $b .M87 2013

082 04 $a 595.703 $2 23

___ 1# $a Murawski, Darlyne, $__ author.

245 10 $__ Ultimate bug-opedia : $__ the most complete bug reference ever $__ by Darlyne Murawski & Nancy Honovich.

246 3# $a National Geographic kids ultimate bug-opedia

264 #1 $__ Washington, D.C. : $__ National Geographic, $__ [2013]

___ ## $a 271 pages : $b color illustrations ; $c 28 cm

336 ## $a text $2 rdacontent

336 ## $a still image $2 rdacontent

337 ## $a unmediated $2 rdamedia

338 ## $a volume $2 rdacarrier

500 ## $a At head of title: National Geographic kids.

___ ## $a Includes bibliographical references (pages 264–265) and index.

650 #0 $__ Insects $v Encyclopedias, Juvenile.

___ 1# $a Honovich, Nancy, $__ author.

CHAPTER SEVEN
Introduction to the RDA Toolkit

Introduction
The RDA toolkit is an integrated set of online resources, providing users with access to a collection of cataloging-related documents. The RDA Toolkit gives you the material you need to implement RDA; to make cataloging decisions based on principles; to increase efficiency; to facilitate collaboration; and to help position the library community for the future by making bibliographic data accessible through online technologies.

What Does the RDA Toolkit Include?
The RDA Toolkit consists of three groups of resources, each on a separate navigation tab:
- **The RDA Instruction Set** provides guidelines for descriptive cataloging.
- **Tools** are additional materials developed by the RDA Toolkit creators. These include examples of RDA records, 'mappings' of RDA elements to corresponding MARC elements, and diagrams illustrating various FRBR/RDA concepts.
- **Resources** are external documents you can refer to when cataloging. These include the text of AACR2 for reference, Policy Statements of the Library of Congress, British Library, German-speaking libraries and the National Library of Australia, and other resources like the MARC standards.

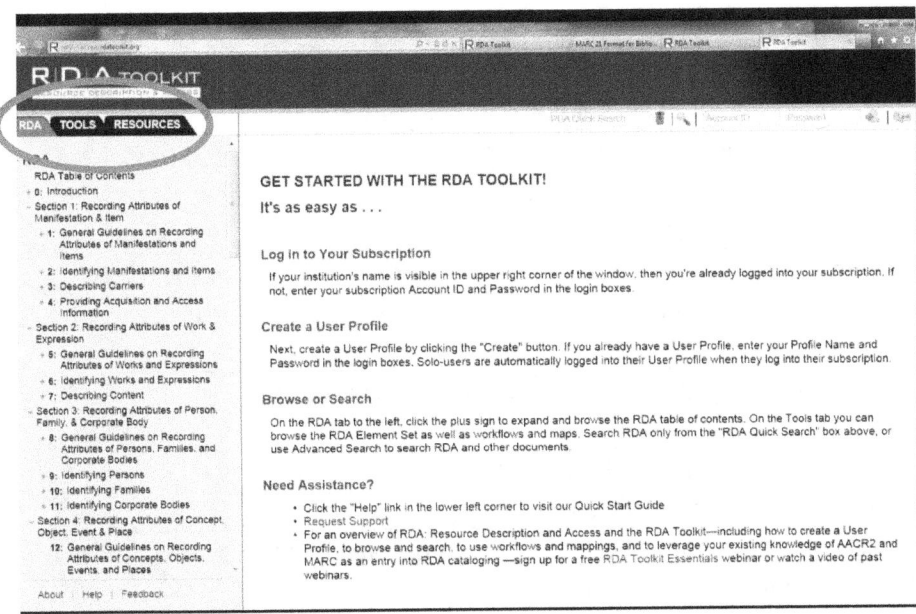

The RDA Instruction Set
The RDA Instruction Set is the part of the Toolkit that provides details of what a cataloger can record in a bibliographic record, an authority record, or for access points. It supersedes and is the replacement for AACR2.

The RDA Instruction Set appears as the Toolkit's first tab in the left navigation pane, and is marked simply 'RDA'.

Although the Instruction Set is also available in a loose-leaf print format, it is designed as an online tool and it is not expected that catalogers will read it in sequence from start to finish. Instead, you are encouraged to use the embedded links found in the Toolkit to take you to specific information. You may find that the same instruction is repeated in a number of places. This is to ensure that the instruction is seen, no matter which set of links you follow.

The RDA Instruction Set is arranged by FRBR concepts (Group One, Two and Three entities, their attributes and their relationships). The Instruction Set consists of 10 sections that hold 37 chapters, Appendices A–L, a glossary and an index.

- Chapter 0 gives an overview of RDA and an introduction to the RDA Instruction Set
- Sections 1–4 cover how to record attributes
- Sections 5–10 cover how to record relationships
- Appendices A to H provide guidelines about presentation, including capitalization, abbreviations, etc.
- Appendices D and E indicate the type and position of ISBD punctuation used in catalog records
- Appendices I to L cover 'relationship designators' (lists of vocabularies indicating various relationships for, between and among entities).

RDA Instruction Set—Appendices

Appendix A.	Capitalization
Appendix B.	Abbreviations
Appendix C.	Initial articles
Appendix D.	Record syntaxes for descriptive data
Appendix E.	Record syntaxes for access point control data
Appendix F.	Additional instructions on names of persons
Appendix G.	Titles of nobility, terms of rank, etc.
Appendix H.	Dates in the Christian calendar
Appendix I.	Relationship designators: Relationships between a resource and Persons, Families, and Corporate Bodies associated with the resource
Appendix J.	Relationship designators: Relationships between Works, Expressions, Manifestations, and Items
Appendix K.	Relationship designators: Relationships between Persons, Families, and Corporate Bodies
Appendix L.	Relationship designators: Relationships between Concepts, Objects, Events, and Places

The chapters are numbered continuously throughout the RDA Instruction Set, so when you quote an RDA instruction number you include only the chapter numbers—not the section number. For example, Chapter 2 is in Section 1 of the RDA Instruction Set. In the RDA instruction number 2.3.1 'Basic Instructions on Recording Titles', the '**2**' refers to Chapter 2 and not Section 2 of the RDA Instruction Set.

CHAPTER SEVEN   RDA Toolkit   55

The following table provides a quick summary of the RDA Instruction Set:

	RDA Section	What's in it
Section 1-4 Recording Attributes	**1—Recording attributes of Manifestations & Items**	Manifestations • Title of manifestation, publisher, date of publication, edition, series Items • Annotations, access, ownership
	2—Recording attributes of Works & Expressions	Works • Authorized access points (uniform titles) • Title of the Work (note this is different from recording the title of a Manifestation) and additions to preferred titles Expressions • Form of notation, content type, illustrations
	3—Recording attributes of Person, Family, & Corporate Body	• Attributes recorded in authority records • Constructing access points for persons, families and corporate bodies NOTE: This is not about *choosing* access points
	4—Recording attributes of Concept, Object, Event & Place	• Data elements that are recorded in subject authority records—Not yet included in RDA
Section 5-10 Recording Relationships	**5—Recording primary relationships Between Work, Expression, Manifestation & Item**	• Relationships between Work, Expression, Manifestation and Item by using identifiers, authorized access points and composite descriptions
	6—Recording relationships to Persons, Families & Corporate Bodies	• *Choice* of access points for persons, families and corporate bodies • Relationships established through 'relationship designators'
	7—Recording relationships to Concepts, Objects, Events & Places	• Not yet included in RDA • *Choice* of subjects
	8—Recording relationships between Works, Expressions, Manifestations & Items	• Relationships between Work and Work; Expression and Expression etc. • Identifiers, access points and descriptions
	9—Recording relationships between Persons, Families & Corporate Bodies	• Relationships between a person and another person, a person and a family etc. • pseudonyms, former and later names, variant names
	10—Recording relationships between Concepts, Objects, Events & Places	• Not yet included in RDA • *Relationships* between subjects

Source: *Teaching RDA: Train-the-trainer course RDA: Resource description and access* presented by the National Library of Australia in 2012 and made available under a Creative Commons Attribution 3.0 Australia License.

EXERCISE 7.1

Use the RDA Instruction Set to answer the following questions.

1. Which section contains instruction number 7.4?

2. Which section contains instruction number 1.7.2?

3. What is instruction number 2.4.3?

4. What information do you find at instruction number 29.1?

5. What does RDA Chapter 33 cover?

6. What is instruction number 3.5.1.4.14?

RDA Instruction Set—Internal Structure

The RDA Instruction Set has a consistent internal structure, to help you navigate through it more easily. General information that applies to all instances of each concept is given first, followed by specific instructions for individual instances. The Table of Contents for the RDA Instruction Set reflects this structure:

1. The first chapter in each section provides general guidelines for the entities discussed in that section.

2. The sectional 'General Guidelines' chapters begin with information about (in this order): the scope of that section, important terminology, functional objectives of that section and, if appropriate, the core elements for the entities in that section.

3. The remaining chapters in each section deal with specific instructions about various aspects or attributes of the entities. These change for each section.

- Section 3: Recording Attributes of Person, Family, & Corporate Body
  - + 8: General Guidelines on Recording Attributes of Persons, Families, and Corporate Bodies
  - − 9: Identifying Persons
    - 9.0 Purpose and Scope
    - + 9.1 General Guidelines on Identifying Persons *(circled)*

- − 2: Identifying Manifestations and Items
  - 2.0 Purpose and Scope
  - + 2.1 Basis for Identification of the Resource
  - + 2.2 Sources of Information
  - + 2.3 Title
  - − 2.4 Statement of Responsibility
    - + 2.4.1 Basic Instructions on Recording Statements of Responsibility
    - + 2.4.2 Statement of Responsibility Relating to Title Proper
    - + 2.4.3 Parallel Statement of Responsibility Relating to Title Proper

4. Each remaining chapter in each section begins with the purpose and scope of the chapter, followed by general guidelines on that chapter. These guidelines look at more detailed information than the sectional guideline chapter, including, for example, instructions on what to use as preferred sources of information for that chapter's attributes.

5. Subsections within each chapter also progress from the general to the specific. For example, RDA Chapter 2 has subsections for each attribute of a Manifestation (title, edition statement, etc.). Subsection 2.4 covers Statements of Responsibility. The subsection begins with basic instructions on recording statements of responsibility, then goes on to provide specific instructions about particular types of statement of responsibility.

RDA instruction Set—Reading What You See

The RDA Instruction Set uses icons, colored text and different fonts to highlight some of its special features. These include:
- definitions
- RDA links
- core elements
- examples
- exceptions, alternatives, and options
- icons.

Definitions are shown with reddish-brown text and a down arrow. The arrow links you to the Glossary entry for that term.
   e.g., **title proper¼**

RDA links will take you to other relevant instructions within the RDA Instruction Set.
   e.g., other title information (see 2.3.4 RDA)

Core elements are the attributes that must be included in a record, if they are applicable to the resource being cataloged, to make it an RDA–compliant record. All core elements are listed in Chapter 0 of the RDA Instruction Set. The General Guidelines chapter of each Section repeats the core elements pertaining to that Section. As you look through the RDA

Instructions, you will also see the core elements clearly marked in blue, CORE ELEMENT below the name of the element. If there are any conditions relating to when the element is core, additional information then follows the term 'Core Element'.

For example,

2.3 Title
CORE ELEMENT
The title proper is a core element. Other titles are optional.

Examples in the Toolkit are presented on a yellow background.

EXAMPLE

International gas report
Source of information reads: International gas report, including World gas report

---

Exceptions to an instruction are noted with the label, 'Exception' and a left margin mark, both in green print.

Exceptions

Introductory words. For instructions on introductory words not intended to be part of the title, see 2.3.1.6 RDA.

Optional information within instructions, such as **Alternatives, Optional Additions** or **Optional Omissions** are labeled and have a left margin mark, both in green print.

Alternative LC-PCC PS NLA PS D-A-CH BL PS

Devise a title in a language and script preferred by the agency preparing the description.

Optional Addition NLA PS D-A-CH BL PS

Record the titles of the individual contents as titles of related works (see 25.1 RDA).

Optional Omission NLA PS D-A-CH

Abridge a long title only if it can be abridged without loss of essential information. Use a mark of omission (...) to indicate such an omission. Never omit any of the first five words.

The **icons** LC-PCC PS NLA PS D-A-CH BL PS in the RDA instructions set link to the Library of Congress—Program for Cooperative Cataloging Policy Statements (LC–PCC PS), the National Library of Australia Policy Statements (NLA PS), Anwendungsrichtlinien für den deutschsprachigen Raum (D-A-CH AWR) and British Library (BL PS) respectively. These policy statements are located in the third tab under 'Resources'. They show the decisions by the Library of Congress, the National Library of Australia, cataloging agencies in Germany, Austria and Switzerland, and the British Library about how they will implement RDA instructions. These icons link you to the relevant policy statement in the 'Resources' tab.

RDA Toolkit—Tools

- RDA: Element Set
- RDA Mappings
- Examples of RDA Records (JSC)
  - MARC Encoding
- Workflows
- Maps
- 2010 Entity Relationship Diagram (Archival)
- Schemas (Archival)

The second tab in the RDA Toolkit is the 'Tools' tab. This tab contains additional materials developed by the RDA Toolkit creators. These include:
- examples of RDA records
- 'mappings' of RDA elements to different schemas, including MARC elements
- diagrams illustrating various FRBR/RDA concepts
- workflows and other procedures that have been created by subscribers. (These can be used individually, shared within an organization or shared globally with all RDA subscribers.)

RDA Toolkit—Resources

The final tab in the RDA Toolkit is the 'Resources' tab. This tab consists of external documents that you can refer to when cataloging. The full text of AACR2, Anwendungsrichtlinien für den deutschsprachigen Raum, the British Library, Library of Congress and National Library of Australia Policy Statements are provided. Policy statements from other national bodies will be added in future.

Links to other resources including the MARC standards, FRBR, Dublin Core Metadata, and LC Cataloger's Desktop are located on this tab.

- AACR2
- Anwendungsrichtlinien für den deutschsprachigen Raum (D-A-CH AWR)
- Library of Congress-Program for Cooperative Cataloging Policy Statements (LC-PCC PS)
- National Library of Australia Policy Statements (NLA PS)
- Other Resources

ACTIVITY 7.1

Access an archived copy of 'RDA Toolkit Essentials' Webinar at the following link http://www.rdatoolkit.org/essentials. This hour-long webinar takes you through each of the features of the RDA Toolkit.

(Note: It is only necessary to view the most recent webinar as any changes that have been made from previous versions are updated in the latest webinar.)

EXERCISE 7.2

Use all the tabs and features of the RDA Toolkit to answer the following questions.

1. Where in the Toolkit will you find information on abbreviations?

2. Which sections of RDA deal with recording attributes?

3. Which sections of RDA deal with recording relationships?

4. Are the RDA to MARC mappings for bibliographic data and authority data in the same file?

5. Where do you find the link to the MARC Standards in the RDA Toolkit?

RDA Toolkit Help

There is a 'Help' link located on the bottom left hand side of each page of the RDA Toolkit. 'Help' provides detailed information to assist you to:
- log on to the Toolkit
- create profiles where you can set preferences, save searches, and create, save, and share workflows and maps
- navigate the RDA Toolkit, with definitions and descriptions of the buttons and navigational options that are available
- search the RDA Toolkit, with tips and instructions on using the Quick Search and Advanced Search options
- develop user-contributed content, with a space to create, share, copy, and modify your own workflows and mappings.

Searching RDA

There are several ways to find the information you require in the RDA Instruction Set. You can find it by:
- navigating, using the consistent internal structure of the Toolkit to work through the sections and chapters
- searching, using the Quick Search or Advanced Search options.

Both Quick Search and Advanced Search use a web search engine that functions in much the same way as Google.

Detailed instructions on how to use Quick Search and Advanced Search are provided in the 'Help' section of the RDA Toolkit, under the title 'Search Tips'. This section also explains how to save a search, and provides information about how to read the Search Results page.

Sorting Search Results
After you have conducted a search, the Toolkit provides two options for sorting your search results:
- by relevancy
- by document order.

Relevancy
Relevancy is calculated on the number of occurrences of a word within a document—the importance of the document itself in relation to other documents in the RDA Toolkit collection is not factored in. Because of this, the results returned may not be ordered by the information that is most important for your cataloging. When sorting by relevancy, you can access glossary and index entries, but only by clicking the button under your results set—which removes the primary search results from view and only gives you access to the glossary and index entries.

Document Order
Document Order lists search results using the numbering of the RDA Instruction Set, so it follows the structure and logic of the Instruction Set. Glossary and Index entries are also incorporated into the 'Document Order' search results set.

The Toolkit search results use 'Relevance' as its default, but a more practical approach is to change this to 'Document Order' listing.

Helpful Hints When Using the RDA Toolkit
- Procedures for logging onto the Toolkit may involve two steps if you have an institutional account:
    - First log into your institutional account
    - Then log into your personal profile if you have created one.
- If you are timed out of the Toolkit, return to http://www.rdatoolkit.org/ and click on the blue 'Access RDA Toolkit' button to return to the Toolkit.
- As you navigate within the Toolkit, don't use the browser's 'Back' and 'Forward' buttons.
- When searching, remember to clear your previous search.
- In Advanced Search, don't limit yourself too much by searching too narrowly or by using too many text filters or instruction types—you may miss some important instructions.

- As you become more proficient at where things are in the RDA Instruction Set, you can search more effectively by using Advanced Search, and only nominating portions of RDA, the Policy Statements, or any other Toolkit documents that you suspect contain the information you need.
- Always check where you are in the Toolkit—be sure you are looking at the RDA Instruction Set (rather than, for example, AACR2 or one of the various policy statements).

EXERCISE 7.3

Use the RDA Toolkit to answer the following questions:

1. Where in RDA Chapter 2 are instructions for recording copyright date?

2. Is 9.2 a core element?

3. Where do you find information about color illustrations? [Hint: navigate to the page if you know the chapter to look for, otherwise do a quick search]

4. Where would you look for instructions on a prominent member of the family?

5. Where would you find the definition for a 'sheet'?

CHAPTER EIGHT
Using the RDA Instruction Set

Introduction
This chapter covers general information about how to use the RDA Instruction Set. Later chapters cover each section of the Instruction Set in detail.

General Approach to Using the RDA Instruction Set
In your early use of RDA, this is a good general approach to the Instruction Set:

1. *Read the introductory information.* Chapter 0 of the RDA Instruction Set is an overview that explains RDA's key features. It gives an idea not only of the practical aspects of RDA (structure, core elements, access points, etc.) but also explains the conceptual models that form the basis of the guidelines.

2. *Choose the Section you require.* The Instruction Set is arranged so that you begin gathering descriptive information at the Manifestation level, because you can do this by looking at the resource in hand. It is a good idea to begin here, and follow the structure of the Instruction Set. First record the attributes of Manifestations and Items (RDA Sections 1–2). Then record the attributes of Works and Expressions in turn (RDA Section 2). Add information about Persons, Families and Corporate Bodies, then subjects (RDA Section 3–4). Finally, record the relationships between and among the FRBR entities (RDA Sections 5–10). As you become more familiar with RDA, you may vary this approach.

3. *Read the General Guidelines chapter for the Section you are working with.* This will give you basic information that applies to that Section. In many cases, the practical information about recording data that is provided in the General Guidelines chapter is not repeated at more detailed levels in subsequent chapters; instead there are links that refer you back to the General Guidelines. So it is useful to be aware of what is in those chapters before you look for specific attributes.

4. *Open each of the Chapters.* Most RDA chapters have subsections dealing with specific aspects of their topic. For example, RDA Chapter 2 has 18 subsections dealing with different attributes; RDA Chapter 3 has 22 subsections on different carriers. You can choose the attribute or aspect you need to describe, and follow its instructions. Don't forget to read the General Guideline for that chapter, before progressing to the specific instructions you want.

5. *Follow all the links in the Instructions.* Initially, it is useful to check all the links you are given, that send you to different parts of the RDA Instruction Set. Some of them will be essential to the data you are recording, others may not be relevant. As you use the Instruction Set more, you will get to know which links need to be checked and which will not be relevant to the resource you are cataloging.

6. *Record the information into your library's preferred cataloging format.* Remember, RDA is a *content* standard, not an *encoding* standard—it tells you what information to gather, but not what order to display it in, or what format to use for coding the data. Most libraries use cataloging software or cataloging databases for presentation purposes. Transfer the information you have gathered using RDA's guidelines into your library's cataloging software or database, using the formats provided.

Additional Aspects of the RDA Instruction Set
Guidelines not Rules
The RDA Instruction Set is a series of guidelines for cataloging, not a set of prescriptive rules. This allows catalogers more flexibility in describing resources, and is consistent with the intention that RDA becomes a cataloging standard for a range of cultural collecting institutions, not just libraries. Therefore, RDA includes *options* for many of its instructions. Library catalogers will have to decide if they intend to implement any options and ensure this is done consistently within their library or within their library sector.

Instructions for Different Types of Resources
The RDA Instruction Set is arranged according to the attributes of the Group entities, rather than by the physical format of the material in hand. Because of this, RDA has been described as 'format-neutral'. This does not mean, however, that it ignores the special characteristics of resources like serials, DVDs, e-resources, websites and other formats. Embedded within many of the RDA Instruction Set chapters are special instructions for different types of resources.

For example,
- RDA Chapter 3.4 provides basic instructions on recording the extent of resources in general, but also provides guidance on how to describe the extent of music, computer formats, three-dimensional forms etc.
- RDA Chapter 6 deals with attributes of Works and Expressions in general, but also with special attributes of musical, legal and religious works.
- RDA Chapter 7 gives guidelines on recording the content of resources, with special instructions about theses, music, film, cartographic resources and other forms of material.

Getting Started with the RDA Instruction Set
Deciding

Before you begin cataloging, it is important to determine broadly what you are cataloging. Is your description about a monograph, a serial, or some other type of resource? Is your description about a whole resource (a book, or journal run, or DVD), a part of a resource like one volume of a set (or part of a part), or the whole *and* its parts (like a monograph in series)?

As our collections have grown and become more varied, we are frequently dealing with these different options. So in RDA, the emphasis is on making this decision *first*, and then approaching the rest of your cataloging from this standpoint. The decision about what type of resource you are cataloging is important because it affects other decisions you will be making when you catalog: choice of title proper, who is responsible for the content, etc.

Mode of Issuance decisions

For decisions about what you are cataloging, RDA specifies and defines four different *modes of issuance* (RDA 1.1.3 and RDA 2.13)

- **Single unit**—a resource issued either as a single physical unit (e.g., a single-volume monograph) or as a single logical unit (e.g., a PDF file on the Web).
- **Multipart monograph**—a resource issued in two or more parts that will be completed in a finite number of parts (e.g., three audiocassettes issued as a set).
- **Serial**—a resource issued in successive parts, usually having numbering, that has no predetermined conclusion (e.g., a periodical, a newspaper).
- **Integrating resource**—a resource that is added to or changed by means of updates that are integrated into the whole and cannot be easily separated out (e.g., a loose-leaf manual that is updated with replacement pages, or a website that is updated continuously).

Throughout the RDA Instruction Set, special instructions are given for how to deal with resources issued in these different modes of issuance. For example, RDA 1.6 indicates when new cataloging descriptions are required if there are changes in the various modes of issuance. RDA 2.3.2 provides instructions on how to record changes in the title proper for different modes of issuance: multipart monographs, serials, and integrating resources.

Type of Description decisions

For decisions about how you will describe a resource, RDA specifies and defines three different *types of description* (RDA1.1.4 and RDA 1.5)

- **Comprehensive description**—describes the resource as a whole (e.g., a monograph, a kit, a collection).
- **Analytical description**—describes a part of a larger resource (e.g., a single volume of a set, an item in a series).
- **Hierarchical description**—combines a comprehensive description of the whole resource with analytical descriptions of one or more of its parts; also known as 'multilevel descriptions'.

The following example illustrates the various types of descriptions:

 Imagine your library owns a collection of sketches made around Paris by a single artist. Each sketch is in a cardboard frame. All the sketches have the artist's name and the year embossed on the cardboard frame. Some of the sketches have the words 'Paris Buildings' added to the right-hand corner of their frames.

- One catalog record for the whole collection, providing information about the collection as a single unit (e.g., a general title, creator, size/s of sketches) would be a **comprehensive** description
- A separate catalog record for each sketch, or for selected sketches, would be an **analytical** description
- A catalog record for the whole collection, that included additional bibliographic details for the 'Paris Buildings' subset on the catalog record, would be a **hierarchical** description. Libraries don't use this type of description as often as they did in the past—automated cataloging systems have made it easier to 'copy and paste' details that are common to the whole collection into individual records, so separate analytical descriptions are now preferred. However, hierarchical descriptions are still used to highlight parts of formed collections like manuscript or archive collections.

 EXERCISE 8.1

For each of these resources, indicate the:
a) mode of issuance
b) type of description

1. *Folk music journal.* London : The English Folk Dance and Song Society 1965–

   a) _____

   b) _____

2. *Bollywood and beyond* / edited by Rachel Dwyer. [Volume 1 of 4 volume set titled *Bollywood : critical concepts in media and cultural studies* / edited by Rachel Dwyer.] Milton, Abingdon, Oxon : Routledge, 2015.

   a) _____

   b) _____

3. *A Guide to the labeling of soft drink products* / prepared by the National Soft Drink Association. Washington, D.C. : National Soft Drink Association., 1982. 1 volume (loose-leaf) ; 28 cm

   a) _____

   b) _____

4. *The Hunger Games.* West Hollywood, Cal : Color Force, 2012. (This is a DVD.)

   a) _____

   b) _____

5. Willingham, Bill. *March of the wooden soldiers.* New York : DC Comics, 2004.

   a) _____

   b) _____

6. *The official Bruce Springsteen website.* [Colts Neck, NJ] : Thrill Hill Productions, Inc, ©2014. Title from title screen (viewed on 24 October 2014). Mode of access: Internet via World Wide Web. At: http://brucespringsteen.net/.

   a) _____

   b) _____

7. *Biodiversity in Aotearoa : walking the talk* / Anne Nicolson and Greenpeace. Auckland : Greenpeace New Zealand, 1997. 1 videocassette (35 minutes) + 1 computer disk (3 ¾ inches) + 1 booklet (42 leaves : illustrations, maps ; 30 cm) ; in container.

   a) _____

   b) _____

Identifying

RDA allows catalogers more flexibility in choosing where they find the information they use in their bibliographic descriptions ('preferred sources of information'). The resource itself is a preferred source for information, and in some cases packaging around the resource, or information in reference works or catalogs, can also be used.

Different sources of information can be used for different types of resources. RDA 2.2 provides guidance on general sources of information that can be used by different categories of resources, and how to record information from other sources (usually with square brackets or coding).

In addition, each attribute in the RDA Instruction Set has specific sources of information that can be used for that attribute. These are listed as part of the chapter subsection covering basic instructions for recording that attribute. For example, RDA 2.4.2.2 lists sources of information that can be used for statements of responsibility relating to a title proper.

 New terminology: *AACR2's 'Chief source of information' is now RDA's 'Preferred source(s) of information'. This reflects RDA's focus as guidelines, not rules.*

Recording

RDA provides instructions on all the elements (i.e., attributes) that can be described in a bibliographic record, and indicates which of these are core (i.e., mandatory if available).

Transcribing and recording (RDA 1.7)
RDA makes a distinction between 'transcribing' and 'recording':

- **Transcribe**—copy as you see the item on the resource (including errors). Many Manifestation instructions are to 'transcribe'.

  However, many elements (e.g., names, title, editions, notes, etc.) are capitalized according to Appendix A, even for 'transcribed' items.

- **Record**—use the information found on the resource or in another source, but you may adjust the information slightly if required for readability or presentation purposes.

 **EXERCISE 8.2**

Find the RDA instruction for dealing with the following. Indicate whether you can transcribe or record the information:

Topic	Instruction Number	Transcribe or record?
1. Edition statement		
2. Inaccuracies		
3. Terms of availability		
4. Production statement		
5. Title proper		
6. Numbering within series		
7. Numbering of serials		
8. Title proper of series		
9. Punctuation		
10. Chronograms		

An RDA–Compliant Catalog Record

Here is an outline of an RDA–compliant record, showing the core elements and using ISBD punctuation:

> Preferred name for the person, family or corporate body.
> Title proper / first statement of responsibility. – Edition statement. – Numbering of serials (for journals) or Scale (for cartographic items). – Place of publication : publisher, date of publication and/or copyright date. - Extent of resource : other physical details ; dimensions. - (Title proper of series; numbering within the series. Title of subseries; numbering within subseries). – Identifier
> [New concepts: Content Type; Media Type, Carrier Type]
> Authorized access points for authors, titles, series and subjects.

Here is the same RDA–compliant outline, shown in a MARC record format:

RDA element (RDA number)	MARC field name	MARC field & subfield
Identifier (RDA 2.15)	ISBN	020 ## $a
Preferred Name for the Person (RDA 9.2.2)	Main entry—personal name	100 1# $a, $d, $e
Title proper (RDA 2.3.2) / Statement of responsibility (RDA 2.4.2)	Title statement / Statement of responsibility	245 10 $a / $c
Edition statement (RDA 2.5)	Edition	250 ## $a
Copyright date (RDA 2.11) *	Copyright date	264 #4 $c ©
Place of publication (RDA 2.8.2) : Publisher (RDA 2.8.4), Date of publication (RDA 2.8.6)	Place of publication : Publisher, Date of publication	264 ## $a : $b, $c
Extent (RDA 3.4.5) : Other physical details (RDA 3.6 to 3.9, 3.11, 3.14 to 3.17) ; Dimensions (RDA 3.5)	Physical description	300 ## $a : $b ; $c
Content type (RDA 6.9)	Content type	336 ## $a $2rdacontent
Media type (RDA 3.2)	Media type	337 ## $a $2rdamedia
Carrier type (RDA 3.3)	Carrier type	338 ## $a $2rdacarrier
Series (RDA 2.12) ; Numbering within series or subseries (RDA 2.12.9, 2.12.17)	Series statement ; Volume/sequential designation	490 0# $a ; $v
Subject access fields (RDA Section 4)	Subject headings	6XX $a
Other authorized access points— (various RDA chapters)	Added entries	7XX $a

*This is not a core element, however some national institutions, including the Library of Congress, require the copyright date to be included in a record when it is known.

Compare this RDA–compliant record with the outline of an AACR2–compliant record on page 34 of this workbook. You will notice that although there are differences in the amount of information making up a core AACR2 vs RDA record, many of the elements in an AACR2 record have been kept in RDA–compliant records. RDA–compliant records require less 'core' information in the title and series areas, and in some cases the terminology used for the element has changed. RDA–compliant records also contain some new information regarding Content, Carrier and Media Types.

Remember that the RDA–compliant outline and MARC format above are only showing core RDA elements—those that are mandatory to include if they are available for your resource. This doesn't mean you should ignore other information. For example, RDA does not consider subtitles to be core elements, but many libraries include subtitles in their catalog records, particularly to differentiate between resources with general titles like *'Dolls : a collector's guide'*, *'Dolls : a complete bibliography'*, *'Dolls : makers and marks'*, etc.

 Your general rule of thumb should be: **when creating an RDA–compliant record, include all the core elements plus any other elements that are useful to your library clients**.

CHAPTER NINE
Attributes of Manifestations and Items

Introduction
In this chapter we will begin working through the RDA Instruction Set in sequence. The Instruction Set begins with the characteristics, or attributes, of the physical elements at the Manifestation and Item level. It then goes on to describe the attributes of the more conceptual Work and Expression levels.

This workbook focuses on those 'core' elements that are the basic information required for an RDA–compliant bibliographic record. Key points for each core element are noted; however, remember that the Instruction Set also includes guidelines on recording other information that is useful for creating fuller and more descriptive catalog records.

Core Elements for Manifestations
The core elements to be described at the Manifestation level are:
- Title proper
- Statement of responsibility
- Edition
- Numbering of serials
- Publication statement
- Copyright date
- Series statement
- Identifiers
- Carrier type
- Extent
- Dimensions

Key points about how to record these elements are given below, with associated RDA instruction numbers. It is still important, however, to refer to the full text of the instruction when cataloging.

 Refer to the RDA Instruction Set for information about describing both core and non-core elements that you might use in a catalog record.

Title Proper (RDA 2.3.2)
- Transcribe the Title Proper as it appears on the resource or source of information.
  - Numbers and symbols should be recorded as is rather than spelled out.
  - Capitalization can be recorded as is, or by following Appendix A guidelines, depending on your library's policy.
- Don't correct errors for monographs, but

- Do correct errors for serials and integrating resources (to ensure stable titles).
- Don't use [sic] or [i.e. ____].
- Use a variant title to indicate the correct (i.e., error-free) title, or a note to explain the error.

 Heirarchy in organizations (Note: Title misspelled)

RDA records this as:
245 10 $a Heirarchy in organizations
246 1# $i Corrected title: $a Hierarchy in organizations

Previous cataloging, using AACR2 (or earlier rules) would have recorded this as:
245 10 $a Heirarchy [i.e. Hierarchy] in organizations
or as:
245 10 $a Heirarchy [sic] in organizations

Statement of Responsibility for Title Proper (RDA 2.4.2)
- Only Statements of Responsibility for Title Proper are core elements.
- Statements of Responsibility for other forms of title (e.g., parallel titles) are not core.
- There is a difference between a single statement of responsibility that includes multiple creators, and multiple statements of responsibility (e.g., for creators, illustrators and translators in a single resource).
- For the Title Proper, in cases when there are multiple statements of responsibility, only the first recorded Statement of Responsibility is required (but others may be included).
- Transcribe Statement(s) of Responsibility as they appear on the preferred source(s) of information.
- If multiple statements of responsibility are recorded, give them in the order found on the preferred source(s) of information.
- For multiple names in a Statement of Responsibility, either list all the names or use 'first named [and x others]'. Do not use '[et al.]'.

RDA 2.4.1.5	RDA 2.4.1.5 (Option)
100 10 $a Pakoa, Kalo	100 10 $a Pakoa, Kalo
245 10 $a Assessing tropical marine invertebrates : $b a manual for Pacific Island resource managers / $c by Kalo Pakoa, **Kim Friedman, Bradley Moore, Emmanuel Tardy and Ian Bertram.**	245 10 $a Assessing tropical marine invertebrates : $b a manual for Pacific Island resource managers / $c by Kalo Pakoa **[and four others].**

 **EXERCISE 9.1**

Provide the title proper and statement of responsibility for each of the following:

a.

Title proper:

_____

_____

_____

Statement of responsibility:

_____

_____

_____

Cover licensed under Creative Commons CC-BY-ND 3.0 DE

b.

Title proper:

_____

_____

_____

Statement of responsibility:

_____

_____

_____

Copyright 2014 Northfield Publishing.
Reprinted with permission.

c.

Title proper:

_____

_____

_____

Statement of responsibility:

_____

_____

_____

Copyright 2011 Lantern. Reprinted with permission.

d.

Title proper:

_____

_____

_____

Statement of responsibility:

_____

_____

_____

Copyright 2014 Little, Brown and Company. Reprinted with permission.

e.

Schrijverschap in de Belgische belle époque
Een sociaal-culturele geschiedenis
CHRISTOPHE VERBRUGGEN
UITGEVERIJ VANTILT · ACADEMIA PRESS

http://www.doabooks.org/doab?func=fulltext&rid=13274

Title proper:

_____

_____

_____

Statement of responsibility:

_____

_____

_____

f.

Title proper:

_____

_____

_____

Statement of responsibility:

_____

_____

_____

Copyright © 2001 M. G. Myriam Hunink, etc..
Reprinted with the permission of Cambridge University Press.

g.

Title proper:

_____

_____

_____

Statement of responsibility:

_____

_____

_____

Copyright 1994 Naxos Audiobooks.
Reprinted with permission

h.

Title proper:

_____

_____

_____

_____

Statement of responsibility:

_____

_____

_____

Copyright 2009 Churchill Livingstone Elsevier.
Reprinted with permission

CHAPTER NINE   Attributes of Manifestations and Items

Edition Statement (RDA 2.5)
- RDA 2.5.1.1 defines an edition statement; RDA 2.5.1.4 gives examples of edition statements.
- RDA 2.5.2.1 defines 'designations' of editions and how to recognize them.
- Transcribe edition statements as they appear on the resource or preferred source of information.
- Don't use abbreviations unless the resource uses them.
- Don't convert numerals to Romanized form.

Second edition
Interactive version
1st standard ed.

EXERCISE 9.2
Provide the edition statements from the following resources in an acceptable RDA format

1. *Cultural diversity : A primer for the human services.* Fifth edition

2. Updated 8th ed. of *Physical geology* by Charles C. Plummer, David McGeary and Diane H. Carlson

3. McCance and Widdowson's *The composition of foods* 6th ed

4. *World music : a global journey* by Terry E. Miller and Andrew Shahriari. Concise edition

5. *M.Y.O.B. Accounting : user guide* Version 19.1

6. *Introduction to Econometrics* 2nd Revised International Edition

Numbering of Serials (RDA 2.6)

- Both enumeration (numbering, e.g., vol 1, no. 1; Part 1, etc.) and chronological designation (dates, e.g., May 2010, Spring 1994, etc.) of the first and last issue of a serial are core elements.
- Record these if available; otherwise supply the information from other sources if available. Enclose this supplied information in square brackets.
- *Transcribe* words and months as they appear on the resource.
- *Record* numerals, using general guidelines from RDA 1.8. Substitute a slash for a hyphen, as necessary, for clarity.

July/August 2005
4th issue
Vol. 1, no. 1
volume 5, number 3

Production Statement (RDA 2.7)

- Production Statements are only used for unpublished material.
- Only date of production is a core element. Place of production and producer's name are optional.
- If using MARC coding, use the 264 field 'Production, Publication, Distribution, Manufacture and Copyright Notice', with the MARC indicator '0' in the second indicator position 'function of entity'.

Publication Statement (RDA 2.8)

- Publication Statements are used for published material.
- Place of publication, publisher's name and date of publication are core elements.
- *Transcribe* places of publication and publishers' names as they appear. Only include larger jurisdictions if they appear on the source of information or if they are important for identification or access. (RDA 2.8.2—2.8.4)
- Only the first place of publication and the first publisher recorded are required elements, others are optional.

On resource: London – New York – Boston
    264 #1 $a London
or: **264 #1 $a London ; $a New York ; $a Boston**

- If place of publication or publisher can't be determined, record '[Place of publication not identified]' or '[publisher not identified]'. Do not use 's.l.' or 's.n.'

264 #1 $a[Place of publication not identified] :$bJ.J. Wilson Publishing Company, $c[2005]
not: 264 #1 $a s.l. :$bWilson Pub. Co.

- *Record* dates of publication (RDA 2.8.6). If a date of publication cannot be determined, supply an approximate date enclosed in square brackets.
- See RDA 1.9 for details about recording dates supplied by the cataloger.

Recording dates of publication not identified in the resource (i.e., supplied by cataloger from other sources)

Year known, but not listed in resource	264 ... $c [1989]
Either one of two consecutive years	264 ... $c [1988 or 1989]
Probable year	264 ... $c [1989?]
Probable range of years	264 ... $c [between 1986 and 1989?]
Earliest and/or latest possible date known	264 ... $c [not before 30 June, 1989]

- If an approximate date cannot be determined for a single-part resource, record as '[date of publication not identified]'. Use this phrase only as a last resort; prefer even a very broad date.
- These instructions about dates only apply to resources with the mode of issuance 'single unit'. If an approximate date cannot be determined for a multipart monograph, serial or integrating resource, do not record a date of publication at all.
- If using MARC coding, use the 264 field 'Production, Publication, Distribution, Manufacture and Copyright Notice', with the MARC indicator '**1**' in the second indicator position 'function of entity'.

Distribution Statement (RDA 2.9)
- Distribution Statements are used for published material.
- A Distribution Statement is only required if publication details are not available.
    - However, some libraries include both Publication and Distribution Statements for their audiovisual materials.
- If publication details are not available, then place of distribution, distributor's name, and date of distribution are core elements.
- If using MARC coding, use the 264 field 'Production, Publication, Distribution, Manufacture and Copyright Notice', with the MARC indicator '**2**' in the second indicator position 'function of entity'.

Manufacture Statement (RDA 2.10)
- Manufacturing Statements are used for published material.
- Manufacturing Statements are only required if neither publication nor distribution details are available.
- If publication and distribution details are not available, then place of manufacture, manufacturer's name, and date of manufacture are core elements.
- If using MARC coding, use the 264 field 'Production, Publication, Distribution, Manufacture and Copyright Notice', with the MARC indicator '**3**' in the second indicator position 'function of entity'.

Copyright Date (RDA 2.11)
- Copyright Date is used for published material.
- Copyright Date is only core if neither the date of publication nor the date of distribution is identified.
- Use Copyright Date in preference to a date of manufacture if publication and distribution dates are not available.
- Precede the date by either the copyright symbol © or the phonogram symbol ℗, or by the words 'copyright' or 'phonogram copyright' (not 'c' or 'p').
- If the resource has multiple copyright dates for various parts (e.g., text, sound, graphics), record only the latest copyright date.
- If using MARC coding, use the 264 field 'Production, Publication, Distribution, Manufacture and Copyright Notice', with the MARC indicator '**4**' in the second indicator position 'function of entity'. Only use **$c** with this indicator.
- *Note:* Many large libraries, including the Library of Congress, make copyright date a mandatory element, even if other dates are present.

eg   *On resource: Published in 1985, copyright 1970*

    Option 1: RDA–compliant   264 #1 $a ... $b ... $c 1985

    Option 2: LC–compliant   264 #1 $a ... $b ... $c 1985
    264 #4 $c © 1970 (*or* 264 #4 $c copyright 1970)
    (use an additional 264 field, only for copyright)

CHAPTER NINE   Attributes of Manifestations and Items   81

 EXERCISE 9.3
Look at the excerpts from resources provided below. Choose the correct form of MARC transcription for the attributes noted:

1. Book

Soil fertility and fertilizers an introduction to nutrient management John L. Havlin Samuel L. Tisdale Werner L. Nelson James D. Beaton Pearson New Jersey	Pearson Upper Saddle River, NJ Eighth edition 2014 Copyright©2014. ISBN 9780135033739

245 field (Title and statement of responsibility)

_____ 245 10 $a Soil fertility and fertilizers : $b an introduction to nutrient management / $c John L. Havlin ... [et al.].

_____ 245 10 $a Soil fertility and fertilizers : $b an introduction to nutrient management / $c John L. Havlin, Samuel L. Tisdale, Werner L. Nelson, James D. Beaton.

_____ 245 00 $a Soil fertility and fertilizers ... / $c John L. Havlin [and others].

250 field (Edition)

_____ 250 ## $a 8th edition.

_____ 250 ## $a Eighth ed.

_____ 250 ## $a Eighth edition

_____ 250 ## $a 8th ed.

264 field (Publication, distribution)

_____ 264 #1 $a Upper Saddle River, N.J. : $b Pearson, $c 2014.

_____ 264 #1 $a Upper Saddle, New Jersey : $b Pearson, $c 2014.

_____ 264 #1 $a New Jersey : $b Pearson Publishers, $c 2014.

2. Sound Recording on CD

```
Enid Blyton's
The
Magic
Faraway
Tree

ABC Audio    Read by Kate Winslet

Text trademark and copyright © 1943 Hodder and Stoughton Ltd. & © 2012 Hodder and Stoughton Ltd. All rights reserved.

First published in 2004 in Australia. Distributed by Bolinda Publishing under exclusive licence from the Australian Broadcasting Corporation.

3 HOURS 50 MINUTES on 1 MP3 CD

Bolinda Audio                    ABC Audio
Bolinda Publishing Pty Ltd       700 Harris Street
17 Mohr Street, Tullamarine 3043 Ultimo, N.S.W. 2007
Victoria Australia

ISBN 9781743149270
```

245 field (Title and statement of responsibility)

_____ 245 10 $a The magic faraway tree $h [sound recording] / $c Enid Blyton ; read by Kate Winslet.

_____ 245 10 $a The magic faraway tree / $c Enid Blyton ; read by Kate Winslet.

_____ 245 10 $a The magic faraway tree / $c Kate Winslet.

_____ 245 10 $a Enid Blyton's the magic faraway tree / $c Enid Blyton ; read by Kate Winslet.

264 field (Publication, distribution)

_____ 264 #1 $a Ultimo, N.S.W. : $b Australian Broadcasting Commission, $c 2012.

_____ 264 #2 $a Tullamarine, Vic. : $b Bolinda Audio, $c ℗ 2004.

_____ 264 #1 $a Ultimo, N.S.W. : $b ABC Audio, $c 2004.

_____ 264 #1 $a [Place of publication not identified] : $b Hodder and Stoughton, $c 2012.

3. **Poster**

> # CROWNS AND DUCATS
>
> Shakespeare's money and medals
>
>
>
> 19 April—25 November 2012
>
> ## BRITISH MUSEUM

This display looks at the role of coins and medals in Shakespeare's works and his world.

245 field (Title and statement of responsibility)

_____ 245 00 $a Crowns and ducats $h [picture] : $b Shakespeare's money and medals.

_____ 245 00 $a Crowns and ducats : $b Shakespeare's money and medals.

_____ 245 00 $a Crowns and ducats : $b Shakespeare's money and medals: $b this display looks at the role of coins and medals in Shakespeare's works and his world.

264 field (Publication, distribution)

_____ 264 #1 $a [London? : $b s.n., $c 2012?]

_____ 264 #1 $a [London] : $b British Museum, $c 2012

_____ 264 #1 $a [London : $b publisher unknown, $c 2012?]

_____ 264 #1 $a [London?] : $b [publisher not identified] , $c [2012?]

Series Statement (RDA 2.12)
- Information about the series can be taken from anywhere in the resource.
- Title proper of series, numbering within series, title proper of subseries and numbering within subseries are core elements.

    eg *Issues in geology ; number 26. Contributions to vulcanology ; no. 4*

- Other information about Series Statements is optional.
- A series title is usually found on the title page, a separate series title page, or the cover of a resource.
- Some series are numbered. That is, each item in the series has a unique number.
- A monograph in series can have an individual ISBN and an ISSN for the series.
- A statement of responsibility is added to the series title where it is needed to distinguish one series from another, for example when a series has a common title like *Occasional papers* or *Research reports*.
- In case of doubt about whether a series title is a subseries or a separate series, treat it as a separate series.

Identifier for the Manifestation (RDA 2.15)
- An Identifier is a standard number or character set that is widely recognized as a means of uniquely identifying a resource.
- Recording one Identifier is core; noting additional Identifiers is optional.
- RDA prefers the use of international schemes (ISBN, ISSN, ISMN, URN), but other Identifiers can also be used.
    - The MARC 024 field is used for Identifiers that cannot be accommodated in other MARC fields.
- *Note:* a URL is not considered a stable Identifier, URNs are preferred.
    - Recording URLs is covered at RDA 4.6.
- When describing a set with an Identifier for the whole as well as for individual parts, it is only necessary to record the Identifier for the whole.
    - The practice of recording both an ISBN for a set or collection and separate ISBNs for each of the parts is now an optional addition.
- If there is a specified display format for the Identifier for the manifestation (e.g., ISBN, ISSN, URN), record it using that format.

    eg ISBN 978–1921844–06–5 *or 9781921844065 (if coding with MARC)*
    ISSN 0363–0277
    ISMN M–705015–05–8 *or M705015058 (if coding with MARC)*
    doi 10.1021/ja016126t
    European Commission: CA–23–99–031–EN–C

REVISION QUIZ 9.4

Use the following questions to revise your understanding of attributes of Manifestations. You do not need to write down the answers.

1. What is a core element? Name two core elements at the Manifestation level.

2. What type of publication statement would you use for each of the following resources?
    a) a music CD distributed by EMI
    b) an unpublished manuscript
    c) a painting created by an artist
    d) a book of poems published in 2013
    e) an electronic version of a printed screenplay
    f) an oral history recorded by the speaker at home, no additional copies were made or distributed

3. Should you use a URL as an Identifier for an online Manifestation? Why or why not?

CHAPTER TEN
Further Attributes of Manifestations and Items

Introduction
Chapters 3 and 4 of the RDA Instruction Set continue to describe characteristics of Manifestations and Items. Key points for core elements are discussed below, as well as important but non-core attributes and the use of notes.

RDA Chapter 3
Chapter 3 of the RDA Instruction Set provides guidelines on recording the attributes of the carrier of the resource. This is where you will find instructions on describing the physical characteristics of the packaging of a resource and any information that is contained in, or stored on, the packaging. The elements in this chapter can be used to distinguish between resources with similar characteristics.

These attributes are recorded in various MARC fields. Some attributes only pertain to particular types of resources, e.g., digital file characteristics. However, the following key attributes apply to most resources:
- 337 – Media Type
- 338 – Carrier Type
- 300 $a – Extent
- 300 $c – Dimensions

Media Type (RDA 3.2)
- Media Type is not a core element according to RDA, but it has been adopted as core by the Library of Congress, the National Library of Australia, and the German speaking libraries that are using RDA.
- Media Type is concerned with the physical characteristics of the resource.
- It is used in conjunction with Carrier Type.
- Media Type describes the type of device needed to view, play or run the resource, e.g., audio, video, computer, unmediated (the terminology used for print material) etc.
- RDA provides a controlled list of terms, with definitions, to record Media Type. (RDA 3.2.1.3, Table 3.1)
- Use as many terms as are appropriate to describe the Media Type (or there is an option to use just the predominant media).
- If none of the terms in the controlled list apply, record the Media Type as 'other'.
- MARC coding has a new field for Media Type, field **337**. Use this in conjunction with 007 field, position 00.
- MARC requires the use of '**$2rdamedia**' as a subfield in field 337, to show that the term used in this field has been taken from a controlled vocabulary—the 'rdamedia' list of controlled terms.

- Some libraries also use the 337 MARC $b subfield. This subfield is found at http://www.loc.gov/standards/valuelist/rdamedia.html and contains 'Media Type' codes for the information provided in MARC 337 $a.

        337 ## $a video $2 rdamedia
Or *337 ## $a video $b v $2 rdamedia*

        337 ## $a unmediated $2 rdamedia
Or *337 ## $a unmediated $b n $2 rdamedia*

Carrier Type (RDA 3.3)
- Carrier Type is a core element.
- This attribute is concerned with the physical characteristics of the resource.
- It is used in conjunction with Media Type and Extent.
- Carrier Type describes the storage medium that houses the resource, e.g., audio disc, slide, volume, online resource, etc.
- RDA provides a controlled list of terms to record Carrier Type. (RDA 3.3.1.3)
- Use as many terms as are applicable to describe the Carrier Type (or there is an option to use just the predominant carrier).
- If none of the terms in the controlled list apply, record the Carrier Type as 'other'
- MARC coding has a new field for Carrier Type, field **338**. Use this in conjunction with 007 field, position 01.
- MARC requires the use of '**$2rdacarrier**' as a subfield in field 338, to show that the term used in this field has been taken from a controlled vocabulary—the 'rdacarrier' list of controlled terms.
- Some libraries also use the 338 MARC $b subfield. This subfield is found at http://www.loc.gov/standards/valuelist/rdacarrier.html and contains 'Carrier Type' codes for the information provided in MARC 338 $a.
- A word of warning—do not confuse 'Carrier Type' with 'Extent'.

        338 ## $a audio disc $2 rdacarrier
Or *338 ## $a videodisc $b vd $2 rdacarrier*

        338 ## $a volume $2 rdacarrier
Or *338 ## $a unmediated $b nc $2 rdacarrier*

CHAPTER TEN   Further Attributes of Manifestations and Items   89

 EXERCISE 10.1
Use the correct MARC fields to record media and carrier types for the following resources:

1. The Chronicles of Narnia by C. S. Lewis : read by an all-star cast of England's brightest talent from the stage and screen.Audio book on CD..

   337 $a _____$2 _____

   338 $a _____$2 _____

Copyright 2014 Tyndale House Publishers. Reprinted with permission.

2. ard copy aerial photograph of Franjo Tudjman Bridge, Dubrovnik, Croatia.

   337 $a _____ $2 _____

   338 $a _____ $2 _____

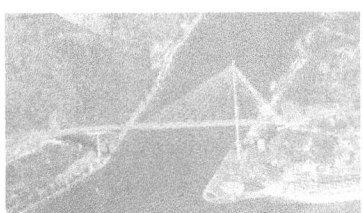

http://commons.wikimedia.org/wiki/File: Aerial_photograph_of_Franjo_Tudjman_Bridge.jpg

3. Hard copy map of Petrogradsky Island, St Petersburg, Russia.

   337 $a _____$2 _____

   338 $a _____$2 _____

http://commons.wikimedia.org/wiki/File: Map_Petrogradsky_Island.png

4. Hard copy sheet music for the song *Hiawatha (His Song to Minnehaha)* words by James O'Dea and music by Neil Moret. Detroit : Whitney-Warner Publishing Company, 1903.

   337 $a _____$2 _____

   338 $a _____$2 _____

http://commons.wikimedia.org/wiki/File: Hiawatha1903.png

90   LEARN CATALOGING THE RDA WAY

5. *The Guardian* Charlottetown newspaper—copy on microfiche.

   337 $a _____ $2 _____

   338 $a _____ $2 _____

6. *The Guardian* Charlottetown newspaper—paper copy.

   337 $a _____ $2 _____

   338 $a _____ $2 _____

Copyright 2014
Transcontinental Media/Charlottetown Guardian.
Reprinted with permission..

7. *The Guardian* Charlottetown online newspaper.

   337 $a _____ $2 _____

   338 $a _____ $2 _____

8. The David Vases (Yuan dynasty, 1351 AD) in Room 95, Chinese ceramics, British Museum (physical object).

   337 $a _____ $2 _____

   338 $a _____ $2 _____

http://commons.wikimedia.org/wiki/File:
Room_95_David_Vases_6747.JPG

Extent (RDA 3.4)
- Extent is a core element, but *only* if the resource is complete, or the total extent is known.
- Extent describes the number and types of units (e.g., a volume) and/or subunits (e.g., a page of a volume) making up the resource.
- In MARC coding, this information is found in the field **300 $a.**
- Use in conjunction with Carrier Type, by giving the number of units and a term from the Carrier Type list, e.g., '2 film reels' or 'approximately 100 slides'.
- If none of the terms in the Carrier Type list apply, use a term in common usage, e.g., '1 USB flash drive' to describe the extent of the resource.
- If the units cannot be named concisely, RDA provides an option to record the units as '*x* various pieces'.

- Specific instructions are given in the RDA Instruction Set for recording the extent of different types of resources and different Carrier Types, and for recording subunits.
- Note that specific instructions for 'Extent of *Text*' appear towards the end of the section, at RDA 3.4.5. This is because instructions are listed according to their Content Type and are filed in alphabetical order.
- When recording 'Extent' information:
  o do not use abbreviations (i.e., use 'pages' and 'volumes', not 'pp.' and 'vols.') unless they are abbreviated that way on the resource itself
  o use 'approximately' (not 'ca.') and 'that is' (not 'i.e.')
  o use 'unnumbered' rather than square brackets enclosing the numeral for unnumbered pages of text.

300 ## $a 254 pages
300 ## $a 1 volume (loose leaf)
300 ## $a xvi, 15 unnumbered pages, 259 pages

Dimensions (RDA 3.5)
- This attribute is not core, but it is an integral part of a MARC record.
- In MARC coding, this is the field **300 $c.**
- The Dimensions attribute provides measurements (height, width, depth, length, gauge, diameter as appropriate) of the carrier and/or container of the resource.
- All dimensions are recorded in metric (although Library of Congress will still use 'inches' for computer discs).
- Note that 'm', 'cm', and 'mm' are not spelled out, as they are considered symbols not abbreviations.
- Record dimensions to the next whole centimeter up (e.g., if the height of a resource measures 17.2 centimeters, record it as '18 cm') unless particular types of material instruct otherwise.
- Detailed instructions are given at RDA 3.5.1.4 for how to measure and record various types of materials (flipcharts, discs, sheets, three dimensional forms, etc.). These carriers are listed in alphabetical order, not in any priority order.
  o Note that different measurements are taken for different types of material, for example print resources measure height and width, while reels and cassettes measure diameter and gauge (i.e., width) of the film or tape.
- Separate instructions are given for cartographic materials (RDA 3.5.2) and for still images (RDA 3.5.3).
- Instructions for volumes (i.e., printed texts) are at RDA 3.5.1.4.14.

Standard text volume:	300 ## $a ... $b ... $c 22 cm
Volume <10 cm, use mm:	300 ## $a ... $b ... $c 75 mm
Film and videotape reels:	300 ## $a ... $b ... $c 18 cm, 25.4 mm
Audiocassettes:	300 ## $a ... $b ... $c 10 x 7 cm, 4mm tape
Globes:	300 ## $a ... $b ... $c 18 cm in diameter

EXERCISE 10.2
*Look at the information provided for this resource. Indicate which of the choices below would satisfy the **minimum** requirement for original cataloging, reflecting core requirements.*

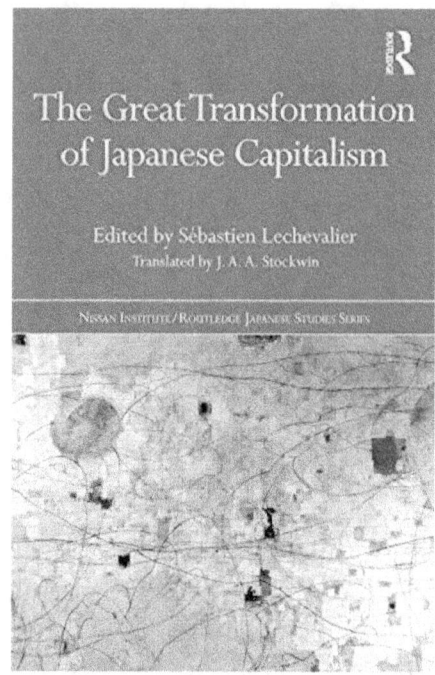

Title page verso information:

First published in French in 2011 as
La grande transformation du capitalism japonais (1980–2010)
By Presses de Sciences Po.

Published 2014
By Routledge
2 Park Square, Milton Park, Abingdon, Oxon OX14 4RN
And by Routledge
711 Third Avenue, New York, NY 10017
© 2014 Sébastien Lechevalier

Other information:
35 introductory pages, last numbered page = 198;
height = 24½ cm

245 field

_____ 245 $a Grande transformation du capitalisme japonais (1980–2010).

_____ 245 $a The great transformation of Japanese capitalism / $c edited by Sébastien Lechevalier ; translated by J. A. A. Stockwin.

_____ 245 $a The Great Transformation of Japanese Capitalism / $c edited by Sébastien Lechevalier.

_____ 245 $a The great transformation of Japanese capitalism / $c edited by Sébastien Lechevalier.

264 field

_____ 264 #1 $a [Paris] : $b Presses de Sciences Po., $c 2011.

_____ 264 #1 $a New York : $b Routledge, $c 2014.

_____ 264 #1 $a Abingdon : $b Routledge, $c 2014.

_____ two 264 fields:
    264 #1 $a Abingdon : $b Routledge, $c 2014.
    264 #4 $c copyright 2014.

300 field

_____ 300 $a 198 p. ; $c 25 cm.

_____ 300 $a xxxv, 198 pages ; $c 25 cm.

_____ 300 $a xxxv, 198 pages ; $c 24½ cm.

_____ 300 $a pages ; $c cm.

Non–core Physical Characteristics (RDA Chapter 3.6 onwards)

In addition to the core elements noted above, RDA Chapter 3 provides extensive instructions on recording other physical characteristics.

These non-core physical characteristics include:
- sound characteristics, such as type of recording, recording medium, playing speed, groove characteristics, track configuration, tape configuration, configuration of playback channels, and special playback characteristics
- video characteristics, such as video format, broadcast standard, resolution, and bandwidth
- equipment or system requirements
- item-specific information, e.g., condition, imperfect holdings of serials.

RDA's instructions for recording non-core physical characteristics can be used as required:
- in describing 'Extent', or
- in the MARC 300 $b field, or
- in the MARC 007 field, or
- as notes in your catalog record.

Note that non-core physical characteristics do **not** include illustrations. Even though MARC 300 $b covers illustrations, these are not mentioned in RDA Chapter 3, because illustrations are an attribute of an Expression, not of a Manifestation. Therefore they are dealt with in Chapter 7 of the RDA Instruction Set (RDA 7.15, 'Illustrative Content').

Notes (Various Chapters)

You may be aware that in AACR2, 'notes' were contained in a separate area of description, and served two purposes: to expand on information recorded in other areas of the catalog record and to provide information that didn't fit into the other areas. In MARC, the 5XX tags are used to record note information.

The expanded and more precise nature of elements in RDA means that many things AACR2 instructed us to record as notes now have their own element. 'Notes' instructions in RDA largely serve as a means of recording extra information about these elements (e.g., source of title, changes in imprint information, complications with serial numbering, etc.). This means there are fewer generic notes, and less to put into the MARC 500 field.

The instructions on notes are within the chapters for the elements to which they relate, e.g.,
- RDA 2.17 deals with making notes relating to Manifestations
- RDA 2.21 deals with making notes relating to Items
- RDA 7.29 deals with making notes relating to Expressions
- RDA 2.14.1.4 deals with making notes about changes in frequency of a resource
- RDA 3.21 and 3.22 deals with making notes relating to describing Carriers
- RDA 5.9 deals with making cataloger's notes.

In summary:
- Many AACR2 'notes' are now RDA 'elements' e.g.,
  - RDA Chapter 4 (Acquisition and Access)
  - RDA Chapter 7 (Describing Content)
- Some notes are still recorded in MARC 5XX.
- Notes vs details: notes information is at the end of relevant chapters of the RDA Instruction Set; 'details' that used to be notes are interspersed throughout the RDA instructions.

Core Elements for Items

There are no core elements in the RDA Instruction Set at the Item level, but libraries often include item information in their cataloging. For example, holdings statements or notes about the condition of an item provide information specific to the individual copy that is held in your library.

Acquisition and Access Information (RDA Chapter 4)

The attributes covered in this chapter are concerned with access to and acquisition of resources, at both the Manifestation and Item level. They cover such things as terms of availability, holdings, access conditions, and URLs for Internet resources.

There are no core elements in RDA Chapter 4. However, details like:
- contact information for resources that are not available through commercial suppliers (RDA 4.3)
- access conditions (e.g., 'not for loan') for individual items in a library collection (RDA 4.4)
- URLs for website resources (RDA 4.6)

may be important information to record for particular resources. Therefore, this chapter should not be overlooked when adding additional information to your catalog record.

CHAPTER TEN   Further Attributes of Manifestations and Items   95

 EXERCISE 10.3
Record the Manifestation attributes of the resource below, using the template provided. MARC codes are provided if you wish to add them to your answers.

© Copyright Datascape Information Pty Ltd 1994

This work is copyright. Apart from any use as permitted under the *Copyright Act 1968*, no part may be reproduced by any process without prior written permission from the publishers. Requests and inquiries concerning reproduction and rights should be addressed to Datascape Information Pty Ltd, GPO Box 1870, Canberra ACT 2601.

ISBN 0- 646-21833-6

Printed by Panther Publishing & Printing, Fyshwick ACT

This resource has viii preliminary pages plus 140 pages, solely of text. It is 14.3 cm wide and 20.5 cm high. It lists bookshops and shop descriptions by region, and includes a names index and a comprehensive subject index.

Foreword

It is hard to surpass the delight of finding the perfect book—whether it be for a gift, special project, or just a plain good read. Part of the excitement comes from browsing through bookshops and discovering the treasures they have to offer. Every bookshop is different. Each has its own flair and style and, to the dedicated browser, none of them are dull!

It is our pleasure to introduce you to the range of bookshops in Canberra and Queanbeyan, and to share with you a number of other sources where you may find books of interest. This guide takes you through bookstores, specialty shops, government departments and warehouse outlets, highlighting the features and specialities of each.

The guide was produced by Datascape Information, a Canberra company which specialises in information databases and information services, to celebrate our tenth year in business. We would like to acknowledge the enthusiastic contributions to this project by Fiona Bray and Cath Murphy, who visited the book sources and laboured over descriptions for each; Caitlin McCoull and Lynn Farkas, who helped edit the entries and compiled the subject index; and Jim Gillespie, who was responsible for the database programming, book design and production of the guide.

Thanks are extended to those colleagues who encouraged us with their support and interest. And a special thanks is due to the shop managers in Canberra and Queanbeyan, who answered our questions and allowed us to browse their bookshelves.

We hope *Browsing Canberra's Bookshops* gives you as much pleasure in its use as we had in its compilation. If you have an additional book source you would like to share, please let us know. Happy browsing!

Lynn Farkas, Director
Datascape Information Pty Ltd

November 1994

RDA number	RDA element	MARC field	Data Recorded
1.7 2.3.1.4 2.3.2	General guidelines Recording titles Title proper	245 __ $a	
2.3.4	Other title information	245 $b	
2.4.2	Statement of responsibility	245 $c	
2.5	Edition statement	250 $a	
2.8.1.4, 2.8.2.3	Place of publication	264 __ $a	
2.8.4	Publisher	264 $b	
2.8.6	Date of publication	264 $c	
2.11	Copyright date	264 04 $c	
2.15	Identifier	020 $a	
3.2	Media type	337 $a $2	
3.3	Carrier type	338 $a $2	
3.4.5	Extent	300 $a	
3.5	Dimensions	300 $c	

CHAPTER ELEVEN
Attributes of Works and Expressions

Introduction
Section 2 of RDA deals with how to record the attributes, or characteristics, of the remaining Group One entities: Works and Expressions.

RDA Section 2
- RDA Section 2 is divided into:
    - instructions for *identifying* Works and Expressions (such as title, date and form) in RDA Chapter 6; and
    - instructions for *describing the characteristics* of Works and Expressions, (such as nature of the content, intended audience, language, etc.) in RDA Chapter 7.

- In RDA Chapter 6:
    - **6.2 to 6.8** deal with how to identify **Works**
    - **6.9 to 6. 13** deal with how to identify **Expressions**
    - **6.14 to 6.26** deal with particular types of Works, namely musical works, legal works and religious works
    - **6.1 to 6.26** give instructions on what identifying information about Works and Expressions should be recorded and how to record it
    - **6.27 to 6.31** describe how to take the information that was recorded above and use it to construct an authorized access point for the Work or Expression.

- For Works and Expressions, the core elements are largely those that *identify* Works and Expressions, and are divided into those that are *always* core and those that are only core if they are needed to distinguish the Work or Expression from another similar Work or Expression.

- RDA Section 2 covers not only physical attributes of Works and Expressions, but also the authorized access points for Works and Expressions. It provides instructions on how to find and describe information that will eventually be used in authority records. These aspects of RDA Section 2 are covered in Chapters Twelve and Thirteen of this workbook.

- Dealing with 'Works' and 'Expressions' also involves the *creators of a Work* and the *contributors to an Expression*. Therefore, you will need to consult the related instructions in RDA Chapter 19, 'Persons, Families, and Corporate Bodies Associated with a Work,' and RDA Chapter 20, 'Persons, Families, and Corporate Bodies Associated with an Expression.'

Core Elements for Works

There are only two core elements at the Work level: Preferred Title for the Work, and Identifier for the Work.

RDA makes a distinction between the Preferred Title for the *Work*, and the Title or Title Proper at the *Manifestation* level. When a resource has only been produced with one manifestation, its title proper will usually be the same as the Preferred Title at the Work level. When there are many manifestations, however, we need some way to group the various publications so that a user will find them all together. In these cases, we choose a title that is either:
 a) in common use or the title by which the Work is commonly known, like 'Bible', or
 b) the first published title of the resource, or
 c) the title in a particular language (perhaps the language of publication, or the cataloger's language).

We call this title the 'Preferred Title for the Work'. A similar but not exactly equivalent concept was known as a **uniform title** in AACR2.

In our current cataloging, if the Preferred Title of a Work differs from the Title Proper of a particular manifestation, the catalog record will include both titles:
- the Title Proper as part of the descriptive catalog record, and
- the Preferred Title for the Work as an authorized access point.

(This may change in future, if we have separate records at the Work, Expression, Manifestation and Item levels.)

Preferred Titles of a Work are used for a monograph when:
1. The Work has appeared under different titles proper, for example:
    - J. K. Rowling's *Harry Potter and the philosopher's stone* was released in the United States as *Harry Potter and the sorcerer's stone* and in France as *Harry Potter à l'école des sorciers* (Harry Potter at the School of Wizards)
2. The Work is translated into different languages. Preferred Titles, therefore, group all translations with the original Work, for example:
    - *The threepenny opera* is the English translation of Bertolt Brecht's *Die Dreigroschenoper*
3. The Work is commonly known as something different from the wording of the Title Proper, for example:
    - Shakespeare's *Macbeth* is actually titled *The tragedie of Macbeth* in the First Folio of his works, published in 1623.

Title of the Work (RDA 6.2)
- Preferred Titles of the Work are core elements, variant titles are not core.
- Preferred Title is roughly equivalent to the AACR2 concept of 'uniform title'.
- RDA has specific instructions on abbreviations, capitalization, initial articles, etc. for titles of Works. (RDA 6.2.1.3—6.2.1.9)
- RDA has specific instructions for recording details of Preferred Titles for special types of Works (links from RDA 6.2.2.8), parts of Works (RDA 6.2.2.9), and compilations of Works (RDA 6.2.2.10).

Identifier for the Work (RDA 6.8)
- The Identifier for the Work is a character string uniquely associated with a Work, for example LC Control number, NLA permalink, ISWC (International Standard Musical Work Code).
- This attribute has been included in RDA for future development. At present there are limited Identifiers available at the Work level, for example the ISWC (International Standard Musical Work Code). It is expected that other Work level Identifiers will be developed as RDA cataloging progresses. Until that time, in most cases you will not be able to include a separate Identifier for the Work.
- Note that the ISSN or ISBN cannot be used as an Identifier at the Work level—they are identifiers for specific Manifestations. For example, the ISBN for the Macmillan Publishing Company's edition of *The great Gatsby* is different from the ISBN for the Arion Press edition.

'Core if Necessary' Elements of Works (RDA 6.3—6.6)
These are additional attributes that can be used if required to differentiate a Work from another Work with the same title. When needed, all of these elements are core:
- form (terms like 'play', 'motion picture', 'computer file', etc. taken from a library's preferred list. RDA does not provide a specific list, but gives examples of possible terms at RDA 6.3.1.3)
- date (earliest date associated with a Work, e.g., date it was first published)
- place of origin (country or territory where the Work originated)
- other distinguishing characteristics of Works.

The 'core if necessary' elements are usually added in brackets after the Preferred Title for the Work. This normally occurs when the Preferred Title is used as an authorized access point.

 Pride and Prejudice (Motion picture)

Core Elements for Expressions
Content type (RDA 6.9)
- Content Type is the form of communication by which the content is expressed, e.g., spoken word, still image, text, etc.
- RDA provides a controlled list of terms, with definitions, to record Content Type (RDA 6.9.1.3, Table 6.1).
- Use as many terms as are appropriate to describe the Content Type (or there is an option to use just the predominant Content Type).
- If none of the terms in the controlled list apply, record the Content Type as 'other'.
- MARC coding has a new field for Content Type, field **336**. Use this in conjunction with Leader position 06.
- MARC requires the use of '**$2rdacontent**' as a subfield in field 336, to show that the term used in this field has been taken from a controlled vocabulary—the 'rdacontent' list of controlled terms.

- Some libraries also use the 336 MARC $b subfield. This subfield is found at http://www.loc.gov/standards/valuelist/rdacontent.html and contains Content Type codes for the information provided in MARC 336 $a.
- *Note:* 'Content Type' is different from 'Content'. 'Content' covers physical size, dimensions, etc. and is dealt with in RDA Chapter 7 (see RDA 7.0—7.29).

EXERCISE 11.1

You have already filled in the fields for media and carrier types for the following resources. Now add the Content Type.

1. The Chronicles of Narnia by C. S. Lewis : read by an all-star cast of England's brightest talent from the stage and screen. Audio book on CD.

    336 ## $a _____ $2 _____

    337 ## $a audio $2 rdamedia

    338 ## $a audio disc $2 rdacarrier

Copyright 2014 Tyndale House Publishers. Reprinted with permission.

2. Aerial photograph of Franjo Tudjman Bridge, Dubrovnik, Croatia.

    336 ## $a _____ $2_____

    337 ## $a unmediated $2 rdamedia

    338 ## $a sheet $2 rdacarrier

http://commons.wikimedia.org/wiki/File:
Aerial_photograph_of_Franjo_Tudjman_Bridge.jpg

3. Hard copy map of Petrogradsky Island, St Petersburg, Russia.

    336 ## $a _____ $2 _____

    337 ## $a unmediated $2 rdamedia

    338 ## $a sheet $2 rdacarrier

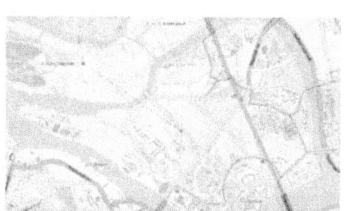

http://commons.wikimedia.org/wiki/File:
Map_Petrogradsky_Island.png

CHAPTER ELEVEN   Attributes of Works and Expressions   103

4. Hard copy sheet music for the song Hiawatha (His Song to Minnehaha) words by James O'Dea and music by Neil Moret. Detroit : Whitney-Warner Publishing Company, 1903.

   336 ## $a _____ $2 _____

   337 ## $a unmediated $2 rdamedia
   338 ## $a volume $2 rdacarrier

   http://commons.wikimedia.org/wiki/File:
   Hiawatha1903.png

5. *The Guardian* Charlottetown newspaper—copy on microfiche.

   336 ## $a _____ $2 _____

   336 ## $a _____ $2 _____

   337##$a microform $2 rdamedia
   338##$a microfiche $2 rdacarrier

6. *The Guardian* Charlottetown newspaper—paper copy.

   336 ## $a _____ $2 _____

   336 ## $a _____ $2 _____

   337##$a unmediated $2 rdamedia
   338##$a volume $2 rdacarrier

   Copyright 2014
   Transcontinental Media/Charlottetown Guardian.
   Reprinted with permission.

7. *The Guardian* Charlottetown online newspaper.

   336 ## $a _____ $2 _____

   336 ## $a _____ $2 _____

   337##$a computer $2 rdamedia
   338##$a online resource $2 rdacarrier

8. The David Vases (Yuan dynasty, 1351 AD) in Room 95, Chinese ceramics, British Museum (physical object).

   336 ## $a _____ $2 _____

   337 ## $a unmediated $2 rdamedia
   338 ## $a object $2 rdacarrier

   http://commons.wikimedia.org/wiki/File:
   Room_95_David_Vases_6747.JPG

Identifier for the Expression (RDA 6.13)
- This is a character string uniquely associated with an Expression, for example LC Control number, NLA permalink, ISWC (International Standard Musical Work Code).
- As with identifiers for Works, this attribute has been included in RDA for future development. At present there are limited Identifiers available at the Expression level.

'Core if Necessary' Elements of Expressions (RDA 6.10—6.12)
These are additional attributes that can be used if required to differentiate an Expression from another Expression of the same Work. When needed, all of these elements are core:
- date (the earliest date associated with the Expression, usually the date of the earliest Manifestation)
- language (in which the Work is expressed, this includes translations of the Work being expressed)
- other distinguishing characteristics such as 'Director's cut', 'Selections' (for selected parts or excerpts), etc.

Describing Content (RDA Chapter 7)
- 'Content' in RDA Chapter 7 differs from 'Content Type' in RDA Chapter 6.
    - *Content Type* describes the form of expression used for the resource
    - *Content* covers the physical characteristics of the resource (color, illustrations, scale, sound etc.)
- 'Content' information is usually recorded in the MARC **300 $b** field, or as a **5XX** note; 'Content Type' information now has its own, new MARC field **336**.
- No Content elements are core, but many are regularly used in descriptive cataloging:
    - illustrations (MARC 300 $b)
    - supplementary content (MARC 500/504 e.g., 'Includes index', 'Bibliography pages 50–55', etc.)
    - color details (MARC 300 $b)
    - intended audience (MARC 521)
    - thesis or dissertation information (MARC 502)
    - summary of contents (MARC 520)
    - scale and other cartographic content details (RDA 7.4–7.6 and 7.25–7.27)
    - sound, music and other recorded media content details (RDA 7.18–7.24).
- RDA Chapter 7 gives detailed instructions about terms to use when recording Content attributes
- The 'alternative' instruction on illustrations (RDA 7.15.1.3) provides a more specific list of terms that can be used for illustrative matter and most libraries use this list.
- Many of the Content attributes can be used by particular types of libraries to further enhance the user's access to information, for example:
    - public libraries may find the 'intended audience' and 'awards' attributes valuable for their clients
    - academic libraries already use Content attributes to good advantage by recording thesis and supplementary content information
    - sound and film collecting agencies or cartographic agencies now have the ability to record more specific content details.

CHAPTER ELEVEN   Attributes of Works and Expressions   105

 EXERCISE 11.2
Note the physical characteristic information for each of the following, and code in MARC. Refer to the appropriate instructions in RDA, and to the MARC codes.

1. A book is 20.5 centimeters high and 14.6 centimeters wide and has 287 pages and 163 illustrations including 55 in full color.

   300 _____

2. A continuing serial is 20.3 centimeters wide and 24.6 centimeters high, the latest issue has 108 pages and a picture on the cover.

   300 _____

3. A computer program has six 12 centimeter computer disks, a large reference manual and a quick reference card, contains color animations and sound.

   300 _____

4. A set of 3 digitally recorded stereo compact discs and a booklet in a cardboard box. The discs are 4 and ¾ inches in diameter, and play for 56 minutes, 58 minutes and 65 minutes.

   300 _____

 REVISION QUIZ 11.3
Use the following questions to revise your understanding of attributes of Works and Expressions. You do not need to write down the answers.

1. What are the core elements for Works?

2. Name the core elements at the Expression level.

3. When would you use 'core if necessary' elements at the Work level?

4. When would you use 'core if necessary' elements at the Expression level?

5. What are six attributes, described in RDA Chapter 7, that you could use to describe the content of a resource? Are any of these core elements?

CHAPTER TWELVE
Access Points

Introduction
This chapter discusses access points, and how to create them for Works and Expressions.

RDA's instructions on recording attributes of Manifestations and Items focus on describing the resource in hand. These instructions are concerned mainly with identifying and noting the physical characteristics of the resource. At the Work and Expression levels we are not dealing with physical entities, so there are fewer physical attributes—as we saw in the previous chapter of this workbook. However, RDA provides instructions at the Work and Expression levels for developing and recording access points to include in catalog records.

RDA also provides instructions for creating access points for Group Two entities (Persons, Families and Corporate Bodies) and for the Group Three entity 'Places'. These access points are covered in Chapter Thirteen of this workbook, as part of the discussion of authority records.

Access Points (RDA 6.27)
An important part of descriptive cataloging is determining and creating access points for the catalog record. Access points are one of the ways that RDA indicates relationships between and among resources. RDA provides guidance on how to create access points in the chapters dealing with recording attributes, and some guidance on what access points to create in the chapters dealing with recording relationships. Other ways of indicating relationships are covered in Chapters Fifteen to Seventeen of this workbook.

Access points in RDA perform the same function as headings (main and added entries) did in AACR2: they provide a name or term under which information pertaining to a specific entity (person, title, etc.) will be found.

Access points in RDA are attributes of Works or Expressions; Persons, Families or Corporate Bodies; and Places.

 New terminology:

AACR2 term	RDA term
Heading / Main entry / Added entry	Access point
Authorized heading	Authorized access point
See reference	Variant access point
Authority control	Access point control
Uniform title	Preferred Title for the Work

What Should be Included as Access Points?

In general, any term that will help a user to find or identify a resource should be added to a catalog record as an access point. These include:

- Principal creator (author, etc.) of the resource (noted in MARC terminology as the 'main entry' and recorded in the MARC 1XX field). This can be a person, family or corporate body.
- Additional creators or contributors to the resource (noted in MARC as 'added entries' and recorded in MARC 7XX fields). These can be persons, families and/or corporate bodies.
- Non-commercial publishers of a resource (noted in MARC as 'added entries' and recorded in MARC 710 field). This is a common practice in some countries, based on the idea that many users will remember that a report was put out by, for example, the Australian Red Cross—but they will not know the names of the author/s of the report. Including an access point for the associated organization will help users find the resource.
    - Commercial publishers are not given access points, since they usually publish over a range of topics and do not have the same strong subject association with their publications.
- Title of the resource.
- Any variations of the title (e.g., different titles on a publication's cover or spine from that on the principal source of information; distinctive subtitles; different spellings; titles in different languages, etc.) that users might search.
- Title of the series which the resource is part of (e.g., the Twilight Saga series of fiction, or an academic series like *Trends in Librarianship*).
- Subject headings that describe the resource.
    - Note that these are not covered in this workbook. For subject heading information, use the *Learn Library of Congress subject access* workbook in the 'Learn Library Skills' series.

It is the cataloger's responsibility to decide what should be an access point and how many access points to include in the catalog record. Some smaller libraries restrict the number of access points, particularly for added authors; however, in general you should add as many access points as you feel are needed to enable effective searching.

Constructing Access Points

RDA makes provision for a number of types of access points:

Name access points:	Title access points:
• Access points for a Person	• Access points for Works
• Access points for a Family	• Access points for Expressions
• Access points for a Corporate Body	

Some of these are **authorized access points**—the term that is accepted as the preferred heading. Alternate, non-preferred access points are called **variant access points**—these constitute *see* or *see also* references in an authority record or a catalog.

RDA provides detailed information about constructing access points for Works and Expressions in RDA Chapter 6, and for Persons, Families and Corporate Bodies in RDA Chapters 9, 10 and 11, and for Places in RDA Chapter 16.

RDA's authorized access points are based on determining a *Preferred Name* for a person or corporate body, or a *Preferred Title* for a resource, and combining that information with additional characteristics or attributes.

Authorized access points for a name are made up of the preferred choice of the name, plus if necessary some additional attributes like dates, fuller form of name, etc. (see RDA 9.19, RDA 10.10 or RDA 11.13 for constructing access points for Persons, Families and Corporate Bodies, respectively).

 Farkas, Lynn, 1951—

Authorized access points for Works are made up of the Preferred Name for the creator, plus the Preferred Title for the Work, or just the Preferred Title for the Work if there is no creator. (RDA 6.27.2)

 Farkas, Lynn, 1951— . MAIS thesaurus
Psycho (Motion picture)

Authorized access points for Expressions are made up of the access point for the Work, plus one or more of the following attributes for an Expression: Content Type, Date of Expression, Language of Expression, or other defining characteristics of an Expression. (RDA 6.27.3)

 Farkas, Lynn, 1951— . MAIS thesaurus. French
Psycho (Motion picture, 1998)

Authorized access points are used as headings in bibliographic records—as their name implies, they allow access (or searching) by that term. Authority records contain details about the authorized access points themselves.

Authority records give details about
- the components that make up authorized access points
- the non-preferred (i.e., variant) forms of the access point
- additional information about the access point, where appropriate, and
- where the cataloger found the information used to construct the access point.

Constructing Access Points to Represent Works (RDA 6.27.1.2)
- Start with the Preferred Title for the Work. (RDA 6.2)
- Precede the Preferred Title for the Work with the creator for that preferred title, if appropriate. (see RDA Chapter 19)
- Make additions to the Preferred Title for the Work, if needed to make it distinct—e.g., form, date, place of Work. (RDA 6.27.1.9)

 Marsh, Ngaio, 1895–1982. *Dead water.*
Obama, Barack. *Dreams from my father.*
Journal of Stamp Collecting (Ballarat, Vic.)

- Instructions on constructing authorized access points can be applied to adaptations, commentaries, parts of work etc. (RDA 6.27.1.5, RDA 6.27.1.6, and RDA 6.27.2)

 Only one creator (with principal responsibility for a Work) is used in an authorized access point. This differs from Manifestation-level statements of responsibility, where all persons associated with the Manifestation can be recorded.

Compilations vs. Collaborations

RDA makes a distinction between compilations (RDA 6.27.1.4) and collaborations (RDA 6.27.1.3). It is an important distinction, and there is a difference in how each is dealt with.
- A **compilation** is a collection of Works by one or more creators.
- A **collaboration** is one Work, developed by more than one creator.

When a resource has more than one creator:
- If it is a compilation, it is identified by the Preferred Title for the compilation.
- If it is a collaboration, it is identified by a combination of the Preferred Name for the principal (or first-named) creator and the Preferred Title.

Coding Access Points

Although 'Work' is a concept, we can provide information about it bibliographically. We can identify attributes of Works that tell us about the concepts AACR2 called 'main entry', 'uniform title', and 'access points'. We can incorporate this information into authority or bibliographic records, using a range of encoding schemas (MARC, Dublin Core, etc.)

For example, MARC has four possibilities for coding the concept 'Title of a Work/Preferred Title of a Work':
- 1XX + 240   ('persons' main entry plus uniform title added entry)
- 1XX + 245   ('persons' main entry plus title added entry)
- 130   (uniform title as a main entry)
- 245   (title as a main entry)

MARC does not have a special tag for coding Works; instead, MARC provides two tags for indicating uniform titles: one when the Work has no known creator, and one (used in conjunction with a 1XX field) when a Work has a known creator.

Creator known?	Use MARC tag/s	Example
No	130 + 245	130 0# $a Bible 245 00 $a Good news Bible.
Yes	1XX + 240 + 245	100 1# $a Jones, Roger 240 10 $a Winning lives. $k screenplay 245 10 $a Winning lives.

 When coding using uniform titles, the catalog record must always also include a 245 title field, even if this is the same as or similar to the 130 or 240 uniform title.

EXERCISE 12.1

Provide the authorized access point for the following Works. Then code in MARC.

a. A journal with the title proper *Trends in evolutionary biology*

   Access point:

   MARC coding:

b. Another journal with the title *Trends in evolutionary biology* that is published in Los Angeles

   Access point:

   MARC coding:

c. A book by Peter Williams with the title *Cooking for fun*

   Access point:

   MARC coding:

d. A book with no known authors with the title *Cooking for fun,* published in 2012 by Culinary Press

   Access point:

   MARC coding:

e. Another book with no known authors with the title *Cooking for fun,* published in 2014 by Household Press

   Access point:

   MARC coding:

f. A compilation of works by different authors with the title *Selected folk tales,* published in Tokyo in 2013

   Access point:

   MARC coding:

g. Another compilation of works by different authors with the title *Selected folk tales*, published in Bangkok in 2014

   Access point:

   MARC coding:

h. A newly-discovered sonnet by Shakespeare, *As you like it* (not to be confused with the better-known play of the same title that your library holds)

   Access point:

   MARC coding:

Constructing Access Points to Represent Expressions (RDA 6.27.3)

Access points for Expressions distinguish different Expressions, or versions, of a Work from each other. They are constructed by adding additional information to the authorized access point for the Work. By starting with the authorized access point for the Work, we ensure that all Expressions are grouped with their overarching Work.

- Start with the Preferred Title for the Work. (RDA 6.2)
- Precede the Preferred Title for the Work with the creator for that preferred title, if appropriate. (see RDA Chapter 19)
- Add one or more of the following:
    - Content Type (RDA 6.9.1.3, using Table 6.1 terminology where possible)
    - Date of Expression
    - Language of Expression, and/or
    - other distinguishing characteristics of the Expression. (RDA 6.12)

Marsh, Ngaio, 1895–1982. *Dead water.* Spanish
Obama, Barack. *Dreams from my father.* Spoken word
Carroll, Lewis. *Alice in wonderland.* French. Spoken word

EXERCISE 12.2

Provide the authorized access point for the following Expressions. Then code in MARC.

a. *Tren dalam biologi evolusi,* an Indonesian translation of the work in Exercise 12.1a (a journal with the title proper *Trends in evolutionary biology*)

Access point:

MARC coding:

b. An audio version of the work in Exercise 12.1c (a book by Peter Williams with the title *Cooking for fun*)

Access point:

MARC coding:

c. *Cucinare per divertimento,* an Italian translation of the work in Exercise 12.1d (a book with no known authors with the title *Cooking for fun*, published in 2012 by Culinary Press)

Access point:

MARC coding:

d. *Cucinare per divertimento,* an Italian translation of the work in Exercise 12.1e (another book with no known authors with the title *Cooking for fun*, published in 2014 by Household Press)

Access point:

MARC coding:

CHAPTER THIRTEEN
Attributes of Persons, Families and Corporate Bodies

Introduction
We now focus on the Group Two entities of Person, Family and Corporate Body. This chapter covers how to identify and record the attributes of Group Two entities in authority records, and how to create their access points to use in bibliographic records. But first, it is important to understand more about how authority records are constructed and used.

RDA Section 3—Attributes of Person, Family and Corporate Body
Even though this Section is titled 'Recording Attributes', you must approach it slightly differently to RDA Sections 1 and 2. When discussing attributes of people, we are no longer dealing with physical properties of a resource, but instead we are dealing with the defining characteristics of a living being or organization.

We record data about resources in our bibliographic records. But we record data about people, families and corporate bodies in two places:
- some of the information goes into bibliographic records, in the form of authorized access points (the concepts of 'main entry' and 'added entries' in AACR2 and MARC)
- the majority goes into authority records, that more fully describe the person, family or corporate body.

Authority Data
RDA includes instructions on what information to collect in order to construct authority data, based on attributes and relationships in the FRAD (Functional Requirements of Authority Data) model.

RDA does not separate these from instructions about bibliographic data, because it sees both as part of the complete entity-relationship continuum.

For example, Chapters 8.12 and 8.13 of the RDA Instruction Set provide details about how to record sources consulted when determining names for Group Two entities, and when and how to make catalogers' notes about this. This information is not included in library bibliographic descriptions. RDA doesn't indicate *where* this information should be recorded, only that it is useful information to record. However, it is currently documented by most libraries in separate authority records and authority files, using the MARC Format for Authority Data.

RDA provides mappings of RDA elements to the MARC formats for bibliographic and authority data, located on the 'Tools' tab of the RDA toolkit. There are also links to these mappings from Appendix E.2 *Record Syntaxes for Access Point Control—MARC 21 Format for Authority Data* and Appendix D.2 *Record Syntaxes for Descriptive Data –MARC 21 Format for*

Bibliographic Data. These mappings help determine where the information RDA suggests you gather should be recorded in a MARC record. They are useful tools, particularly in the early stages of using the RDA Instruction Set.

Core Elements for Authority Data
RDA Chapter 9 details all the attributes that can be recorded for a person. The core elements are:
- Preferred name for the person
- Dates associated with the person
- Title of the person
- Identifier for the person
    - As with Identifiers for Works and Expressions, this attribute has been included in RDA for future development. At present there are limited Identifiers available for persons.

'Core if necessary' elements are used when needed to differentiate two people with the same name. These elements are:
- Fuller form of name
- Other designation associated with a person, e.g., 'Reverend', 'Sir', etc.
- Profession or occupation
- Period of activity of the person

There are three meanings of 'Core' when it comes to authority data:
- Core to record (can be either in an access point or elsewhere in the authority record)
    - e.g., *Dates of birth and death*
- Core in an access point
    - e.g., *Title of person, Conference dates*
- Core only if needed to resolve conflict in an access point
    - e.g., *fuller form of name, Profession or occupation*

Additional attributes to record as authority data include gender, place of birth and/or death, country associated with the person, place of residence (i.e., city or state), address of the person (including email addresses), professional affiliations, language of the person, field of activity of the person, and biographical information (RDA 9.7 to RDA 9.18).

Dates in Authority Records
Dates are important elements for authority records. They are core to record somewhere in an authority record for conferences, people and families, and core when needed to resolve a conflict for corporate bodies.

For those dates that are not required as part of the access point to resolve a conflict, catalogers can decide whether to record them as separate elements in the authority record (i.e., in a different MARC field like MARC 046), or as part of the access point, or as both.

The following dates can be recorded in an authority record:
- birth and death dates for persons, e.g., *Hemingway, Ernest, 1899–1961*
- establishment and termination dates for corporate bodies, e.g., *Ansett Australia (1936–2002)*
- conference dates (required in the access point), e.g., *Canadian Conference on Artificial Intelligence (27th : 2014 : Montréal (Québec))*
- significant dates in the history of a family, or the dates of existence of the family, e.g., *Romanov (Dynasty : 1613–1917); Farkas (Family : 1917—   )*

Note the different punctuation used for recording dates for people, families, corporate bodies and conferences. Punctuation details for Persons, Families and Corporate Bodies are given in Appendix E.1, *Record Syntaxes for Access Point Control, 'Presentation'*.

Differences between AACR2 Authorities and RDA Authorities

Just as library catalogs contain many bibliographic records created using AACR2 rules, their authority files also contain AACR2 legacy records. The points below indicate changes in the way certain data is recorded in RDA that can impact on access points and authority records.

- *Abbreviations*
  RDA's move away from the use of abbreviations affects authorized access points and authority records as well as bibliographic data. The most notable of these is the word 'Department', which is no longer abbreviated. This constitutes a significant change in practice when recording the preferred name for corporate bodies.

- *Bible Headings*
  Authorized access points for books of the Bible are different from their AACR2 counterparts. When creating authorized access points for the whole of the Old or New Testaments of the Bible, abbreviations O.T. and N.T. are now spelled out, e.g., 'Bible. Old Testament' (RDA access point) *not* 'Bible. O.T.' (former AACR2 heading). In addition, references to the Old and New Testaments are no longer used when naming books of the Bible, e.g., 'Bible. Genesis' (RDA) *not* 'Bible. O.T. Genesis' (AACR2). These changes may require significant conversion of records in some library catalogs.

- *Forms of Names*
  There are minor changes in choosing the preferred form of name that may result in differences between AACR2 and RDA headings, such as the reduction in English language bias, choices among different forms of the same name etc.

- *More Information*
  There is more information you can record in authority records. RDA provides guidelines for recording not only names, dates and titles for people, but also additional attributes like gender, place of residence, language of the person, and professional affiliations that were not part of an AACR2 authority record. New MARC fields have been created for many of these additional attributes.

Here are two authority records for a person, created using RDA guidelines and AACR2 rules. The differences between them are highlighted in bold in the RDA record, and explained below the example. Note the additional elements in the RDA-compliant data, and the MARC coding used.

AACR2–compliant Authority Record	RDA–compliant Authority Record
000 01187cz a2200301n 450	000 01187cz a2200301n 450
001 1425509	001 1425509
005 20020814172756.0	005 20141022005104.0
008 790816n| acannaabn |b aaa	008 790816n| **a**zannaabn |b aaa
010 __ |a n 79073589	010 __ |a n 79073589
035 __ |a (OCoLC)oca00306330	035 __ |a (OCoLC)oca00306330
040 __ |a DLC |b eng |c DLC	**040** __ |a DLC |b eng **|e rda** |c DLC |d DLC |d OCoLC |d ICrlF
053 _0 |a PS3562.O923	**046** __ |f 19370320
100 1_ |a Lowry, Lois	053 _0 |a PS3562.O923
370 __ |a Honolulu (Hawaii) |e Maine |e Massachusetts	100 1_ |a Lowry, Lois
670 __ |a Looking back, 2000: |b t.p. (Lois Lowry) p. 11, etc. (b. 1937, in Hawaii; author of A summer to die; writes books for children and adults)	370 __ |a Honolulu (Hawaii) |e Maine |e Massachusetts
	374 __ **|a Children's author |a Photographer**
	375 __ **|a female**
	377 __ **|a eng**
	670 __ |a Looking back, 2000: |b **title page** (Lois Lowry) **page** 11, etc. (**born** 1937, in Hawaii; author of A summer to die; writes books for children and adults)
	670 __ |a Wikipedia, Oct. 20, 2014 |b (Lois Lowry was born on March 20, 1937, in Honolulu, Hawaii ; degree in English literature from the University of Southern Maine ; her specialty was child photography ; homes in Massachusetts and Maine)

008—in position 10, use z for 'other' descriptive cataloging rules, not 'c' for AACR2 rules
040—$e indicates this is an RDA record (note the order of subfields: $a, $b, $e, $c, $d)
374—New MARC field for Occupation, RDA 9.16
375—New MARC field for Gender, RDA 9.7
377—New MARC field for language, RDA 9.14 (RDA instructs us to record the language used by a person in their activity. MARC makes provision for this by using a code from the MARC language code lists in the $a field, or the full language in the $l field, or both.)
670—no abbreviations used, words are spelled out in full

Recording Attributes of Person, Family, Corporate Body (RDA Section 3)

As noted earlier, the data recorded for the entities in Section 3 of the RDA Instruction Set can be used in bibliographic records and in authority records. In dealing with RDA Section 3 we will also touch on some information about relationships (in RDA Section 6) and using the relationship designators in the appendices (RDA Appendices I and K).

RDA Section 3 focuses on how to describe, record, and construct access points for the Group Two entities. RDA Section 6 focuses on how to incorporate these into a bibliographic record, by showing their relationship to the resource (as a creator, compiler, publisher, owner, etc.). Chapters Fifteen and Sixteen of this workbook explain RDA Section 6 relationships.

The approach of RDA towards Persons, Families and Corporate Bodies is very similar.
- Each entity (Person, Family, Corporate Body) has a separate chapter devoted to it.
- The early parts of the chapters deal with attributes that can be identified and recorded.
- The final numbered point in each chapter explains which of these attributes can be used to construct an authorized access point.

Choosing and Recording Personal Names (RDA Chapter 9)

It is important to become familiar with the instructions in RDA Chapter 9. Distinguishing and recording a name so that it can be used consistently by other catalogers is a basic, and very important, cataloging skill.

RDA 9.2 gives instructions on choosing and recording names of persons. Key points include:
- Choose the name by which the person is most commonly known, and which is most frequently used, e.g., Lady Gaga *not* Stefani Germanotta. (RDA 9.2.2.3)
- If a person has changed their name, choose the latest form of the person's name, e.g., Bill Clinton *not* William Jefferson Blythe III. (RDA 9.2.2.7)
- If a person has more than one identity (that is, if they use pseudonyms on some of their works), choose the name associated with each identity as the preferred name for that identity. (RDA 9.2.2.8)
- RDA treats 'real' names and 'alternate' names the same, so if Charles L. Dodgson wrote *Alice in Wonderland* under the pseudonym 'Lewis Carroll', RDA records the author as 'Carroll, Lewis', *not* 'Carroll, Lewis (pseudonym)'.
    - The link between Lewis Carroll and Charles L. Dodgson is not shown in bibliographic records—this information is given in authority records. There will be one authority record for Charles L. Dodgson that indicates he has an alternate identity Lewis Carroll, and another authority record for Lewis Carroll that indicates his real identity is Charles L. Dodgson. RDA Appendix K.2.1 provides the terminology to describe this relationship. RDA Chapter 30 gives guidance on recording the relationship.
    - However, if a person never uses their real name for their Works, choose their pseudonym as the preferred name. Record the individual's real name as a variant name, or non-preferred name, in the authority record. (RDA 9.2.2.8)

- If a name includes a surname or an element that can be considered a surname, invert the name so that the surname is the first element of the name access point (e.g., X, Malcolm *not* Malcolm X). (RDA 9.2.2.9.1)
- If a name includes a term (Junior, Senior or equivalent in other languages) or numbers (III, IV) indicating family sequence relationships, include these following a person's given name or names, preceded by a comma, e.g., Gates, Bill, III or Downey, Robert, Jr. (RDA 9.2.2.9.5)
- Fictitious characters are now considered 'persons' (e.g., Poirot, Hercule), and follow the same rules for choosing and recording names as 'real' people. (RDA 9.0)
- Add birth and (when appropriate) death dates as core elements to a person's name.
- If a person commonly uses a form of name that is not their full name (for example, their surname and initials only), you can add the fuller form of name in brackets after their preferred name, e.g., Lawrence, D. H. (David Herbert). (RDA 9.5 and 9.19.1.4)
- You can add an occupation to a common name to distinguish between multiple people with the same name. (RDA 9.16.1.3).

RDA Chapter 9 includes many more instances of how to deal with particular name issues, and provides extensive examples for each. At the end of the chapter, RDA 9.19 provides instructions for putting name details together to create authorized access points and variant access points to represent people.

CHAPTER THIRTEEN   Attributes of Persons, Families and Corporate Bodies   119

 EXERCISE 13.1
Use RDA Chapter 9 and its associated links to give the correct form of the following personal names. Instruction numbers have been provided to assist in your decisions.

1. Ian Harrison – RDA 9.2.2.9

2. Stevan Eldred-Grigg – RDA 9.2.2.12

3. Tomie de Paola, an American writer of Italian descent – RDA 9.2.2.9 + 9.2.2.11.1 or 9.2.2.10.2

4. Maurice Gough Gee who prefers not to use his middle name – RDA 9.2.2

5. Mao Zedong (Mao is the surname) – RDA 9.2.2.9

6. Pelham Grenville Wodehouse's name appears on his title pages as P. G. Wodehouse. He is commonly known by his initials. – RDA 9.5

7. Michael O'Leary who wrote on risk management. His middle name Peter distinguishes him from other creators called Michael O'Leary. – RDA 9.5.1

8. Michael O'Leary who wrote on rail travel. His middle initial 'D' distinguishes him from other creators called Michael O'Leary. – RDA 9.5.1

9. Kathleen Mansfield Beauchamp married John Murray and always wrote under the pseudonym Katherine Mansfield. – RDA 9.2.2.8

10. José Maria Escrivá de Balaguer (Escrivá de Balaguer is a Spanish compound surname); born 1902, died 1975. – RDA 9.2.2.10

Key Points for Creating Authorized Access Points for Persons (RDA 9.19)

- All the RDA Chapter 9 attributes for a Person (preferred name, life dates, title, fuller form of name, profession, period of activity, gender, place of birth/death, country associated with the person, address and place of residence, language, field of activity and biographical information) can be recorded in an authority record.
- However, only six of these attributes are used to create an authorized access point, and are seen in a bibliographic record. They are used when required, in the following order:
    - *Title or other designation associated with the Person* (RDA 9.19.1.2, RDA 9.4 and RDA 9.6)
        - Required for certain names, e.g., royalty, nobility, religious rank, saints and spirits.
    - *Other term of rank, honor or office* (RDA 9.19.1.6 and RDA 9.4.1.9)
        - For example, 'Sir' or 'Captain', added after the Preferred Name. Core if needed to differentiate people, optional otherwise.
    - *Fuller form of name* (RDA 9.19.1.4 and RDA 9.5)
        - Add only if needed to differentiate people, and when life dates are not available (but there are options to use both the fuller forms of name and life dates, even if not required for differentiation).
    - *Profession or occupation* (RDA 9.19.1.6 and RDA 9.16)
        - Required for names "not conveying the idea of a person", e.g., *Sting (Musician)*. Can also be added to common names to differentiate people, if no other attributes are available, e.g., Smith, John (Pilot).
    - *Date of birth and/or death* (RDA 9.19.1.3, RDA 9.3.2 and RDA 9.3.3)
        - Core to include if available.
    - *Period of activity of person* (RDA 9.19.1.5 and RDA 9.3.4)
        - Add to differentiate only when life dates or fuller forms of name are not available (but there are options to add even if not needed).
- There are a number of new fields in the MARC Authority Format that cater for the RDA identifying attributes for Persons. These include the MARC Authority 040, 368, and 370–378 fields.

RDA terminology: **Preferred Name** *for a person is the form of name chosen to identify the person. It is also the basis for the* **authorized access point** *representing that person.*

CHAPTER THIRTEEN   Attributes of Persons, Families and Corporate Bodies   121

 EXERCISE 13.2
The following is an RDA–compliant personal name authority record.

LC control no.: nb 90173911

LCCN permalink: http://lccn.loc.gov/nb90173911

HEADING: Mackay, Hugh, 1952—

000 01151cz a2200253n 450

001 5828710

005 20130329051012.0

008 010215n| azannaabn |a aaa

010 __ |a nb 90173911

035 __ |a (Uk)004031200

040 __ |a Uk |b eng |e rda |c Uk |d Uk

046 __ |f 19521010

100 1_ |a Mackay, Hugh, |d 1952—

372 __ |a Sociology |a College teaching |2 lcsh

373 __ |a Open University. Faculty of Social Sciences |2 naf

374 __ |a Sociologists |a College teachers |2 lcsh

375 __ |a male

377 __ |a eng

400 1_ |a Mackay, Alistair Hugh, |d 1952—

400 1_ |a McKay, Hugh, |d 1952—

670 __ |a The media reader, 1999: |b t.p. (Hugh Mackay) back cover (Senior Lecturer and Staff Tutor in Sociology, Open Univ., Wales) BL AL sent 15 Feb. 2001

670 __ |a E-mail from author, 17th Dec. 2002 |b (Alistair Hugh Mackay, born 10th Oct. 1952. Author seldom uses Alistair, not used in authorship)

670 __ |a Doing cultural studies, 2013: |b t.p. (Hugh McKay [i.e. Mackay])

670 __ |a Open University www site, 28 March 2013: |b Faculty of Social Sciences staff profile (Dr. Hugh Mackay; co-author of Doing cultural studies; co-editor of The media reader)

Fill in the template on the following page, using the 'MARC Authority to RDA Mapping' file in the RDA Toolkit. Name each of the MARC fields and subfields from the authority record above and indicate the RDA instruction numbers that tell you how to record this data. The first MARC code has been done for you:

MARC code	RDA instruction number	MARC field and subfield name
010	9.18	Library of Congress Control Number
035		
040		
046		
100		
372		
373		
374		
375		
377		
400		
670		

Identifying Families (RDA Chapter 10)

Under RDA guidelines, families can now be considered creators and contributors, not just subjects. This will be important for family histories, family reunion publications, special collections, archives etc. There is a new MARC Authority field for family information—Authority field 376—as well as existing MARC authority fields for family place (field 370) and family history (fields 665 or 678).

Core elements for Families are:
- Preferred Name for the Family
- Type of Family
- Date Associated with the Family
- Identifier for the Family (if available).

The **Preferred Name for the Family** is the name by which the family is most commonly known. (RDA 10.2.2)
- This can be the family surname, the name of a clan, the name of a royal house or dynasty, etc.
- If a family changes its name, record the earlier name as the preferred name for use with resources associated with the earlier name, and the later name as the preferred name for resources associated with the later name. (RDA 10.2.2.7)
    - Authority records are created for each name, and each authority record will indicate the relationship between earlier and later names of the Family. (RDA Chapter 31)
    - Your library catalog, therefore, may have a number of different authorized access points for the same family.
- When developing an authorized access point, start with the Preferred Name for a Family and include the Type of Family in parentheses at the end of the preferred name.

Type of Family (RDA 10.2)
- Use terms like (Family), (Clan), (Dynasty), (Royal house).
- There is no controlled vocabulary, so the cataloger chooses an appropriate term, e.g., 100 3# $a Ming (Dynasty).
- Note that Type of Family is a separate element to the name of the family. The two are combined to create the authorized access point for the family, e.g., Dean (Family).

Date Associated with the Family should be a significant date or dates associated with the history of a family. (RDA 10.4)
- Significant dates can include the date a royal household began or finished, or the date when the family became prominent historically, or the date of an important event for the family.
- Dates can be recorded as:
    - part of the authority record in the MARC 046 field
    - or added after the Type of Family in an authorized access point, e.g., Dean (Family : 1880–1925)
    - or both.

Identifier for the Family (RDA 10.10)
- As with identifiers for Persons, the attribute 'Identifier for the Family' has been included in RDA for future development. At present there are limited Identifiers available for Families.

'Core when needed' elements are used to distinguish between two families with the same name. Core when needed elements are:
- Place Associated with the Family
- Prominent Member of the Family.

A **Place Associated with a Family** can be a city, town, state or province, or country in which the family normally resides or has some connection. (RDA 10.5)

A **Prominent Member of the Family** can be any well-known individual in the family (RDA 10.6.1), e.g., *Austen (Family : Austen, Jane, 1775–1817)*.

- In this example, Jane Austen is added to the family access point because, without a prominent member, the entry would be simply 'Austen (Family)' and that might not be enough to distinguish Jane Austen's family from another family group with the same surname.
- Prominent members of a family can be coded into the MARC 376 field (Family Information), subfield $b. This is a repeatable field, so any number of prominent family members can be named. However, only one prominent member can be used as part of the authorized access point for the family.
- When using a prominent member of a family as part of the authorized access point for the family, the entire authorized access point for that person (including their preferred name and dates of birth/death) is used, not just the name component.

Other attributes of families are hereditary titles for a family, the language or languages a family uses in its communication, and a history of the family. None of these attributes are core elements but some, like a history of the family, can be useful for distinguishing the family from others with the same name.

Note that identifying and recording data about families relies more heavily on the cataloger's interpretation of significant incidents than does identifying data about people and to some extent data about corporate bodies. Significant dates and places associated with a family can change over time, as can the most prominent member of a family.

Key Points for Creating Authorized Access Points for Families (RDA 10.11)

As with RDA Chapter 9, the final portion of RDA Chapter 10 provides instructions for putting family details together to create authorized access points and variant access points representing families.

Begin an authorized access point with the Preferred Name for the Family, then add in parentheses after it the following elements in the following order (RDA 10.11.1.2 to RDA 10.11.1.5):

- Type of family—required for all authorized access points, e.g., Minar (Family).
- Date associated with the family—can be included even if not needed to distinguish between families with the same name, e.g., Minar (Family : 1883–   ).
- Place associated with the family—add only if needed to distinguish one family from another, e.g., Minar (Family : Fiji).
- Prominent member of the family—add only if needed to distinguish one access point from another, and if a place associated with a family is not available, e.g., Minar (Family : Minar, Joseph, 1925–1998).

EXERCISE 13.3

Use this passage about the Barrymore family to gather the information needed to create an authorized access point for the family. Record this in the template provided on the following page. Note: not all fields in the template may apply.

> The Barrymore family is notable for their success in the acting world, both on stage and on the screen. The Barrymore family has been called a multi-generation theatrical dynasty and were the inspiration for the Broadway and West End play called *The Royal Family*.
>
> Maurice Barrymore (orig. Herbert Blythe; 1847/49–1905) made his stage debut in London before moving to New York City (1875), where he adopted Barrymore as his stage name. He joined Augustin Daly's company and in 1876 married Georgiana Drew, of the theatrical Drew family.
>
> Their eldest child, Lionel Barrymore (orig. Lionel Blythe; 1878–1954), became a leading Broadway actor in plays such as *Peter Ibbetson* (1917) and *The Copperhead* (1918) and then moved to Hollywood in 1926, where he appeared in films such as *A Free Soul* (1931, Academy Award) and *Grand Hotel* (1932). Famous as a character actor, he made some 200 films, including 15 Dr. Kildare pictures.
>
> His sister Ethel Barrymore (orig. Ethel Blythe; 1879–1959) appeared in London in *Peter the Great* (1898) and on Broadway in *Captain Jinks of the Horse Marines* (1901). She opened the New York theatre named for her in 1928 in *The Kingdom of God* and later starred in *The Corn Is Green* (1940). She appeared in more than 30 films, including *None but the Lonely Heart* (1944, Academy Award) and *The Spiral Staircase* (1946).
>
> Their brother John Barrymore (orig. John Blythe; 1882–1942) was acclaimed in plays such as *Justice* (1916), *Richard III* (1920), and especially *Hamlet* (1922). His films include *Dr. Jekyll and Mr. Hyde* (1920) and *Dinner at Eight* (1933). An alcoholic, he was known for his flamboyant behavior.
>
> His son, John Blyth Barrymore III (born May 15, 1954) is an American former film and television actor known for his role as Zeke in the 1970s television series, *Kung Fu*.
>
> John's granddaughter Drew Blythe Barrymore (born February 22, 1975) is an American actress, screenwriter, film director, producer, model and author. Drew first appeared in an advertisement when she was eleven months old, and made her film debut in *Altered States* in 1980. She won notice at age seven in the film *E.T.* (1982). She has gone on to star in, and produce, many films since that time. A recipient of a star on the Hollywood Walk of Fame, Barrymore appeared on the cover of the 2007 *People* magazine's '100 Most Beautiful' issue. She is also the god-daughter of director Steven Spielberg and Sophia Loren.

(Source: Adapted from Encyclopedia Brittanica website, http://www.britannica.com/EBchecked/topic/1365389/Barrymore-family , viewed 25 Oct 2014)

RDA Element	Data Recorded
10.2.2 Preferred name for the family	
10.3 Type of family	
10.4 Date associated with the family	
10.5 Place associated with the family	
10.6 Prominent member/s of the family	
10.8 Language of the family	
10.9 Family history	
10.10 Identifier for the family	
10.11 Authorized Access point	
10.11.2 Variant access point/s	
8.12 Source/s consulted	

Identifying Corporate Bodies (RDA Chapter 11)

In RDA, Corporate Bodies include associations, institutions, business companies, non-profit enterprises, governments and government agencies, schools, projects and programs, religious bodies, church groups, ad hoc events (e.g., athletic contests, expeditions), vessels (e.g., ships, aircraft and spacecraft), and conferences.

Conferences include conferences, congresses, meetings, exhibitions, fairs and festivals. They use slightly different naming conventions and we will discuss them later in this chapter.

Core elements for corporate bodies are:
- Corporate Body name
- significant dates in the history of the body—core if needed to distinguish from another body with the same name
- location and number of a conference
- Identifier (if available).

Dates are core for conferences, and core if needed to resolve a conflict for other corporate bodies. Use significant dates in the history of the Corporate Body, e.g., date of establishment or of termination, or if these are unknown, a range of dates to indicate when the Corporate Body was active.
- Record significant dates for Corporate Bodies in the 046 field of a MARC authority record, and in the 110 $d MARC field if needed as part of the authorized access point.
- Record conference dates in the 111 $d MARC field, and in the 046 field if desired.

Choosing and Recording Corporate Body Names (RDA 11.2.2)
- Choose the name by which the Corporate Body is commonly known. (RDA 11.2.2.3)
  - This can be its official name, or a conventional name (i.e., the name by which that body has come to be known, e.g., Westminster Abbey, not its official name 'Collegiate Church of St. Peter in Westminster'). (RDA 11.2.2.5.4)
  - Corporate Body names are usually recorded in direct order e.g., National Archives of Scotland *not* 'Scotland, National Archives of'.
- Choose the conventional name of a government (that is, the name of the area over which the government exercises jurisdiction), be it a country, province, state, county or municipality, e.g., Fiji, *not* 'Republic of Fiji'; Australia *not* 'Commonwealth of Australia', Great Britain, *not* 'United Kingdom of Great Britain and Northern Ireland'. (RDA 11.2.2.5.4)
- If the Corporate Body's name does not convey the idea that it is an organization, add a term in parentheses to indicate the type of Corporate Body, e.g., 'Apollo 11 (Spacecraft)' or 'Klaus Gardiner (Firm)'. (RDA 11.7 and RDA 11.13.1.2)
- If a Corporate Body changes its name, use the name associated with the Corporate Body in the resource being cataloged. (RDA 11.2.2.6)
  - Authority records are created for each new name change. Each authority record indicates the relationship between earlier and later names. (RDA Chapter 32)
  - Your library catalog, therefore, may have a number of different authorized access points for the same corporate body.

- Omit adjectival terms and abbreviations that indicate incorporation, e.g., 'Pty. Ltd.', 'Inc.', 'Incorporated' etc., unless they are an integral part of the name, e.g., Films Incorporated. (RDA 11.2.2.10)
- Include initial articles in a Corporate Body name, e.g., The Library Association. (RDA 11.2.2.8)
  - *Note:* this is a change from previous cataloging rules that omitted initial articles, and RDA has an option to follow the earlier practice.
  - The Library of Congress, British Library, and the National Library of Australia have decided to follow the earlier practice and omit initial articles.
  - The libraries in the Anwendungsrichtlinien für den deutschsprachigen Raum consortium, however, will follow the new RDA guideline.
  - Note that you can access all the Policy Statements on this topic by clicking on the green 'LC–PCC PS', yellow 'NLA PS', purple 'D-A-CH AWR', or red 'BL PS' icons at RDA instruction 11.2.2.8.

EXERCISE 13.4

Use the instructions in RDA Chapter 11.2.1 to 11.2.2.12 to choose the best form of name for the following Corporate Bodies:

1. Colonial Sugar Refinery Limited, usually known by its initials, CSR Limited
   - ____ Colonial Sugar Refinery
   - ____ CSR Limited
   - ____ CSR Ltd.
   - ____ CSR
   - ____ Colonial Sugar Refinery Limited

2. The Lao People's Democratic Republic
   - ____ Lao People's Democratic Republic
   - ____ The Lao Democratic Republic
   - ____ Laos
   - ____ Lao Republic

3. Tourism Industry Association of Canada, formerly the Canadian Tourist Association
   - ____ Tourist Association of Canada
   - ____ Tourism Industry Association of Canada
   - ____ Canadian Tourist Association
   - ____ CTA
   - ____ TIAC

4. United Nations Educational, Scientific and Cultural Organization, or UNESCO (Unesco is the formally presented version on most publications)
   - ____ UNESCO
   - ____ United Nations Educational, Scientific and Cultural Organisation
   - ____ United Nations Educational, Scientific and Cultural Organization
   - ____ Unesco

5. One for All, a jazz group
   ____ One for All
   ____ 1 for All
   ____ One for All (Musical group)
   ____ 1 for All (Musical group)

6. Canadian Federation of Musicians (CFM), formerly referred to as AFM Canada
   ____ AFM Canada
   ____ Canadian Federation of Musicians
   ____ Canada. Federation of Musicians
   ____ CFM

Subordinate and Related Corporate Bodies (RDA 11.2.2.13—11.2.2.15)
A subordinate body is a part, section or division of a larger Corporate Body. It is normally identified by referring to the parent body. For example, a department or branch is usually named by placing the parent body first, then adding the department or branch name, e.g., *MyStore. Complaints Department*.

If the name of a subordinate Corporate Body is distinctive, and does not need the name of the parent body to identify it, it can be recorded directly under its own name. This is what RDA 11.2.2.13 says, and the examples provided bear this out—the *Association of College and Research Libraries* is a division of the American Library Association, but its name is distinctive and readily identified without referring to its parent body. In the same way, 'Transport NI' and 'Northern Ireland Water' are subordinate bodies of the Department for Regional Development in Northern Ireland, but will be recorded under their distinctive names: *Transport NI*, and, *Northern Ireland Water*.

Many subordinate bodies' names, however, cannot stand alone. RDA 11.2.2.14 lists six types of subordinate bodies whose names must be recorded under the name of their parent body. These cover names that:
- imply that the body is an administrative part of its parent, e.g., *Department, Branch, Committee, Working Group, Office*
- are general in nature, e.g., *Research Institute, Annual Meeting, Region 3, Library*
- do not convey the idea of a Corporate Body, e.g., *Human Resources*, or
- already include the entire name of the higher or related body.

RDA 11.2.2.15 covers how to record names of bodies that are not directly subordinate to their parent (i.e., within their organization's hierarchy there are other departments, divisions or sections between them and the top level parent body). There are instructions for two types of recording:
- *Direct subdivision*—if the subordinate body in question comes under an organizational unit whose name can stand alone, the subordinate body is recorded by using the name of the organizational unit, followed by its own name, e.g., *World Health Organization. Programme, Budget and Administration Committee* not 'United Nations. World Health Organization. Programme, Budget and Administration

Committee'. (In this case, the World Health Organization is distinctive and unique enough not to have to be named under its parent body.)

- *Indirect subdivision*—Where the subordinate body comes under an organizational unit whose name cannot stand alone, only use the parts of the organizational hierarchy that are needed to identify the subordinate body uniquely. In most cases, this means recording the parent body plus the lowest subordinate body (omitting other subordinate bodies in the organizational hierarchy), e.g., *American Bar Association. Committee on Nonprofit Corporations* not 'American Bar Association. Section of Business Law. Committee on Nonprofit Corporations'.

Note that in both cases, the full hierarchies should be recorded in authority records as variant names.

Similar guidelines are provided on recording names of government bodies. The same instructions at RDA 11.2.2.14.1—11.2.2.14.6 about including the name of the parent body (i.e., the name of the government) apply, as well as additional ones (RDA 11.2.2.14.7—11.2.2.14.12 and RDA 11.2.2.1—11.2.2.24) covering governments, government agencies, government officials, courts and armed forces.

- If a government body is subordinate only to the government and not to a subdivision of the government, record it after the jurisdiction (i.e., government) name, e.g., *South Africa. Department of Home Affairs.*

- If a government body has a name that is distinctive and identifiable, record it under its own name, e.g., *IP Australia.*

- Subsections of government departments and agencies are recorded using RDA 11.2.2.15 instructions about direct or indirect subdivision. As with corporate bodies, only the elements needed to distinguish the government body are recorded, e.g., *New Zealand. Local Government Commission* not 'New Zealand. Department of Internal Affairs. Local Government Commission'.

- If in doubt about whether to include a department name as part of the access point for a subordinate government body, ask yourself: Is there likely to be another body of this name within another government department? If so, keep the department name. If not, omit the department name from the hierarchy, and record the subordinate body directly under the name of the government.

As with other types of Corporate Bodies, the full hierarchies for government organizations should be recorded in authority records as variant names.

RDA instructions 11.2.2.25 to 11.2.2.29 also provide information on recording names of religious bodies, religious officials, dioceses and synods, and papal diplomatic missions.

EXERCISE 13.5

Use the instructions in RDA Chapter 11.2.2 to choose the best form of name for the following Corporate Bodies:

1. The Committee on Manpower Resources for Science and Technology of the Department of Education and Science of the United States government

2. The Australian Nuclear Science and Technology Organisation (ANSTO) of the Department of Industry of the Australian government

3. The Agricultural Division of Imperial Chemical Industries

4. Faculté de médicine Saint-Antoine (part of the Université Pierre et Marie Curie)

5. The United Nations Children's Fund, most commonly referred to as UNICEF

6. The Federal Aviation Administration, an agency of the U.S. Department of Transportation

7. Ministry of Agriculture, Fisheries and Food (located in Britain)

8. University of the South Pacific, in Suva, Fiji

9. The United Nations Department of Public Information's Education Information Programmes

10. Facebook, the company founded by Mark Zuckerberg

Key Points for Creating Authorized Access Points for Corporate Bodies (RDA 11.13)

The final portion of RDA Chapter 11 provides instructions for creating authorized access points and variant access points to represent Corporate Bodies.

Begin an authorized access point with the Preferred Name for the Corporate Body, then add in parentheses after it the following elements in the following order (RDA 11.13.1.2 to RDA 11.13.1.7):

- Type of Corporate Body—add if needed to distinguish between two corporate bodies, or if the name does not suggest that it is a corporate body, e.g., Bounty (Ship).
- Place associated with the Corporate Body—add a country, state, province, city or other local place if it is needed to distinguish one organization from another.
- Associated institution—for example, if a Corporate Body is associated with, but not part of, a nearby university.
    - Add an associated institution only if needed to distinguish one access point from another, although there is an option to include this information if it helps identify the Corporate Body, even if there is no other with a similar name.
    - If an institution's name is commonly associated with the name of the Corporate Body, prefer using it as an addition instead of a local place name.
- Date associated with the Corporate Body—only add when an associated place or associated institution are not available.
- Type of jurisdiction—add to a place name to indicate its political administrative area (e.g., Kingdom, Duchy, State, Province, etc.), or to the name of a government other than a city or a town.
- Other designation associated with the Corporate Body—if none of the elements above can distinguish between two bodies, add your own suitable designation, e.g., 'World Cup (Cricket)' as opposed to 'World Cup (Soccer)'.

If a combination of elements are needed to distinguish two corporate bodies, separate the elements with a space, colon, space—e.g., St. Mary (Church : Cardiff, Wales).

EXERCISE 13.6

The table below represents the data collected for creating a Corporate Body authority record.

a) Use the 'RDA to MARC' mappings to identify the MARC tags and subfields for the RDA elements recorded

b) Construct the authorized access point and the variant access point/s.

RDA Element	MARC tag and subfields	Data Recorded
11.2.2 Preferred name for the corporate body		Red Hot Chili Peppers
11.2.3 Variant name		Red Hot Chilli Peppers Chili Peppers RHCP
11.3 Place		Los Angeles, USA
11.4.3 Date of establishment		1983
11.4.4 Date of termination		
11.7 Other designation		Musical group
11.8 Language		English
11.10 Field of activity		Music
8.12 Source consulted		Wikipedia entry, viewed 25 February 2014. (Red Hot Chili Peppers (also known as "Chili Peppers" or "RHCP") are an American funk rock band formed in Los Angeles in 1983. Currently, the band consists of founding members Anthony Kiedis (vocals) and Michael "Flea" Balzary (bass), longtime drummer Chad Smith, and guitarist Josh Klinghoffer, who joined in late 2009, following the departure of John Frusciante. Red Hot Chili Peppers have won seven Grammy Awards, and have become one of the best-selling bands of all time, selling over 80 million records worldwide. In 2012, they were inducted into the Rock and Roll Hall of Fame. The band's original line-up featured guitarist Hillel Slovak and drummer Jack Irons, alongside Kiedis and Flea.) http://en.wikipedia.org/wiki/Red_Hot_Chili_Peppers
11.13.1 Access point		
11.13.2 Variant access point		

Conferences (RDA Chapter 11, various parts)

Instructions for recording information about conferences are contained in various parts of RDA Chapter 11:

- RDA 11.3.2 covers location of conferences.
- RDA 11.4.2 deals with dates associated with conferences.
- RDA 11.6 covers numbering in conferences.
- RDA 11.13.1.8 provides instructions on constructing an authorized access point for a conference.

Core elements for conferences are:

- Conference name
- Date
- Location and number of conference
- Identifier (if available).

Determining the name of a conference follows the same general rules as for other types of corporate bodies. However, some additional guidance on conference names can be found in the 'exceptions' to RDA 11.2.2.5.4, that cover different forms of a conference name:

- Choose the form of name that includes the name of the associated body.
- For annual meetings of an association, apply the instructions at RDA 11.2.2.14.6.
- If a conference has a specific name and a more general name as part of a series of conferences, choose the specific name as the preferred name.

As with identifiers for Persons, Families and other types of Corporate Bodies, the attribute 'Identifier' for a conference has been included in RDA for future development. At present there are limited Identifiers available for conferences.

Authorized access points for conferences take the form:
Conference name (number : date : location)

World Library and Information Congress (75th : 2009 : Milan, Italy)

- Numbers of conferences are recorded as ordinal numbers, e.g., 1st, 2nd, etc (RDA 11.6)
- Record the year the conference was held as the date. Only add more specific dates (i.e., months and days) to distinguish between conferences with the same name held in the same year. (RDA 11.4.2.3)
    - Record conference dates in the 111 $d MARC field, and in the 046 field if desired.
- For conferences located in cities or smaller areas, add the name of the larger area or jurisdiction to which it belongs, following the rules for recording place names in RDA Chapter 16, e.g., Beijing, China. (RDA 11.3.2 and RDA 16.2.2.4)

Conferences are coded in the MARC 111 tag.

111 2# $a World Library and Information Congress $n (75th :$d 2009 :$c Milan, Italy)

 Note where the subfield codes are located when a parenthesis is used—its first code is always outside the parentheses.

CHAPTER THIRTEEN   Attributes of Persons, Families and Corporate Bodies   135

 EXERCISE 13.7
Create the authorized access points for the following conferences. Then code in MARC.

1. World Library and Information Congress, August 2013, Singapore

   Access point:

   MARC coding:

2. The 113th Annual Meeting of the American Anthropological Association held in Washington, DC in 2014

   Access point:

   MARC coding:

3. XII International Conference on Sport Medicine and Sport Science held at Cape Town, South Africa, November 6–7, 2014

   Access point:

   MARC coding:

4. International Conference on Secure Knowledge Management 2014, Dubai, 8–9 December 2014

   Access point:

   MARC coding:

5. Seventh Annual Green Building Convention was held at Cape Town International Convention Centre, Cape Town, South Africa from 10–12 September 2014

   Access point:

   MARC coding:

6. 36th International Conference on Software Engineering, Hyderabad, India, held May 31 to June 7, 2014

   Access point:

   MARC coding:

7. General Assembly Meeting of the tenth International Congress of Aerobiology, held in September 2014 at the School of Medicine, University of Western Sydney in Campbelltown, N.S.W.

   Access point:

   MARC coding:

EXERCISE 13.8

Use the template below to create an authority record for the 'Second Annual Illustration, Comics, and Animation Conference', held at Dartmouth College in Hanover, New Hampshire, February 28— March 2, 2014
https://sites.dartmouth.edu/illustrationcomicsanimationconference/
Note: use ABCD as your library symbol in the 040 field.

040		$a $b eng $e rda $c
046		$s [earliest date] $t [latest date]
111		$a [name of conference] $n (number : $d date : $c place)
368		$a [type of corporate body]
370		$c [associated country] $e [headquarters] $f [other associated place]
377		$a [language code] $l [language term]
670		$a [source consulted] $b [data found] $u [URL of source]

CHAPTER FOURTEEN
Attributes of Concepts, Objects, Events and Places

Introduction
AACR2 (our previous cataloging rules) did not address subject cataloging. However, because RDA is based on the conceptual model of FRBR, which includes the Group Three attributes of Concepts, Objects, Events and Places (i.e., subject information), RDA incorporates subjects into its Instruction Set.

Catalogers use a variety of thesauri, subject heading lists and classification schemes for subject cataloging. They select a scheme according to its appropriateness to describe the subjects of the resources in their collection. These subject descriptors are firmly established within each library's cataloging procedures. They work well with all types and formats of resources. Therefore, the need to revise them in order to cope better with modern material—a major consideration for revamping descriptive cataloging practices—was not as strong for subject cataloging. In recognition of this, the developers of RDA decided to work within current cataloging practices rather than place constraints on the subject schemes that are being used. For this reason, RDA provides only basic guidance on subject cataloging.

Subjects in RDA
RDA Section 4, 'Recording Attributes of Concept, Object, Event & Place', discusses how to record Group Three attributes. In effect this section deals with the subject access aspects of cataloging.

Section 4 contains RDA Chapter 12 to RDA Chapter 16:
- RDA Chapter 12—general guidelines for all Group Three entities
- RDA Chapter 13—identifying concepts
- RDA Chapter 14—identifying objects
- RDA Chapter 15—identifying events
- RDA Chapter 16—identifying places.

Except for RDA Chapter 16, none of these chapters provides any information but the message 'To be developed after the initial release of RDA'. The chapters are included merely as placeholders for the future.

Throughout the RDA Instruction Set, all chapters that focus on Group Three entitles simply provide the message 'To be developed after the initial release of RDA'. These chapters, like those in Section 4, are there as placeholders for the future.

You will see this 'placeholder' message when you look at:
- Section 7: Recording Relationships to Concepts, Objects, Events, & Places
  - RDA Chapter 23: General Guidelines on Recording the Subject of a Work
- Section 10: Recording Relationships between Concepts, Objects, Events, & Places
  - RDA Chapter 33: General Guidelines on Recording Relationships between Concepts, Objects, Events, and Places
  - RDA Chapter 34: Related Concepts
  - RDA Chapter 35: Related Objects
  - RDA Chapter 36: Related Events
  - RDA Chapter 37: Related Places
- Appendix L: Relationship Designators: Relationships Between Concepts, Objects, Events, and Places

Identifying Places (RDA Chapter 16)

RDA Chapter 16, 'Identifying Places' is the only chapter in Section 4 that contains information.
- RDA 16.2.2 provides extensive instructions on how to record place names when they are used as jurisdiction names, or as qualifiers in person, family and corporate body names.
- RDA 16.2.2.9 and RDA 16.2.2.10 set out the special treatment given to certain countries and cities, including those in Australia, the United States, Canada, the former U.S.S.R., the former Yugoslavia, and Britain.
- RDA 16.2.3 covers variant forms of place names.

Instructions for constructing authorized access points for places are 'to be added in a later release', except for instructions on the use of place names as part of government jurisdictions. These refer back to RDA Chapter 11 (RDA 11.13.1.1).

In summary, RDA Chapter 16 instructs catalogers to:
- Spell out any abbreviations.
- Use definite articles as part of the geographic name for certain names.
- Give the next larger jurisdiction, when necessary, to break a conflict.
- Give the jurisdiction type, when necessary, to break a conflict.

It does not:
- Provide instructions on choosing or identifying Identifiers for a Place.
- Provide instructions for constructing authorized access points for a Place.
- Provide instructions for constructing variant access points for a Place.

CHAPTER FOURTEEN   Attributes of Concepts, Objects, Events and Places   139

 EXERCISE 14.1
Use the Library of Congress Authorities (http://authorities.loc.gov/) or another authority file to determine the correct form of name for the following places.

1. Washington, D.C.

2. Washington State

3. Milan (city in Italy)

4. Vancouver Island, British Columbia, Canada

5. Antarctic regions

6. Addis Ababa

7. Mount Isa (western Queensland)

8. Kiev in the Ukraine

9. Ayrshire, a county in Scotland

10. Southern Ocean

CHAPTER FIFTEEN
Recording Relationships

Introduction
Relationships are a key aspect of the FRBR conceptual model, on which RDA is based. The RDA Instruction Set devotes more sections to recording relationships than it does to recording attributes. This indicates how significant RDA believes relationships should be in our catalog records.

This chapter outlines relationships and their importance in RDA cataloging. It introduces the basic concepts involved in recording relationships. These are explained in detail in the chapters that follow.

What are Relationships?
In a bibliographic record we identify the attributes of the resource we are cataloging. We then describe how these attributes are associated with one another. It is these connections and associations that demonstrate relationships. Relationships are able to show how a resource is linked to another resource, or show the responsibility a Person, Corporate Body, or Family has for a particular Work, Expression, Manifestation or Item.

Expressing relationships in bibliographic and authority records makes it easier for users to find what they want and tells them about other resources that are available in the catalog.

 Relationships provide patrons with pathways to related materials.

Relationships in RDA
Relationships in the RDA Instruction Set consist of two parts:
1. The entities being related: Work, Expression, Manifestation, Item, Person, Family, and Corporate Body
2. The type or nature of the relationship.

Relationships are recorded using an authorized access point for the entity and are coded in 1XX, 2XX, and 7XX MARC fields.

RDA Sections 2 and 3 told us how to construct authorized access points for entities. RDA Section 6 gives us instructions on how to *choose* the access points to use—in other words, what headings (authorized access points) will show us the relationship of that entity to the resource.

The type of relationship existing between an entity and a resource is stated in a term or code that says what the relationship is, or what role a Person, Corporate Body, or Family plays with respect to a particular Work, Expression, Manifestation or Item.

Relationships may be shown by:
- using relationship designators that are listed in the appendices to RDA
    - eg 100 1#$aFitzgerald-Jones, Sandra, $d1938—   , *$e interviewer.*

- relationship codes in MARC 21, particularly through the 7XX linking fields
    - eg 100 1# *$aVerdi, Giuseppe, $d1813–1901.*
        245 10 *$aOtello :$bin full score /$cGiuseppe Verdi.*
        700 1# **$i Libretto based on (work)** *$aShakespeare, William, $d1564–1616.
            $tOthello.*

- notes that identify the entities and provide information about the type of relationship.
    - eg 500 ## **$a Formerly known as:** *The unidentified soldier.*

RDA Sections 5—10

There are six main categories of relationships in RDA and each one is explained in its own section of the RDA Instruction Set. The key differences between them are emphasized in bold text below.
- Section 5: Recording **Primary Relationships** between Works, Expressions, Manifestations, and Items
- Section 6: Recording Relationships **to** Persons, Families, and Corporate Bodies
- Section 7: Recording Relationships **to** Concepts, Objects, Events, and Places
- Section 8: Recording Relationships **between** Works, Expressions, Manifestations, and Items
- Section 9: Recording Relationships **between** Persons, Families, and Corporate Bodies
- Section 10: Recording Relationships **between** Concepts, Objects, Events, and Places

Chapters Sixteen and Seventeen of this workbook deal with each of these categories of relationships, and their respective relationship designators.

Relationship Designators

Relationship designators are terms used to show relationships among and between resources, persons, families, and corporate bodies. They describe a wide range of relationships and allow users to see exactly what relationships exist.

The RDA relationship designators are located in four appendices (RDA Appendix I, J, K and L). Each Appendix covers different categories of relationships:

Appendix	What it does	Where it is used
Appendix I. Relationship designators for relationships between a resource and Persons, Families, and Corporate Bodies associated with the resource	relates resources to Group Two entities	only used in bibliographic records
Appendix J. Relationship designators for relationships between Works, Expressions, Manifestations, and Items	relates Group One entities to each other	used in both bibliographic and authority records
Appendix K. Relationship designators for relationships between Persons, Families, and Corporate Bodies	relates Group Two entities to each other	only used in name authority records (formerly known as 'see also' references)
Appendix L. Relationship designators for relationships between Concepts, Objects, Events, and Places	will deal with Group Three entities	not yet incorporated into RDA

- There is no equivalent to relationship designators in AACR2, although some MARC relator codes in the 7XX fields parallel some of the relationship designators, as do some Dublin Core metadata elements.
- All relationship designators are non-core; libraries can create their own policies on whether to use them or not.
- The lists of relationship designators in Appendices I—L are not closed vocabularies. If no term exists to describe a relationship, it is permissible to add your own term.
    - However, using terms not included in the list of relationship designators will reduce consistency and searchability across library catalogs.
- Relationship designators are added to the following MARC subfields:
    - $e in 100–110 and 700–710
    - $j in 111 and 711
    - $i in 700–730
    - $i in 76X–78X linking entry fields.

EXERCISE 15.1

Choose three relationship designators from Appendix I that you might find useful to include in the type of catalog records your organization creates. Use them to complete the table below.

Relationship Designator	Description from Appendix I	Associated WEMI entity

EXERCISE 15.2

Add relationship designators to the authorized access points in the resources shown below.

1. French translation of Wind in the Willows

   > Le vent dans les saules / Kenneth Grahame; illustrations d'Ernest H. Shepard ; traduit de l'anglais par Jacques Parsons.
   >
   > Published: [Paris] : Gallimard, c1993.
   >
   > ISBN: 2070583120

   100 1# $a Grahame, Kenneth,$d1859–1932,$e _____

   700 1# $a Parsons, Jacques,$e _____

   700 1# $a Shepard, Ernest H,$e _____

2. Book published by the Australian War Memorial

   > Reality in flames : modern Australian art & the Second World War / Warwick Heywood, exhibition curator ; [foreword by Dr Brendan Nelson]
   >
   > 'An Australian War Memorial travelling exhibition'
   >
   > 99 pages : illustrations ; 30 cm.
   >
   > Canberra, ACT: Australian War Memorial, 2014.

   700 1# $a Heywood, Warwick,$e _____

   700 1# $a Nelson, Brendan,$d1958–   ,$e _____

   710 2# $a Australian War Memorial,$e _____

3. CD of Clara Schumann's Piano Concerto

> **Clara Schumann: Piano Concerto, Trio, Romances / Jochum**
>
> Composed by: Clara Wieck Schumann
> Artists: Veronica Jochum, Joseph Silverstein, Colin Carr
> Conducted by: Joseph Silverstein
> Orchestra/Ensemble: Bamberg Symphony Orchestra
> Number of Discs: 1
> Recorded in: Stereo
> Length: 0 Hours 58 Mins.

100 1# $a Schumann, Clara,$d1819–1896,$e _____

700 1# $a Jochum, Veronica,$e _____

700 1# $a Silverstein, Joseph, 1932—   ,$e _____

700 1# $a Silverstein, Joseph, 1932—   ,$e _____

CHAPTER SIXTEEN
Entities Related to Resources

Introduction
The most common relationships that catalogers use in their records are those that show the connection between a resource and the people associated with it. These are the relationships shown between Group One entities (Work, Expression, Manifestation and Item) and Group Two entities (Persons, Families and Corporate Bodies).

Group One to Group Two Entities (RDA Section 6)
RDA records Persons, Families and Corporate Bodies (Group Two) relationships to Work, Expression, Manifestation and Item (Group One) entities in the following ways:

Relationship to the Work = Creator
Relationship to the Expression = Contributor
Relationship to the Manifestation = Publisher
Relationship to the Item = Owner

Or in more detail:

Entity	Group Two relationships	RDA chapter	RDA appendix	MARC field
Work	Creators (e.g., authors, composers, inventors, programmers, etc.)	RDA Chapter 19	Appendix I, relationship designators at 1.2	1XX $e (100, 110, 111) and 7XX $e
Expression	Contributors (e.g., editors, translators, illustrators, etc.)	RDA Chapter 20	Appendix I, relationship designators at 1.3	7XX $e
Manifestation	Publishers, Producers, Distributors, Manufacturers	RDA Chapter 21	Appendix I, relationship designators at 1.4	7XX $e
Item	Owners, Custodians, Curators, Donors, Annotators, etc.	RDA Chapter 22	Appendix I, relationship designators at 1.5	7XX $e

Creators of Works (RDA Chapter 19)

The relationship between a creator and a creator's work is core. Remember, though, in RDA, the relationship is only core for the Person or Family or Corporate Body that has *principal* responsibility for the work. Your library can choose to omit any other Persons, Families or Corporate Bodies who have some responsibility for the Work (RDA 19.2).

Multiple creators can be equally responsible for a resource, and RDA makes provision for creating authorized access points for all of them. However, if using MARC as an encoding scheme we must still name one of them as the principal creator in the 1XX field, and the others in the 7XX fields.

Corporate Bodies

Corporate Bodies can be creators but only under certain circumstances, as explained in RDA 19.2.1.1.1. In brief, a Corporate Body can be a creator if the Work:

- is of an administrative nature dealing with the Corporate Body itself
    - or its internal policies, procedures, finances, and/or operations
    - or its officers, staff, and/or membership (e.g., directories)
    - or its resources (e.g., catalogs, inventories)
- records the collective thought of the body as in the report of a commission, committee, etc. or official statement of position on external policies
- reports the proceedings of a conference, expedition, event, etc.
- records hearings conducted by legislative, judicial or governmental bodies
- is a specified type of legal or religious Work, such as a law, decree, constitution, treaty, or court rules or court decisions
- results from the collective activity of a performing group where responsibility goes beyond just performance
- is a named individual work of art by two or more artists acting as a corporate body
- is a cartographic resource emanating from a corporate body that does more than just publish, distribute, etc.

The Library of Congress Policy Statement (LC–PCC PS for 19.2.1.1.1) provides more detail about how to judge whether a Corporate Body can be considered the creator of a Work. If the Corporate Body is not considered the creator, it may still be an access point in the MARC 7XX fields. In these cases, MARC main entry will be under Title (245 field, first indicator '0').

RDA 19.2.1 also covers other special instances of when to consider corporate bodies, religious officials and families as creators.

EXERCISE 16.1
Indicate the authorized access point for the Corporate Body in each of the following resources. Then indicate whether the Corporate Body can be considered the creator of the Work, according to RDA 19.2.1.1.1.

1. Membership directory of the American Bar Association

    a. Authorized access point:

    b. Creator? (Y/N)

2. The annual report of the Trinidad Netball Association

    a. Authorized access point:

    b. Creator? (Y/N)

3. The Anarchist Federation Program in London / by the London Section of the Anarchist Federation

    a. Authorized access point:

    b. Creator? (Y/N)

4. Standards for air quality developed by the Standards Committee of the American Antipollution Society

    a. Authorized access point:

    b. Creator? (Y/N)

5. The The National Advisory Council on Ageing's discussion paper 'Euthanasia: an issue for your consideration'. (Note: the Council is in Canada)

    a. Authorized access point:

    b. Creator? (Y/N)

6. A room-by-room guide to the Cleveland Museum of Art by Melissa Cranshaw

    a. Authorized access point:

    b. Creator? (Y/N)

Other Group Two Relationships (RDA Chapters 20—22)

RDA Chapter 19 dealt with 'creator' relationships—those Persons, Families and Corporate Bodies associated with a resource at the Work level. We now look at RDA Chapters 20 to 22, that deal with 'contributor' relationships—those Persons, Families and Corporate Bodies associated with a resource at the Expression, Manifestation and Item levels.

The Group Two entities at the Expression level include contributors such as editors, translators, performers, etc. At the Manifestation level, relationships are identified for publishers, manufacturers, book designers, etc. The Item level shows owners, custodians, binders, restorationists, etc.

The relationship designators in Appendix I provide the terms that may be used with these Persons, Families and Corporate Bodies to indicate their relationship to the resource. This appendix is divided into separate sections for relationships at the Work level, Expression level, Manifestation level and Item level, to make these relationships clearer.

*While a creator may be recorded in a MARC 1XX field, contributors are only recorded as 7XX access points. Contributors **may not** be recorded in the 1XX field.*

EXERCISE 16.2
Refer to the URL http://comicbookdb.com/issue.php?ID=251902 for credits for the graphic novel, "Inherit the wind", that is part of the Fables series.

What relationship designators would you choose for:

1. Jim Fern　　　　　　_____

2. Adam Hughes　　　　_____

3. Lovern Kindzierski　_____

4. Todd Klein　　　　　_____

5. Joao Ruas　　　　　_____

6. Bill Willingham　　　_____

[Hint: check Wikipedia for definitions of the terms used on this website.]

In summary, when expressing relationships in RDA:
- RDA Chapters 19 to 22 provide instructions on when to record relationships between entities and their resources.
- The chapters provide instructions on creating the authorized access points to use when recording these relationships.
- Appendix I provides the terminology that explains the relationship.

CHAPTER SEVENTEEN
Entities Related to Each Other

Introduction
The concept of relationships is an integral part of RDA. It goes far beyond simply explaining how people are connected to resources. RDA makes provision for recording relationships between *all* of its entities. Some of these are already used in cataloging, for example, the linking relationships for serials found in the MARC 75X—78X fields. When fully implemented, RDA's relationships will allow library catalogs to link associated materials much more easily, and to describe those associations.

Primary Relationships (RDA Section 5, Chapter 17)
RDA Chapter 17 covers how Group One entities fit together at the catalog record level; that is, the hierarchical relationship of a Work to its Expression or Manifestation, and how this translates into a catalog record.

This category of relationships indicates 'primary relationships'; that is, the way that a single Work relates to all of its bibliographic 'family'. These are relationships:
- between a Work and its Expressions
- between an Expression and its Manifestations
- between a Manifestation and its Items.

This can be shown as:

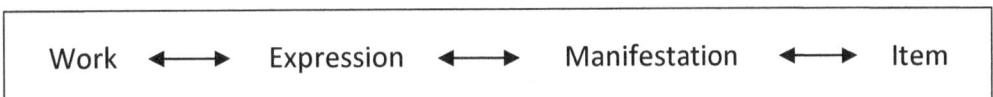

It is not very easy to record these relationships in our current MARC system. Section 5 of RDA outlines the expected future catalog, where there may be separate records for each entity, i.e., Work record, Expression record etc. (as opposed to the composite records we have now).

> **Current scenario:**
> Bibliographic record = Manifestation + elements of Work, Expression, Item
> **Future scenario:**
> Separate record for each WEMI entity, with links to each other

Core Elements for Primary Relationships

There are two core elements for primary relationships:

- **Work manifested** (RDA 17.8)—but if there is more than one Work manifested, only the first-named or the predominant Work is core. Recording any others is optional.

    RDA defines a Work Manifested as 'a work embodied in a manifestation'—in other words, a conceptual idea, or Work, has reached the stage where it has become a physical entity, or Manifestation. In these cases, RDA instructs the cataloger to indicate the Work in the Manifestation record. This is done either by including the Preferred Title for the Work in the bibliographic record (using MARC coding for Uniform Titles) or by a note or linking fields.

    Sometimes a Manifestation includes a number of Works—for example, many music CDs contain pieces by various musicians. In these cases, RDA permits us to record just the first named or major Work.

- **Expression manifested** (RDA 17.10)—is only core if there is more than one Expression. If there is more than one Expression manifested, only the first-named or the predominant Expression must be recorded. Recording any others is optional.

    RDA defines an Expression Manifested as 'an expression embodied in a manifestation'—in other words, a version of the Work (i.e. an Expression) has reached the stage where it has become a physical entity, or Manifestation. In these cases, RDA instructs the cataloger to indicate the Expression in the Manifestation record. This is done either by including the Authorized Access Point for the Expression in the bibliographic record (using MARC coding for Uniform Titles) or by a note or linking fields.

    Sometimes a Manifestation includes a number of Expressions—for example, a book containing the text in a number of different languages. In these cases, RDA permits us to record just the first or major Expression.

Many national libraries, including the Library of Congress, have decided to not implement the instructions on recording primary relationships at this stage. Instead they use the RDA Chapter 6 instructions for identifying and recording Works and Expressions. Using either of these chapters produces the same results in our current MARC records because MARC is not designed to record primary relationships.

Since the relationships between a Work, Expression, Manifestation, and Item are inherent in the FRBR definitions of those entities, relationship designators are not used for primary relationships.

Relationships Between Group One Entities (RDA Section 8, Chapters 24—28, and Appendix J)

RDA Section 8 deals with a range of structural relationships, and entities related at the same level:
- Whole/part
- Part-to-part
- Sequential (e.g., 'continued by')
- Accompanying
- Adaptations (e.g., 'based on')
- Work-to-Work
- Expression-to-Expression, etc.

Work-to-Work and Expression-to-Expression relationships can be recorded using any one or more of the following:
- Identifier
- Authorized access point
- Description (in the form of a note).

Manifestation-to-Manifestation and Item-to-Item relationships can only be recorded using an Identifier or a description.

Appendix J lists relationships between Group One entities. Like Appendix I, it provides relationship designators at the Work, Expression, Manifestation and Item levels. It then subdivides each of these categories into the following types of relationships:

Relationship	Explanation	Applies to	RDA appendix
Derivative relationships	those based on, adapted from, indexed by etc. another	Works, Expressions	J 2.2, J 3.2
Descriptive relationships	those that analyze, evaluate or review another	Works, Expressions, Manifestations, Items	J 2.3, J 3.3, J 4.3, J 5.3
Whole-part relationships	those contained in or part of another, including series and subseries	Works, Expressions, Manifestations, Items	J 2.4, J 3.4, J 4.4, J 5.4
Accompanying relationships	those that augment, supplement, are appended to, catalog etc. another	Works, Expressions, Manifestations, Items	J 2.5, J 3.5, J 4.5, J 5.5
Sequential relationships	those that precede, continue, supersede, merge or separate from another	Works, Expressions, Manifestations	J 2.6, J 3.6,
Equivalent relationships	those that are issued as, reproduce, reprint or act as mirror sites for another	Manifestations, Items	J 4.2, J.5.2

All the President's men the screenplay has a Work-to-Work relationship with *All the President's men* the novel:
- RDA Chapter 25 gives guidelines for recording related Works.
- RDA Appendix J provides the relationship designator terms.
- This is a derivative relationship ('based on'), so RDA J.2.2 uses the terminology:
  - *Screenplay based on: All the President's men*

 EXERCISE 17.1

Look at the relationship designators located in Appendix J. Based on the explanations provided below, what is the relationship designator described and what type of relationship is it? The first one has been done for you.

Explanation	Relationship designator	Type of relationship
An expression of a larger work of which the expression is a discrete component.	*Contained in (expression)*	*Whole-Part Expression Relationships*
An item that exemplifies a manifestation that embodies the same expression of a work.		
A work that enlarges upon the content of the source work.		
An expression of a work that came together with one or more expressions to form the new expression.		
An item that is contained on the same microform with the item being described.		
An expression of a work that has been updated, corrected, or expanded.		
A work that split into two or more separate works with new titles. Apply generally to serials.		
A manifestation that reproduces another manifestation.		
A work that contains a critical evaluation of the described work.		
A serial or newspaper containing a single issue or a supplementary section devoted to a special subject, with or without serial numbering, such as an anniversary number of a periodical or newspaper.		

EXERCISE 17.2
Use the relationship designators in Appendix J to record the history of the following serial:

The journal *Coin News* was published in 1954 in Kingston, Jamaica. In 1989 it changed its name to *Numismatics Jamaica*. In 1991 the journal *Jamaican Coins Monthly* was incorporated into it. This journal, incorporating *Jamaican Coins Monthly*, was published with a new title *Coin News Jamaica* in 1995. In 2003 the journal moved to Montego Bay and expanded its coverage, changing its name to *Caribbean Coin News*.

Coin News (1954–1989)

Numismatics Jamaica (1989–1995)

Jamaican Coins Monthly (1930–1991)

Coin News Jamaica (1995–2003)

Caribbean Coin News (2003—   )

Relationships Between Group Two Entities (RDA Section 9)

RDA Section 9 provides instructions about recording data used in authority records.

- RDA Chapter 30 covers different identities of Persons, (e.g., pseudonyms, creators using multiple names, alternate and real identities) and how to make notes about them in authority records.
- RDA Chapter 31 covers Families, and when to record information that clarifies the relationship between a Family and a resource in an authority record.
- RDA Chapter 32 covers Corporate Bodies and when and how to record their relationships in an authority record (e.g., former and later bodies, subsidiary bodies, mergers etc.)

This section only instructs on when and how to make notes about the various relationships. It refers you to other chapters that deal with how to construct the authorized access points for the entities (RDA Section 3), and what relationship designators to use to describe the relationship (RDA Appendix K).

None of the relationships between Persons, Families and Corporate Bodies are core in RDA. Most of these relationships are recorded as notes in an authority record.

- Persons: use MARC fields 500 $w and 663.
- Corporate Bodies: use 510 $wa, $wb.
- Persons, Families and Corporate Bodies: use 500, 510, $wr, $i.
- Incorporate the relationship designator from Appendix K into subfield $i of the 5XX note field.

Here are two examples of Persons related to another Group Two entity.

a) *Excerpt from authority record for the musical group Aerosmith, showing the band's relationships to its individual members (Joey Kramer, Joe Perry, Steven Tyler and Brad Whitford). Note that each band member will also have an authority record that shows a reciprocal relationship to the group.*

    110 2_ $a Aerosmith (Musical group)
    500 1_ $w r $i Member: $a Kramer, Joey
    500 1_ $w r $i Member: $a Perry, Joe, $d 1950—
    500 1_ $w r $i Member: $a Tyler, Steven, $d 1948—
    500 1_ $w r $i Member: $a Whitford, Brad, $d 1952—

b) *Excerpt from the authority record for Bill Gates, indicating that he founded the Microsoft Corporation and the Bill and Melinda Gates Foundation. This authority record indicates the relationship between the corporate bodies (the Microsoft Corporation and the Bill & Melinda Gates Foundation) and the person (Bill Gates).*

    100 1_ $a Gates, Bill, $d 1955—
    510 2_ $w r $i Founded corporate body: $a Microsoft Corporation
    510 2_ $w r $i Founded corporate body: $a Bill & Melinda Gates Foundation

Entities Related to Each Other: Group Three Entities (RDA Sections 7 and 10)

In Chapter Fourteen of this workbook, we looked at Section 4 of the RDA Instruction Set *Recording Attributes of Concept, Object, Event & Place*, and found that its chapters did not provide information but were there as placeholders for the future.

The same is true for RDA Section 7 *Recording Relationships to Concepts, Objects, Events & Places* and its general guidelines chapter (RDA Chapter 23), as well as RDA Section 10 *Recording Relationships between Concepts, Objects, Events & Places* and its chapters (RDA Chapters 33–37). Each of these chapters consists of the note 'To be developed after the initial release of RDA'.

In the future, RDA Section 7 will focus on the 'has as subject' relationship between a Work and the other entities. It is expected that it will cover the general topic of recording subject relationships, and may constitute a general discussion of subject analysis.

It is expected that RDA Section 10 will look at relationships between the Group Three entities of Concept, Object, Event and Place, and consider Concept-to-Concept, Concept-to-Object, etc. relationships.

As with the other relationships sections, specific relationships for Group Three entities will be recorded, in the future, using relationship designators. Appendix L will provide the list of relationship designators for subject relationships. At this stage, Appendix L is a placeholder with the note 'To be developed after the initial release of RDA'.

 In summary, important aspects of recording relationships in RDA include:

- Relationships indicate links between a resource and its creators, and also between a resource and its bibliographic family.
- Relationships work between, and among, each of the FRBR entities.
- Indicating relationships provides a richer catalog record.
- RDA provides more flexibility in the number of relationships that can be recorded, by using relationship designators.
- Relationship designators are used in bibliographic records, not authority records.
- Relationship designators make it easier to identify different types of relationships and the specific nature of relationships.

CHAPTER EIGHTEEN
Putting It All Together

Introduction

This chapter will consolidate what you have learned about cataloging by having you fully catalog a resource in an RDA–compliant manner, using MARC coding.

You will use this workbook, *Learn cataloging the RDA way*, as the resource to catalog. First gather and record bibliographic information at each WEMI level, then transfer the data to a MARC cataloging template. Note that all the information you need for your MARC record should be gathered on the WEMI templates. If you wish to add other information, you must identify which WEMI entity and element is involved, and add the data to that WEMI template as well as to your MARC record.

After completing the MARC record, use the authority templates to gather and record information about the authors of *Learn cataloging the RDA way*. You may code this in MARC if you wish, but be sure to use the MARC Authority format, not the MARC Bibliographic format.

 It is extremely useful to look regularly at RDA–compliant records and use them as a guide to correct cataloging practice. The examples on the RDA Toolkit/JSC site are designed for this purpose. They cover different formats of material, providing both RDA details and their corresponding MARC records.

 EXERCISE 18.1
Using this workbook as your resource to catalog, and the templates provided:
1. *Identify and record the attributes of the original Work.*
2. *Identify and record the attributes of the Expression of the Work.*
3. *Identify and record the attributes of the Manifestation.*
4. *Put all the attributes into a MARC bibliographic record. Note which WEMI template provided the information.*
5. *Gather information to create authority records for the authors.*

You can use additional resources to find further information as needed, particularly for author information.

Be sure you check the RDA instructions and use the RDA/MARC mappings.

1. Work record

Record attributes of the *Work* using the template below. Use the RDA instruction numbers as a guide.

- 6.2 to 6.8 – Recording the attributes of the Work
- 19.2 – Recording creator associated with the Work and Appendix I
- 6.27 – Constructing the authorized access point for the Work
- 7.2 to 7.9 – Describing content of the Work

RDA Reference	RDA Element	Data Recorded
6.2.1	Preferred title for the Work	
6.2.3	Variant title	
6.3.1	Form of Work	
6.4.1	Date of Work	
6.5.1	Place of origin	
6.6.1	Other distinguishing characteristics	
6.7.1	History of the Work	
6.8	Identifier	
19.2.1.3 Appendix I	Creator associated with the Work	
6.27	Authorized access point for the Work	
7.2–7.3	Nature of content; coverage of content	
7.7	Intended audience	

2. Expression record

Record attributes of the *Expression* using the template below. Use the RDA instruction numbers as a guide.
- 6.9 to 6.13 – Recording attributes of the Expression
- 7.10 to 7.29 – Describing content of the Expression
- RDA Chapter 20 – Person, family and corporate body associated with Expression, and Appendix I

RDA Reference	RDA Element	Data Recorded
6.9	Content type	
6.10	Date of Expression	
6.11	Language of Expression	
6.12	Other distinguishing characteristic of the Expression	
6.13	Identifier for the Expression	
7.10	Summarization of content	
7.12	Language	
7.15	Illustrative content	
7.16	Supplementary content	
7.17	Colour content	
20.2 Appendix I.3	Contributor to the Expression	

3. Manifestation record

Record attributes of the *Manifestation* using the template below. Use the RDA instruction numbers as a guide. *Note*: include attributes of the *Item* if necessary.
- RDA Chapter 2 – Recording attributes of manifestation and items
- RDA Chapter 3 – Describing carriers

RDA Reference	RDA Element	Data Recorded
2.3	Title proper of Manifestation	
2.3.4	Other title information	
2.3.6	Variant title of Manifestation	
2.4.2	Statement of responsibility	
2.5	Edition statement	
2.8.2	Place of publication	
2.8.4	Name of publisher	
2.8.6	Date of publication	
2.11	Copyright date	
2.12	Series	
2.13	Mode of issuance	
2.15	Identifier for the Manifestation	
3.2	Media type	
3.3	Carrier type	
3.4.5	Extent	
3.5	Dimensions	

4. MARC bibliographic record

Use this template and transfer information from the previous records into correct MARC format. Note that you should have already recorded all the information that you need for this template on the previous Work, Expression and Manifestation templates. You may need to add additional fields, or repeat fields, as required.

MARC field	Subfield	Data Recorded	Template Used (W,E, or M)
020	$a		
040	$e		
041	$a		
046	$k		
100 1#	$a $d $e		
240	$a		
245 1x	$a $b $c		
250	$a		
264	$a $b $c		
300	$a $b $c		
336	$a $2		
337	$a $2		
338	$a $2		
490	$a		
5XX			
5XX			
5XX			
520	$a		
7XX	$a		

5. Authority record for author #1

Record authority data using the template below. Use the RDA instruction numbers as a guide. Use the MARC Format for Authority Data to indicate an appropriate MARC field.
- 9.0 to 9.18 – Recording attributes for the person
- 9.19 – Constructing the access point for the person

RDA Reference	RDA Element	Data Recorded	MARC Field
9.2	Name of the person		
9.3	Dates associated with a person		
9.4	Title associated with a person		
9.5	Fuller form of name		
9.6	Other designation associated with a person		
9.7	Gender		
9.8	Place of birth		
9.9	Place of death		
9.10	Country associated with a person		
9.11	Place of residence		
9.12	Address of a person		
9.13	Affiliation		
9.14	Language		
9.15	Field of activity		
9.16	Profession or occupation		
9.17	Biographical information		
9.18	Identifier		
9.19	Authorized access point		
8.12	Sources consulted		

CHAPTER EIGHTEEN   Putting it All Together   165

Authority record for author #2
Record authority data using the template below. Use the RDA instruction numbers as a guide. Use the MARC Format for Authority Data to indicate an appropriate MARC field.
- 9.0 to 9.18 – Recording attributes for the person
- 9.19 – Constructing the access point for the person

RDA Reference	RDA Element	Data Recorded	MARC Field
9.2	Name of the person		
9.3	Dates associated with a person		
9.4	Title associated with a person		
9.5	Fuller form of name		
9.6	Other designation associated with a person		
9.7	Gender		
9.8	Place of birth		
9.9	Place of death		
9.10	Country associated with a person		
9.11	Place of residence		
9.12	Address of a person		
9.13	Affiliation		
9.14	Language		
9.15	Field of activity		
9.16	Profession or occupation		
9.17	Biographical information		
9.18	Identifier		
9.19	Authorized access point		
8.12	Sources consulted		

CHAPTER NINETEEN
Copy Cataloging

Introduction

While most of this workbook has been devoted to original cataloging, staff in cataloging departments also **copy catalog**. This is sometimes called cloning a record, or close cataloging. In simple terms, copy cataloging is the process of cataloging resources using existing bibliographic records.

This chapter focuses on the practical aspects of copy cataloging. For background information about the processes involved, see *Learn basic library skills* by Helen Rowe and Trina Grover.

What is Copy Cataloging?

Copy cataloging involves:
- finding an existing bibliographic record that matches the item in hand
- editing the record to improve or upgrade the information it contains
- attaching appropriate holdings information to the bibliographic record, including location, classification and circulation status.

The Copy Cataloging Process

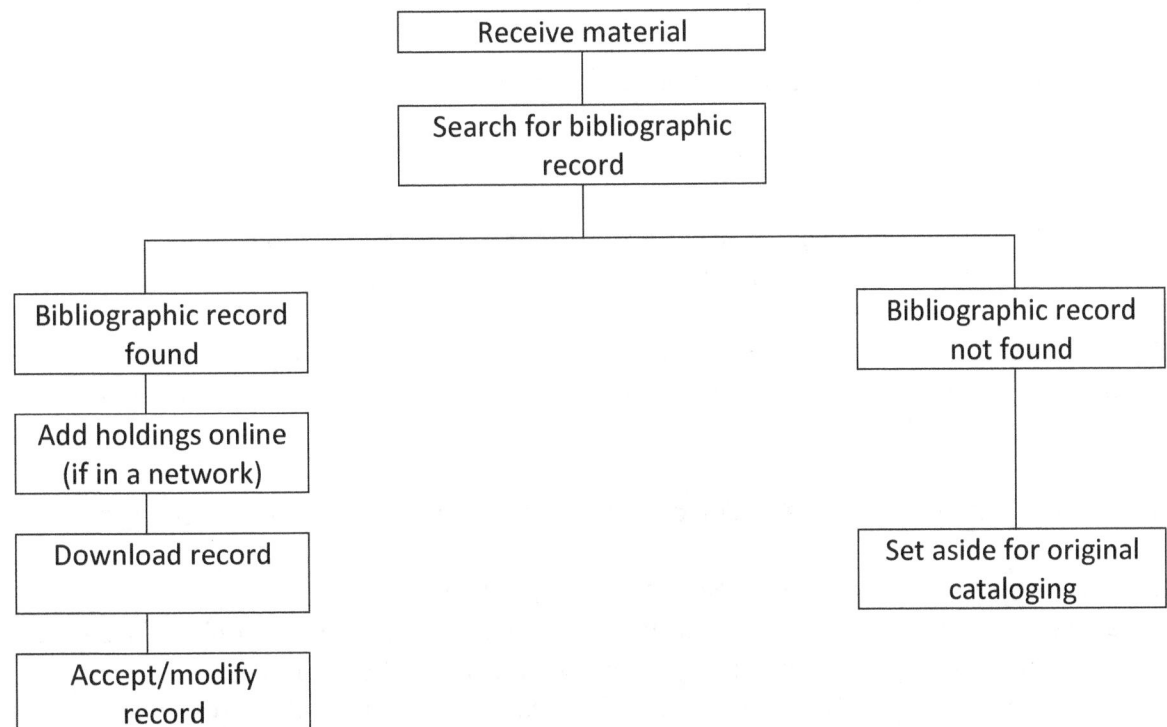

Source: Rowe, Helen and Trina Grover. *Learn basic library skills*. International edition. Friendswood, Texas : TotalRecall Publications, Inc., 2015, page 50.

Sources of Copy Cataloging Records

There are several options for obtaining copy cataloging records, including:
- manual copy cataloging by finding a record in another catalog. Once found, these records can be downloaded, or copied and pasted into your library's catalog
- using Cataloging-in-Publication (CIP) records
- using catalog subscription services that find or create records and sell them to libraries. These services are provided on a commercial basis, offering original and copy cataloging
- purchasing MARC records when you purchase resources from suppliers
- copying a record from a network or consortium that your library belongs to, like OCLC, Libraries Australia, etc.
- 'triggering' an automatic download by adding your holdings to a record.

Steps in Copy Cataloging

1. Search the library's catalog for a bibliographic record that matches the item to be cataloged
   a. Search standard numbers (e.g., ISBN/ISSN/Control number)
   OR
   b. Search title (if no record was found with the standard number search).

2. If a catalog record is found:
   a. check that the copy cataloging record and the item in hand are the same
      - Same title and author
      - Same date of publication and/or edition
      - Same record control number (e.g., LC number from CIP, or ISBN/ISSN)
   b. If all these fields match
      - Check the correctness of the copy for:
        1. descriptive cataloging
        2. classification number
        3. subject headings
      - Accept the copy; or modify it to suit the needs of your library
      - Attach holdings information for the new resource.

3. If no record is found, search another source such as a major library's catalog (like Library of Congress) or a union catalog (like WorldCat), using the same process as in Steps 1 and 2 above.

4. If a record is not found in any catalog, set the resource aside for original cataloging.

5. You will need to create new catalog records if you have:
   a. copies of the same resource in print, as an e-book and in microfilm. These would need three separate records—one for each format of the resource
   b. a new edition—as there would be differences in the content of the resource
   c. a new publisher—even if everything else about the resource was the same, a new publisher would have different publication details.

Copy Cataloging Basics

When you select a bibliographic record to copy catalog, it must match the resource you wish to catalog in its form, its content and its publication details.
- Ensure the new record correctly reflects the resource in hand (e.g., correct edition)
- Check that the access points in the copied record are correct, by searching for name or subject authority records and creating or modifying them as needed
    - Access points should be constructed according to RDA guidelines
- Check the call number and, if necessary, adjust it so that it is consistent with similar resources in your collection.

 On a MARC record you will need to match the following MARC tags with the resource:

Must match: Field	Description
020/022 (if present)	ISBN/ISSN
245	Title Statement
250 $a	Edition Statement
264	Publication, Distribution, etc.
300	Physical Characteristics
490 $a (if present)	Series Statement
505 (if present)	Contents Notes
538 (if present), for AV material	System Details Notes

Editing Copy Cataloging Records

It is not always appropriate to accept a copied record exactly as it appears. In many cases it is necessary to edit parts of the record. Common reasons for editing records when copy cataloging are:
- there are transcription errors, e.g., misspelling, or the number of pages is incorrect
- some information is missing—e.g., statement of responsibility or publication details
- ISBD punctuation is missing or incorrect
- local policy is to use the current descriptive cataloging guidelines (RDA) but the record was created using the old cataloging rules (AACR2)
- local policy is to include access points for all authors but the record does not include them all
- local policy is to include at least one subject heading but there are none in the record
- there are differences relating to local holdings, e.g., the library may have only partial holdings on a record for a multivolume work.

What to Edit

An important decision for copy catalogers is what to accept in a record and what to change.
- In general, accept what is given in the copied record
- Only delete information that is inaccurate or misleading. Limit changes to those that relate to accuracy, substance, or retrievability.

Specific areas to consider for editing include:

Factual Errors—unless there is a guideline to the contrary for a particular field, correct any factual errors.

Typographical Errors for Monographs—ensure that the title has been transcribed *exactly* as it appears on the resource. For RDA-compliant records, do not accept any 245 field 'corrections' of typographical errors that are provided in the copied record. Accept 246 fields in the copied record that address such typographical errors, or add 246 fields for this purpose. Accept notes about the corrected data, according to cataloger judgment.

For a resource with the title 'Ditigal imaging'
If the copied record has:
    245 14 $a Ditigal [sic] imaging   or
    245 14 $a Ditigal [i.e., digital] imaging   or
    245 14 $a Digital imaging

Change to:
    245 14 $a Ditigal imaging
    246 1# $i Corrected title: $a Digital imaging

Typographical Errors for Serials—correct typographical errors in the title proper for serials and integrating resources—i.e., if the issue of a serial or the update of an integrating resource that has been used to create the catalog record contains a typographical error in its title, record the correct title, without explanation, in the 245 field. This ensures that the serial or integrating resource as a whole has a correct, stable title.

Punctuation and Spacing—make changes relating to:
- ISBD punctuation and spacing
- punctuation and spacing in headings

to ensure they are compliant with RDA guidelines and consistent within your catalog.

Capitalization—generally accept capitalization as found. However, make changes relating to:
- any failure to capitalize a proper name
- any failure to follow the instructions in RDA Appendix A.4 regarding words in the title of a resource.

Abbreviations—in transcribed fields, use only the abbreviations that appear on the resource. In other fields, minimize the use of abbreviations as per RDA guidelines. When in doubt, check RDA Appendix B for acceptable abbreviations in a catalog record.

Numerals—in transcribed fields, accept the form of numerals as found on the resource.

Square Brackets—Data only needs to be enclosed in square brackets if it is taken from outside the preferred sources of information or outside the resource itself.

Classification and Subject Matching—ensure that the first subject heading reflects the classification number. Other subject headings (6XX) can be in any order.

CHAPTER NINETEEN   Copy Cataloging   171

 EXERCISE 19.1
Look at the OPAC records displayed below. Identify what is wrong with each of these records by highlighting errors and/or noting missing information. Correct the record where possible.

1. Book

008 131206s2014   dcuab   bc f001 0 eng c

020 ## $a 9780934686259 (pbk.)

040 ## $a NNFr/DLC $c NNFr $d DLC

050 00 $a NK4695.S76 $a C49 2014

082 00 $a 738.3/8 $a 23

245 00 $a Chigusa and the art of tea / $c Louise Allison Cort and Andrew M. Watsky, editors ; with Takeuchi Jun'ichi ... [et al.].

260 ## $a Washington, DC : $b Freer Gallery of Art and Arthur M. Sackler Gallery, Smithsonian Institution ; $a Seattle ; $a London : $b Distributed by the University of Washington Press, $c c2014.

500 ## $a Published by the Freer Gallery of Art and the Arthur M. Sacler Gallery on the occasion of the exhibition Chigusa and the Art of Tea, February 22–July 27, 2014. Organized by the Arthur M. Sacler Gallery, the exhibition travels to the Princeton University Art Museum, September 13, 2014–January 4, 2015.

504 ## $a Includes bibliographical references (p. 273–279) and index.

630 00 $a Chigusa $v Exhibitions

650 #0 $a Pottery, Chinese $v Exhibitions.

650 #0 $a Storage jars $z Japan $v Exhibitions.

650 #0 $a Tea containers $z Japan $v Exhibitions.

650 #0 $a Japanese tea ceremony $x Utensils $v Exhibitions.

650 #0 $a Poetry, Chinese $z Japan $v Exhibitions.

700 1# $a Cort, Louise Allison, $d 1944–

700 1# $a Watsky, Andrew Mark, $d 1957–

710 2# $a Freer Gallery of Art

710 2# $a Arthur M. Sackler Gallery (Smithsonian Institution)

710 2# $a Princeton University. $b Art Museum

2. Map

008		131004t20132013wea ca a s 0 eng d
040	##	$a ANL $b eng $e rda $d ANL
043	##	$a u-at-we
050	#4	$a G9021.H2 2013
100	2#	$a Geological Survey of Western Australia, $e issuing body.
245	10	$a Iron ore deposiits of the Yilgarn Craton - 2013 / $c Geological Survey of Western Australia ; compiled by R W Cooper ; cartography by A K Jones ; edited by B Striewski and K Greenberg.
255	##	$a Scale 1:1,500,000 $b Albers equal area projection with Central meridian 121° and standard parallels 17°30' and 31°30 $c (E 114°00'—E 123°00'/S 25°00—S 35°00').
264	#1	$a East Perth, Western Australia :$b Geological Survey of Western Australia, $c 2013.
264	#1	$c ©2013
300	##	$a 1 map : $b colour ; $c 84 x 68 cm, on sheet 101 x 71 cm.
337	##	$a unmediated $2 rdamedia
338	##	$a sheet $2 rdacarrier
500	##	$a Logos at head of scale bar: Government of Western Australia Department of Mines and Petroleum and Geological Survey of Western Australia.
500	##	$a Includes locality map and data directory with data curreny dates ranging from 1998–2013.
650	#0	$a Iron mining and mining $z Western Australia $z Yilgarn Craton $v Maps.
651	#0	$a Yilgarn Craton (W.A.) $v Maps.
700	1#	$a Cooper, R. W. $q (Roger William), $d 1949— , $e compiler.
700	1#	$a Jones, A. K., $e cartographer.
700	1#	$a Striewski, B., $e editor.
700	1#	$a Greenberg, K., $e editor.
710	1#	$a Western Australia. $b Department of Mines and Petroleum.

3. Conference

008		130402s2013 be a 101 0 eng d
020	##	$a 9789066050693
020	##	$a 9066050691
040	##	$a VXG $c VXG $d ORE $d OCLCO
082	04	$a 634.6 $2 23
111	2#	$a International Symposium on Tropical and Subtropical Fruits ($n 4th : $d 2008 : $c Bogor, Indonesia)
245	10	$a Proceedings of the IVth International Symposium on Tropical and Subtropical Fruits : $b Bogor, Indonesia, November 3–7, 2008 / $c convener R. Poerwanto ; [editors: Endah Retno Palupi, Krisantini, I.J. Warrington].
246	14	$a Proceedings of the Fourth International Symposium on Tropical and Subtropical Fruits.
246	18	$a Fourth IS on Tropical and Subtropical Fruits.
264	#4	$c ©2013
300	##	$a 680 p. : $b ill. ; $c 24 cm.
336	##	$a still image $2 rdacontent
337	##	$a unmediated $2 rdamedia
338	##	$a volume $2 rdacarrier
490	1#	$a Acta horticulturae, $x 0567–7572 ; $v no. 975.
520	##	$a Includes bibliographical references and author index.
650	#0	$a Tropical fruit $v Congresses.
700	1#	$a Poerwanto, R. $q (Roedhy)
700	1#	$a Palupi, Endah Retno.
700	1#	$a Warrington, I. J. $q (Ian J.)
710	2#	$a International Society for Horticultural Science. $b Section Tropical and Subtropical Fruits.
710	2#	$a International society for horticultural science. $b commission education, research training and consultancy.
710	2#	$a International Society for Horticultural Science. $b Commission Molecular Biology and In Vitro Culture.
830	#0	$a Acta horticulturae ; $v no. 975.

4. Serial

008		130822c20139999enkar 0 a0eng
022	0#	$a 2053–6267
040	##	$a Uk $b eng $c Uk $e rda
050	14	$a BX9450 $b .H7
082	04	$a 284.5092 $2 23
222	#4	$a The Huguenot Society journal
245	04	$a The Huguenot Soicety journal.
264	#1	$a London $b Huguenot Society of Great Britain and Ireland $c 2013–
300	##	$a v. : $b illustrations (black and white, and colour) ; $c 24 cm.
310	##	$a Annual
336	##	$a text $2 rdacontent
336	##	$a unmediated $2 rdamedia
338	##	$a volume $2 rdacarrier
362	1#	$a Began with vol. XXX, no. 1 (autumn 2013).
525	##	$a Volume 30, no. 2 (2014) is accompanied by a booklet with title: By-laws.
588	##	$a Description based on: Vol. XXX, no. 1 (autumn 2013); title from title page
588	##	$a Latest issue consulted: Vol. XXX, no. 1 (autumn 2013)
610	20	$a Huguenot Society of Great Britain and Ireland $v Periodicals.
650	#0	$a Huguenots $z England $v Periodicals.
650	#0	$a Hugonots $v Biography $v Periodicals.
650	#0	$a Huguenots $v Periodicals.
710	2#	$a Huguenot Society of Great Britain and Ireland, $e issuing body.
740	02	$a By-laws (Huguenot Society of Great Britain and Ireland).
780	00	$t Proceedings of the Huguenot Society of Great Britain and Ireland $x 0957–0756

Cloning Records

Sometimes you will find a record for a resource that is similar to yours but in a different format (e.g., a record for a book when you want to catalog the spoken word version). In these cases, you can use the existing record as the basis for your cataloging since many of the details will be the same. Creating a new catalog record based on a record for a similar resource (e.g., the spoken word version of a monograph, or a new edition of the monograph) by copying the original record and making appropriate changes, is called **cloning** or **close cataloging**.

The process for cloning is similar to copy cataloging but more care is needed to ensure that only the information in the existing record that matches your resource is retained. Areas that may change in cloned records include:
- format of the resource (may need to change leader and control fields)
- 264 field (if cloning a new edition)
- 3XX fields (for different physical formats, or different editions).

Specific changes that should be made to a cloned record include:
- Change 000 (Leader) field as appropriate, particularly check positions 06, 07, 17 & 18.
- Delete 001 and 003 fields, as these refer only to the original resource.
- Change 008 field to reflect the resource in hand. Particularly, amend date (positions 07–10) and publication (positions 15–17) details for changes in editions. Change positions 18–34 if the type of material has changed.
- Change 020 or 022 fields to the ISBN or ISSN of the new resource.
- Delete 035 or other system record numbers that refer only to the original resource.
- Delete 040 (cataloging source field) and all its subfields, since these refer only to the original resource. Add a new 040 field with your details for this resource. Include $erda if appropriate.
- Ensure the record contains a 050 field and/or a 082 field (classification numbers) as appropriate.

Upgrading Copy Cataloging Records

Because of the large number of AACR2 records in library catalogs, many potential records for copy cataloging or cloning will only be available in this older format. It will be a library policy whether to accept these and add old records to the catalog, or to upgrade the records to make them RDA–compliant.

Accepting an AACR2 record may seem easier, however it does require the cataloger to know the AACR2 rules in order to ensure the information is correctly presented. In the long term, it may be more efficient and cost-effective to simply upgrade records to RDA. This will result in a more consistent catalog. It can also be a better use of cataloging time, since cataloging staff will not have to juggle two sets of rules and guidelines.

Upgrading copy cataloging records requires attention to detail. It may take more time to catalog a resource but adds value to the catalog and makes the catalog a more effective tool for users.

Copy Cataloging Checklist

The chart below highlights the main areas to be checked when accepting a record for copy cataloging, and indicates any changes to be made. Information in the chart includes details on both how to accept an RDA record and how to upgrade an AACR2 record to make it RDA–compliant.

Data Element	Name	RDA Action
Leader/18	Descriptive cataloging form	Should be **i** (for ISBD), not **a** (for AACR2)
020 022	ISBN ISSN	Ensure the ISBN or ISSN matches the resource in hand. If not, do not use for copy cataloging. Instead, clone the record and use the appropriate number for the resource being cataloged
040	Cataloging source	Use appropriate code for your language e.g., **$b eng**, **$b fre**, etc. RDA records should contain **$e rda**. If adding to existing 040 field, insert immediately before $c
082	DDC number	If more than one classification number is given, use the number from the most recent edition. Editions are noted in the **$2** subfield, e.g., **$223** Do not accept/include a library's book number or location symbol in this field; add these in the holdings field
1XX	Creator (MARC 'main entry')	The 1XX field should generally end with a **$e relationship designator** (e.g., author, compiler, filmmaker, etc.) Add a creator if missing (this may happen with AACR2 records if more than three persons or bodies are named in a single statement of responsibility) For a collaboration (all creators jointly responsible for the work), put the first-named creator in a 1XX field and others in 7XXs For a compilation (creators responsible for different sections of the work), put all creators in 7XXs (i.e., no 1XX, use 245 'title main entry')
245	Title proper, etc.	Delete '[sic]' or '[i.e., ___]' Remove $h if present Only abbreviations found on the resource itself should be included in the title Transcribe statements of responsibility exactly as on the resource, including titles and terms of address (e.g., Mrs, Dr, Rev). Qualifications and affiliations after names are optional In an existing statement of responsibility, replace '[et al.]' with a full transcription of the statement, or use '[and x others]'

Data Element	Name	RDA Action
246	Variant title	If '[sic]' or '[i.e., __]' was removed from the 245 title proper, add a 246 field for the corrected form
250	Edition statement	Transcribe the edition statement exactly as on the resource, e.g., Third edition, 3rd edition or 3rd ed. Record numerals as found on the resource. Only abbreviations found on the resource itself should be used
260 vs. 264	Publication statement	Replace 260 field with **264** field and use the appropriate **second indicator (0–3)**, based on the content of the resource
264	Publication statement	**$a** The first place of first publisher is transcribed as found anywhere on the resource. Replace '[S.l.]' with a supplied place if possible, or use '**[Place of publication not identified]**' **$b** The first publisher is transcribed as found anywhere on the resource. Use the full form of name as on the resource (not an abbreviated form of name). If the publisher is unknown, use '**[publisher not identified]**' (not '[s.n.]') **$c** For monographs, ensure that a date of publication is given, even if only an estimate. Replace incomplete dates in the format '[19—?]' with an estimated date or date range, e.g., '[1978?]' or '[1978 or 1979]' or '[between 1978 and 1985]'. If no publication date can be supplied, record '**[date of publication not identified]**'. If a date cannot be determined for a multipart monograph, serial or integrating resource, do not record a date of publication
264 #4	Copyright statement	Record copyright date in a separate 264 field, using **4** as the second indicator Only record a **$c** subfield in this field. Use the form **$c copyright 2014** or **$c © 2014**. For sound recordings use the form **$c phonogram copyright 2014** or **$c ℗ 2014**
300	Physical description	Don't use any abbreviations. Spell out words like pages, volumes, approximately, illustrations, etc., in full. However, 'cm' and 'mm' are considered symbols and can be used Use '34 unnumbered pages', 'not [34] p.'

Data Element	Name	RDA Action

33X	Content type, Media type, Carrier type	Always include 33X fields, e.g.,
		– Book
		    336 ## $a text $2 rdacontent
		    337 ## $a unmediated $2 rdamedia
		    338 ## $a volume $2 rdacarrier
		– Film on DVD
		    336 ## $a two-dimensional moving image $2 rdacontent
		    337 ## $a video $2 rdamedia
		    338 ## $a video disc $2 rdacarrier
		$b codes can be retained if present
		337 fields are not mandatory but are usually included
		All 33X fields are repeatable

490	Series statement	If a **440** field exists on an old record, delete it and transfer information to a **490** field Transcribe series name and numbering as they appear on the resource. Only abbreviate numbering if it appears that way on the resource
5XX	Notes fields	Generally, accept the notes in the copied record Change notes only if they contain typographical errors; are factually incorrect; or their meaning is not clear
6XX	Subject access fields	Check the second indicator to ensure the source of the subject headings is the same thesaurus used in your library (usually **'0' for LCSH**, or **'7'** with **'$2lcgft' for LC genre headings**). If not, delete these and add your own subject headings
7XX	Added entry fields	7XX fields should include **relationship designators**, especially $e designators for personal names and corporate bodies For AACR2 records with more than three persons or bodies named in a single statement of responsibility, ensure the first-named is moved to the 1XX field and the others are recorded as 7XX
830	Series added entry—Uniform Title	Check library policy as some libraries do not use this field. Add if necessary. If required: • Use in conjunction with a 490 field • Use when the preferred title of the series differs from what was transcribed from the resource in the 490 field, or when the series title is required as an access point
9XX	Local fields	These fields were previously used for library-specific information and are no longer supported in the MARC format. They may still appear on some records. Delete these fields

CHAPTER NINETEEN   Copy Cataloging   179

 EXERCISE 19.2
Below are three records that you have found for earlier versions of the resources that you have in hand. Use these as the basis for new, cloned records, and code using MARC. Details of the resources you hold are given.

1.

FIRST INTERNATIONAL EDITION

LIBRARYSPEAK

a glossary of terms in librarianship
and information management

Compiled by
Lynn Farkas

TotalRecall Publications, Inc.
1103 Middlecreek
Friendswood, Texas 77546
281-992-3131   281-482-5390 Fax
www.totalrecallpress.com
All rights reserved. Except as permitted under the United States Copyright Act of 1976, No part of this publication may be reproduced, stored in a retrieval system, or transmitted in any form or by any means electronic or mechanical or by photocopying, recoding, or otherwise without prior permission of the publisher. Exclusive worldwide content publication / distribution
by TotalRecall Publications, Inc.

Copyright © 2014 by Lynn Farkas
Based on the original works by Mary Mortimer

ISBN: 978-1-59095-454-6
UPC: 6-43977-64548-7
Printed in the United States of America with simultaneous printings in Australia, Canada and United Kingdom.

FIRST EDITION
1 2 3 4 5 6 7 8 9 10

This resource has v preliminary pages, 187 pages of text and 4 pages without numbering at the end. It is 14.8 cm wide and 20.5 cm high. There is a bibliography on page 186 and no index. There are no illustrations. The compiler was born in 1951.

Catalog record for the 2007 edition:
000 01309cam a2200337 a 4500
001 000047366360
003 AuCNLKIN
005 20121019194656.0
008 110720s2007   txu   d   000 0 eng d
020 ## $a 9781590958100
020 ## $a 1590958101
035 ## $a (OCoLC)184715529
040 ## $a FVC $c FVC $d OCLCQ $d BTCTA
050 #4 $a Z1006 $b .L5 2007
082 04 $a 020.3 $2 22
245 00 $a LibrarySpeak : $b a glossary of terms in librarianship and information management / $c compiled by Mary Mortimer.

246 14 $a Library speak : $b a glossary of terms in librarianship and information management.
246 30 $a Glossary of terms in librarianship and information management.
250 ## $a 1st North American ed.
260 ## $a Friendswood, TX. : $b TotalRecall, $c 2007.
300 ## $a 235 p. ; $c 23 cm.
504 ## $a Includes bibliographical references (p. 234)
650 #0 $a Library science $v Dictionaries.
650 #0 $a Library science $v Terminology.
650 #0 $a Information science $v Dictionaries.
650 #0 $a Information science $v Terminology.
700 1# $a Mortimer, Mary, $d 1944—

MARC coding for cloned record:
(Note: use ABCD as your library symbol in the 040 field.)

2.

Additional information:
ISBN: 9781743178539
ISBN-10: 1743178530
Audience: Children
For Ages: 6 - 10 years old
For Grades: 1 - 4
Format: 2 Audio CDs, digital, stereo, 12 cm (i.e., 4 ¾ inch)
Playing Time: 2 hours, 7 min
Language: English
Published: 1st September 2013, ℗2013
Publisher: Bolinda Audio, Tullamarine, Victoria (taken from Back cover)
Summary: (taken from Back cover)
'Join Andy and Terry in their newly expanded 39-storey treehouse, featuring 13 brand-new, surprising, crazy and fun-packed storeys!'

About the authors: Andy Griffiths and Terry Denton are a creative partnership. They have won numerous children's choice awards. Andy was born in 1961; Terry in 1950.

Catalog record for the book:
000 01941cam a2200457   4500
001 000052472444
003 AuCNLKIN
005 20140910110013.0
008 130812s2013   at a   000 1 eng d
020 ## $a 9781742612379
020 ## $a 1742612377
035 ## $a (OCoLC)864774391
040 ## $a AUGEN $b eng $c AUGEN $d OCoLC
042 ## $a anuc
082 04 $a A823.3 $2 23
100 1# $a Griffiths, Andy.
245 14 $a The 39–storey treehouse / $c Andy Griffiths ; illustrated by Terry Denton.
246 3# $a Thirty nine storey treehouse
260 ## $a Sydney : $b Pan, $c 2013.
300 ## $a 344 pages : $b illustrations.
336 ## $a text $2 rdacontent
336 ## $a still image $2 rdacontent
337 ## $a unmediated $2 rdamedia
338 ## $a volume $2 rdacarrier

520 8# $a Andy and Terry's amazing treehouse has 13 new levels including a chocolate waterfall, a non-erupting active volcano, an opera house, a baby-dinosaur petting zoo, Andy and Terry's Believe it or Else! museum, a not-very-merry merry-go-round, a boxing elephant called the Trunkinator, an X-Ray room, a disco with light-up dance floor, the world's scariest roller-coaster and a top secret 39th level that hasn't even been finished yet. (Publisher's website).
650 #0 $a Tree houses $v Juvenile fiction.
650 #0 $a Tree houses $v Fiction.
650 #0 $a Australian fiction.
655 #0 $a Short stories
700 1# $a Denton, Terry, $d 1950—
830 #4 $a The treehouse books ; $v 03

MARC coding for cloned record:
(Note: use ABCD as your library symbol in the 040 field.)

3.

LEARN LIBRARY SKILLS SERIES

Learn
LIBRARY OF CONGRESS
SUBJECT ACCESS

INTERNATIONAL EDITION

by
Lynn Farkas

TotalRecall Publications, Inc.
2015

This resource has vi preliminary pages and 116 pages of text. It is A4 size (i.e., 21 cm x 30 cm). There is a bibliography on page 113 and an index on page 115. The resource includes several tables and a chart. The ISBN is 9781590954393. The author was born in 1951.

Catalog record for a previous edition:
000 01287cam a2200361 a 4500
001 000026832644
003 AuCNLKIN
005 20130518005913.0
008 050322s2004   aca   f b   001 0 eng
020 ## $a 1876283173
035 ## $a (OCoLC)155672911
040 ## $a ANL $b eng $d ANL
042 ## $a anuc
082 04 $a 025.49076 $2 22
100 1# $a Ganendran, Jacki, $d 1959—
245 10 $a Learn subject access / $c by Jacki Ganendran ; edited by Lynn Farkas.
250 ## $a 3rd ed.
260 ## $a Canberra : $b DocMatrix, $c 2004.
300 ## $a 106 p., [2] ; $c 30 cm.
490 1# $a Library education series
500 ## $a Includes index.
500 ## $a Reprinted with corrections 2004.
504 ## $a Bibliography: p. [105]
521 ## $a Tertiary students.
650 #0 $a Subject cataloging.
650 #0 $a Subject cataloging $v Problems, exercises, etc.
650 #0 $a Subject headings, Library of Congress.
650 #0 $a Subject headings, Library of Congress $v Problems, exercises, etc.
700 1# $a Farkas, Lynn.

MARC coding for cloned record:
(Note: use ABCD as your library symbol in the 040 field.)

REVISION QUIZ 19.3
Use the following questions to revise your understanding of copy cataloging. You do not need to write down the answers.

1. Name three sources of copy cataloging.

2. Define cloning. How does it differ from copy cataloging?

3. What are the advantages of upgrading an AACR2 copy cataloged record to make it RDA–compliant? What are the disadvantages?

CHAPTER TWENTY
More Practice

Introduction
This chapter presents a variety of resources for you to catalog. It includes examples of the wide range of materials you may encounter in your library cataloging.

Some of the exercises are challenging. They were designed to give practice to students completing this workbook, and to experienced catalogers using the workbook to transition to RDA cataloging. Therefore, all the answers provide full bibliographic records, including classification numbers and subject headings.

In cases where the cataloger can choose to record data in different ways in a MARC record (as, for example, in using $b in a MARC 336, 337 or 338 field), some of the answers contain the different options. It is worthwhile, therefore, studying all the answers to see different ways that cataloging data can be expressed.

We suggest that you create descriptive catalog records for each resource, and if possible add as much additional information as you can from the tools available to you (and from your level of training) to develop a full bibliographic record. Cataloging tools to use in formulating your answers include the MARC bibliographic format; LC Authorities, WorldCat Authorities, Libraries Australia Authorities or other authority files; LC Subject Headings; and LC or DDC classification.

Students new to cataloging are encouraged to consult other publications in the 'Learn Library Skills' series—*Learn Dewey Decimal Classification (Edition 23)*, *Learn Library of Congress Classification,* and *Learn Library of Congress Subject Access*—for comprehensive practical introductions to classification and subject analysis.

EXERCISE 20.1

Create full RDA–compliant catalog records for the resources below and code in MARC. Use the library symbol ABCD in the 040 field. If you prefer, you can use the templates from Chapter Eighteen of this workbook to assist in your cataloging.

1. Book

SPLIT VISION

THE PORTRAYAL OF ARABS IN THE AMERICAN MEDIA

Edited by EDMUND GHAREEB

Published by the AMERICAN-ARAB AFFAIRS COUNCIL

The book has xvii preliminary pages, 402 pages of illustrated text, a bibliography and index, and is 24 cm. high and 15 cm. wide.

SPLIT VISION: THE PORTRAYAL OF ARABS IN THE AMERICAN MEDIA
Edited by Edmund Ghareeb
Copyright © 1983
by the American-Arab Affairs Council, Washington, D.C.

All rights reserved.

Printed in the United States of America

The American-Arab Affairs Council is a nonprofit organization whose goal is to promote a better understanding between the United States and the Arab countries through publications and other educational programs.

American-Arab Affairs Council
1730 M Street, N.W., Suite 411
Washington, D.C.

Revised and expanded edition

ISBN 0-943182-00-X
ISBN 0-943182-01-8 (pbk.)

2. Audiobook

```
┌─────────────────────────────────────────────┐
│           JOHN C. MAXWELL                   │
├─────────────────────────────────────────────┤
│ ABRIDGED, REVISED & UPDATED 10TH ANNIVERSARY EDITION │
├─────────────────────────────────────────────┤
│                                             │
│           THE 21 IRREFUTABLE                │
│                                             │
│             LAWS OF                         │
│                                             │
│           LEADERSHIP                        │
│                                             │
├─────────────────────────────────────────────┤
│             *Follow Them*                   │
│          *and People Will*                  │
│             *Follow You*                    │
├─────────────────────────────────────────────┤
│      FOREWORD BY STEPHEN R. COVEY           │
│         READ BY JOHN C. MAXWELL             │
└─────────────────────────────────────────────┘
```

The audiobook was published in 2013 on 1 CD by Brilliance Audio, Inc., whose headquarters are known to be in Grand Haven, Michigan (although this is not noted on the audiobook). The ISBN is 9781480554030 and the playing time is 3 hours, 28 minutes. The publication provides insights and observations on the laws of leadership that govern personal and organizational effectiveness.

3. Serial

Title page

> # The Histochemical Journal
> *February 1969*
> VOLUME ONE • NUMBER THREE
>
> ## Contents
> ### Papers
> ....
>
> ### Review Articles
> ....
>
> ### Letters to the Editor
> ....
>
> *Published quarterly by*
> CHAPMAN AND HALL
> *11 New Fetter Lane, London EC4*

Facing title page

> **The Purpose of the Journal**
> To publish original research papers, brief communications and review articles in the fields of histochemistry.
>
> **Subscription Rates**
> *The Histochemical Journal* is published quarterly.
> A volume consists of six quarterly issues.
> Subscription rate is £12 (US $28.80) a volume.
>
> All enquiries about subscriptions and back numbers should be sent to:
>
> R. D. Welham
> The Histochemical Journal
> Chapman and Hall
> 11 New Fetter Lane, London EC4, U.K.

This serial is 22.7 cm. high, illustrated, with ISSN 0018-2214. It was a quarterly journal until January 1973 when it became bimonthly. In January 1983 its frequency changed to monthly. It ceased with volume 34, no. 11/12 (2002/2003) and was continued by the Journal of Molecular Histology.

4. Map

Front cover

```
European Route Planning Series

           AA
    South–East Europe

Bulgaria • Greece • Hungary
Romania • Yugoslavia

           ★

20 miles to 1 inch      No. 5
```

Back cover

```
European Route Planning Series

AA European Route Planning Series:

       1. France
    2. Spain and Portugal
   3. Benelux and Germany
 4. Austria, Italy and Switzerland
     5. South East Europe
        6. Scandinavia
   7. Great Britain and Ireland


       20 miles to 1" scale

Produced in the United Kingdom by the
Cartographic Services Department of the
Automobile Association, Basingstoke, Hants RG21
2EA, and distributed overseas by the British Tourist
Authority, 64 St James Street, London SW1A 1NF.

         ISBN 0 86145 072 8
```

This map is colored, 52 cm. high and 136 cm. wide, folded to 26 x 13 cm. It was bought in London in 1986.

5. Series

THE INSPECTOR LYNLEY MYSTERIES: 14

ELIZABETH GEORGE

WHAT CAME BEFORE HE SHOT HER

HarperLargePrint
New York, N.Y.

This is the large print edition published in 2006. It has 1028 pages and is 19½ cm. high. The ISBN is 9780061145919 or 0061145912.

The author was born in 1949.

Back cover text: 'New York Times bestselling author Elizabeth George delivers an explosive new novel. The brutal, inexplicable death of Inspector Thomas Lynley's wife has left Scotland Yard searching for answers. Who is the twelve-year-old boy who pulled the trigger? What were the circumstances that led to his horrific act? That story begins on the other side of London, where the three mixed-race Campbell children are sent to live with their aunt. The oldest, fifteen-year-old Ness, is headed for trouble as fast as her high-heeled boots will take her. That leaves the middle child, Joel, to care for the youngest, Toby. But before long, Joel has his own problems with a local gang. To protect his family, he makes a pact with the devil—a move that leads straight to the front doorstep of Thomas Lynley.'

6. Book

The ISBN for this 2014 publication is 9780935302356. It has ix preliminary pages, 230 pages of text and an index, and is 26 cm in height. The title page verso notes this publication was 'prepared by the Joint Committee on Standards for Educational and Psychological Testing of the American Educational Research Association, American Psychological Association and National Council on Measurement in Education'.

It was published in Washington, DC with a copyright date of 2014.

7. Newspaper

This weekly newspaper began on Thursday, October 24, 2013, continuing Bracknell Forest Standard (ISBN 1758-9134). It is 20 cm x 36 cm in size. Some of its photographs are in black and white, some color.

8. e–book
Stolen future, broken present: the human significance of climate change can be downloaded at http://openhumanitiespress.org/stolen-future-broken-present.html

9. e–serial
Access *Smart science* at http://www.taeti.org/journal/index.php/smartsci/index

10. Report of a Conference

Prospects for adult education

and development

in Asia and the Pacific

Report of a Regional Seminar
Bangkok, 24 November - 4 December 1980

UNESCO REGIONAL OFFICE FOR EDUCATION IN ASIA AND THE PACIFIC
Bangkok, Thailand, 1981

Verso of the title page

©☐Unesco 1981

Published by the Unesco Regional Office for Education in Asia and the Pacific
920 Sukhumvit Road
G.P.O. BOX 1425
Bangkok, Thailand

Printed in Thailand

Opinions expressed in this publication are those of the participants of the Regional Seminar and do not necessarily coincide with any official views of Unesco. The designations employed and the presentation of the material herein do not imply the expression of any opinion whatsoever on the part of Unesco concerning the legal status of any country, or of its authorities, or concerning the delimitations of the frontiers of any country or territory.

This publication reports on the 1980 Regional Seminar on Adult Education and Development in Asia and Oceania, held in Bangkok, Thailand. It has 69 pages, includes a list of the participants, and is 26.5 cm. high.

11. Book on CD

CAMBRIDGE UNIVERSITY PRESS	ENDORSED BY CAMBRIDGE INTERNATIONAL EXAMINATIONS

Mike Wooster, Lawrie Ryan and Roger Norris

Cambridge international AS and A level

Chemistry

Teacher's resource

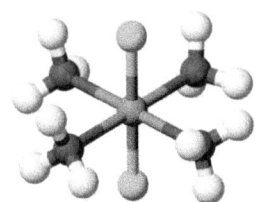

Second edition
Version 1.00

CD-ROM for Windows and Mac OSX

Completely Cambridge

The ISBNs for this CD are 9781107677708 and 110767770X. It was published by Cambridge University Press in 2015.

Search Library of Congress Authorities (Name Authority Headings) http://authorities.loc.gov for the correct forms of names for each of the authors. Hint: if you find more than one authorized name heading, look for information in the 6xx fields that indicate a connection to science or chemistry.

12. Conference

Cover

> # Musical Theatre in America
>
> Conference on the Musical Theatre in America
> Papers and Proceedings
>
> 1981
> C.W. Post Center

Title page

> Sponsored jointly by
> The American Society for Theatre Research
> The Sonneck Society
> The Theatre Library Association
>
> ## Musical Theatre in America
>
> Papers and Proceedings
> of the
> Conference on the Musical Theatre in America
>
> Edited by Glenn Loney
>
> Greenwood Press • Westport, Connecticut • 1984
>
> ISBN 0 3132 3524 4

Facing title page

> Contributions in Drama and Theater Studies
> Number 8
>
> ISSN 0163-3821

This publication has xxi preliminary pages and 441 pages, with black and white illustrations. There is a bibliography on pages 415 to 420, and it contains an index. It is 25 cm. high.

13. Map

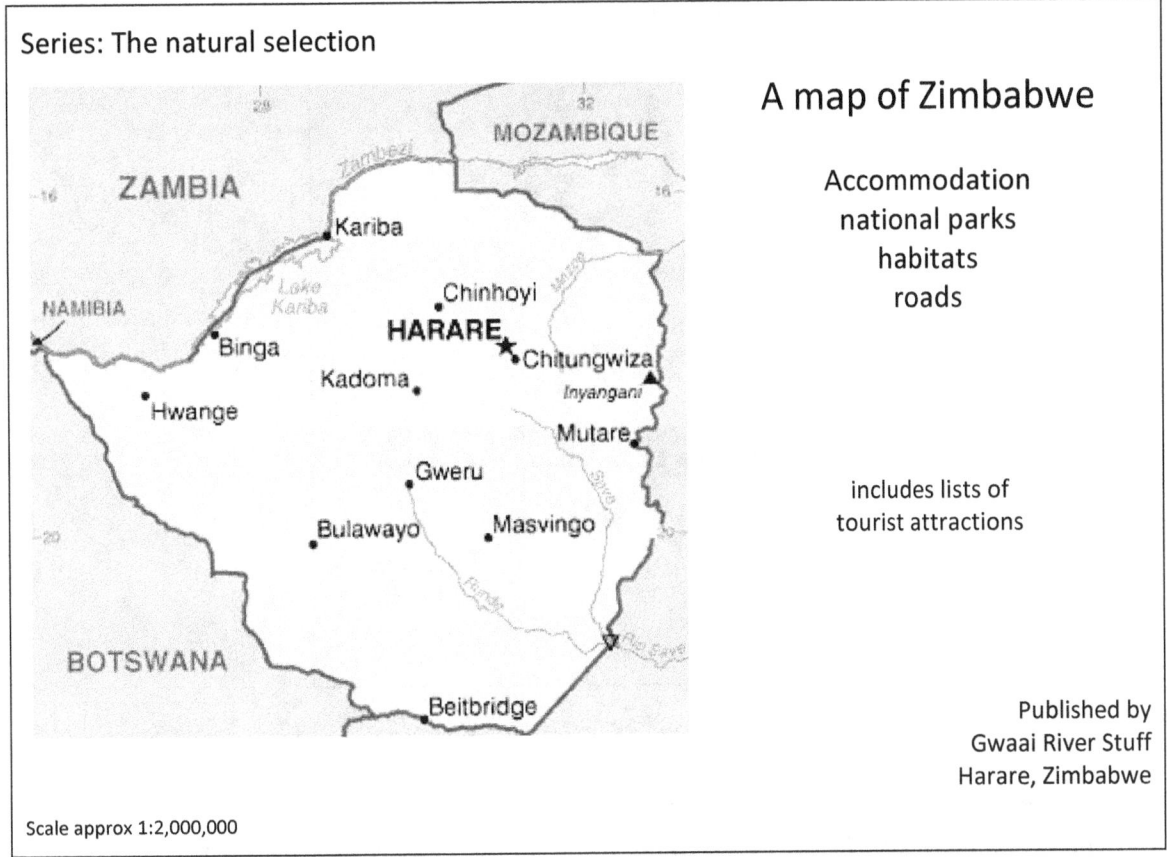

Map size is 43 x 60 cm, folded to 22 x 15 cm. On the verso is a distance table, text, and color illustrations. Information in the text indicates the map was probably produced in 2000.

14. Computer Game

X-BOX 360

2014 FIFA WORLD CUP Brazil

Published by EA Sports

Censorship Classification: G
Product code: 5030944112403

EA Sports is located in Geneva in Switzerland. The game is in English and Spanish, with sound and color. It includes a DVD and a booklet. FIFA is the acronym for Féderation international de football association (check LC Authorities http://authorities.loc.gov for full details).

Release Date: April 15, 2014. Available for 1–4 players ; 2 online multiplayer. System requirements: Xbox 360; 20 MB to save game ; HDTV 720p/1080i/1080p; in-game Dolby digital.

Summary: Lead your country to FIFA World Cup glory while experiencing all the fun, excitement and drama of soccer's greatest event.

15. Series

Title page

> National Campaign Against Drug Abuse
>
> ## Karralika
>
> An Evaluation of a
> Therapeutic Community
> for Drug Users in the
> Australian Capital Territory
>
> *Monograph Series No. 6*
>
> RUTH A. LATUKEFU, M.A. (SYD.), PH.D. (Columbia)
>
> November 1987
>
> Australian Government Publishing Service
> Canberra

Verso of the title page

> © Commonwealth of Australia
> ISSN 0818-8882
> ISBN 0 644 07644 5
>
> ...
>
> This publication is funded by the Commonwealth Department of Community Services and Health for the National Campaign Against Drug Abuse. Inquiries should be directed to the Editor, NCADA Monograph Series, PO Box E84, Queen Victoria Terrace, Parkes, ACT 2600.
>
> Opinions expressed in this publication are the views of the author and do not necessarily represent the views of the governments and groups involved in the National Campaign Against Drug Abuse.

This book has black and white photographs, is 25 cm. high, and has vi preliminary pages and 166 pages of text, including a bibliography on pages 164 to 166.

16. Music CD

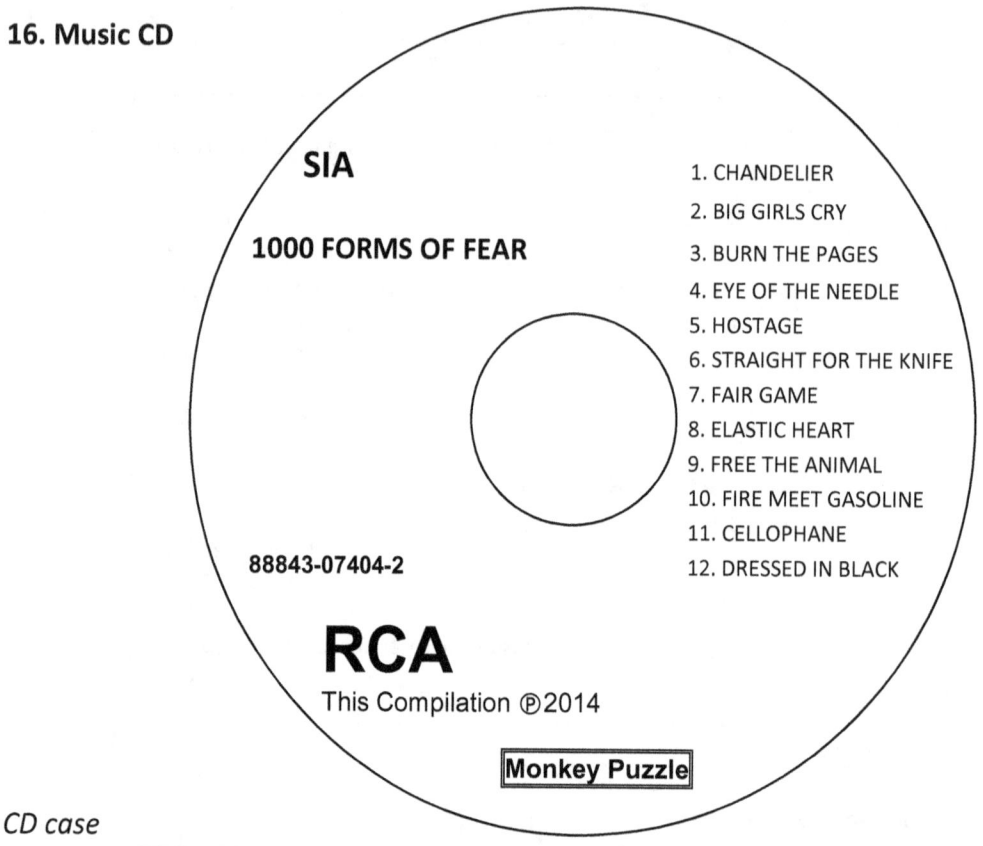

CD case

Compact discs are recorded digitally.

17. USB
Rainforest plants of Australia is accessible at http://rainforests.net.au/product/rainforest-plants-of-australia/
The USB is 6 cm long and in the shape of a key, packaged in a DVD container.

18. Kit

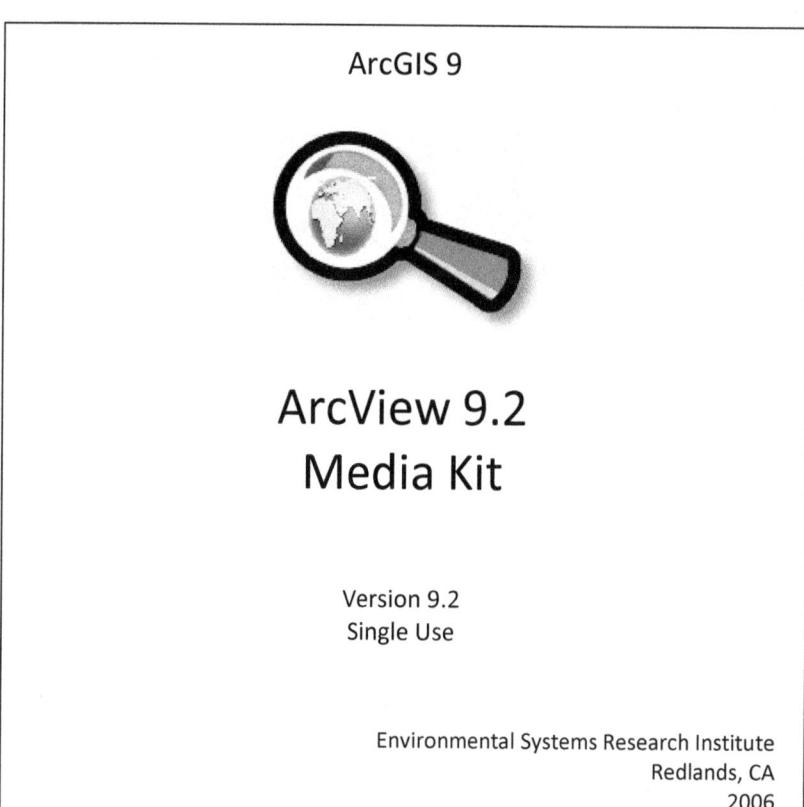

ArcGIS 9

ArcView 9.2
Media Kit

Version 9.2
Single Use

Environmental Systems Research Institute
Redlands, CA
2006

This kit consists of a DVD of the GIS software plus 2 manuals, 1 quick start guide, 1 desktop short cut booklet, 1 memo and 5 DVDs of ESRI data & maps.

System requirements: PC-Intel, Windows 2000 or XP (Home and Professional edition), 512 MB RAM, 1 GHz processor

'ArcView is full-featured GIS software for visualizing, analyzing, creating, and managing data with a geographic component' – information from ESRI website.

19. Book

FIFTH EDITION	TABLE OF CONTENTS
Guidelines for Cardiac Rehabilitation and Secondary Prevention Programs **AACVPR** American Association of Cardiovascular and Pulmonary Rehabilitation *Promoting Health & Preventing Disease*	Cardiac rehabilitation, secondary prevention programs, and the evolution of health care providing optimal care for all patients The continuum of care: from inpatient and outpatient cardiac rehabilitation to long-term secondary prevention Behavior modification and risk factor reduction: guiding principles and practices Nutrition guidelines dietary patterns Cardiac rehabilitation in the inpatient and transitional settings Medical evaluation and exercise testing Outpatient cardiovascular rehabilitation and secondary prevention Modifiable cardiovascular disease risk factors Special populations Program administration Outcomes assessment and utilization Management of medical problems and emergencies

This resource was published by Human Kinetics, Champaign, Illinois with a stated copyright date of 2013. It has xii pages of introductory text and 323 pages of text. The publication is 28 cm in height and contains illustrations, maps, bibliographic references and an index. Its ISBN is 9781450459631 or 1450459633. (Hint: check LC Authorities http://authorities.loc.gov for the correct form of name for AACVPR)

20. Book on CD-Rom

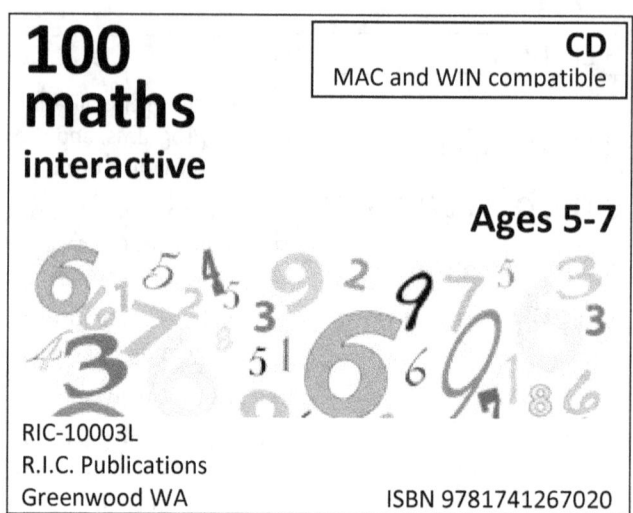

This publication is designed for use with an electronic whiteboard, computer, or projector. It was published in 2014 and includes sound and color. The publisher is in Western Australia, not Washington State, USA.

Contents: Calculating; Handling data; Using and applying mathematics; Understanding shape; Knowing and using number facts; Measuring; Counting and understanding number.

Minimum requirements PC: Operating system Windows XP onwards; 1GB of RAM; Intel Core Duo 2.0 processor or faster.

Minimum requirements MAC: Operating system OSX 10.1 onwards; 1GB of RAM; Power PC G5 processor or better. (For optimum viewing, your screen resolution should be set to 800 x 600 or higher).

21. Website

The dataZoa website is at https://www.datazoa.com/

Details for cataloging can be found in the 'About' section.

22. Book

```
...delivering on the vision


20 years of
modern recreational trails
in Western Australia
1994–2014
```

```
Department of Sport and Recreation
October 2014
```

The book has viii preliminary pages and 66 pages of text with mostly colored illustrations and colored maps. It is 21 cm wide and 30 cm in height. There are bibliographical references on page 66. The ISBN is 9781921648427. It was published by the Department in Perth, WA. It includes the following note "A trail is a journey that takes people into unmodified environments". The chapters are: Introduction; Development of the Bibbulum Track; Development of the Munda Biddi Trail; The Cape to Cape Track; Trails - more than just walking; Management of our long distance trails network; The value of world-class trails; Personal journeys from some trails champions; The role of volunteers in managing our trails; Passionate trails people in government and the wider community; The current agenda; Down the track; Modern trails timeline; Appendices.

23. Music CD

```
                    DVD & CD

              TIBOR RUDAS PRESENTS
          CARRERAS DOMINGO PAVAROTTI with MEHTA

                   The 3 TENORS
                   IN CONCERT 1994

                                            20TH
                                        ANNIVERSARY
                                        CELEBRATION

                                        INCLUDES THE
                                        WORLD FAMOUS
          WARNER                        "NESSUN DORMA"
          CLASSICS
```

THE LEGENDARY CONCERT ON **DVD** AND **CD**

José Carreras • Plácido Domingo • Luciano Pavarotti • Zubin Mehta
Los Angeles Philharmonic • Los Angeles Music Center Opera Chorus

On Saturday July 16 1994, The 3 Tenors performed at the Los Angeles Dodger Stadium. To celebrate the 20th anniversary Warner Classics presents a joint CD and DVD of this concert, including a documentary of "The Vision The Making Of The Three Tenors".

Lyrics sung in English, French, German, Italian, and Spanish.

DVD: Total Duration: 172 mins – NTSC 4:3 Colour Dolby 2.0 Stereo + Dolby 5.1
CD: Total Duration: 73 mins – Digital Recording

This Set: ℗ & © 2010 Warner Music Netherlands BV, revised 2014 Warner Classics, Warner Music UK Ltd., A Warner Music Group Company.
All rights of the producer and of the owner of the work reproduced reserved. Manufactured in the EU. This DVD is copy-protected.

825646337378

24. DVD

M War violence and themes   DVD

Based on the Tony award-winning Broadway play, and set against the sweeping canvas of World War I, this deeply heartfelt story begins with the remarkable friendship between a horse named Joey and his young trainer Albert. When they're forced apart by war, we follow Joey's extraordinary journey as he changes and inspires the lives of everyone he meets.

Based on the novel by Michael Morpurgo

DREAMWORKS PICTURES AND RELIANCE ENTERTAINMENT PRESENT AN AMBLIN ENTERTAINMENT, KENNEDY/ MARSHALL COMPANY PRODUCTION • A STEVEN SPIELBERG FILM • DIRECTED BY STEVEN SPIELBERG • SCREENPLAY BY LEE HALL AND RICHARD CURTIS• PRODUCED BY STEVEN SPIELBERG, KATHLEEN KENNEDY • EXECUTIVE PRODUCERS, FRANK MARSHALL, REVEL GUEST

DVD REGION 4 COLOUR RECORDING SYSTEM **PAL** SURROUND SOUND

5.1 DOLBY DIGITAL   Approx 141 mins

EMILY WATSON DAVID THEWLIS PETER MULLAN NIELS ARESTRUP TOM HIDDLESTON JEREMY IRVINE BENEDICT CUMBERBATCH TOBY KEBBELL DAVID KROSS EDDIE MARSAN NICOLAS BRO RAINER BOCK PATRICK KENNEDY LIAM CUNNINGHAM

©2012
E15940   (Buena   Vista   Australia)
9398521594032
South Yarra, Vic.
DREAMWORKS 2012

DreamWorks Pictures is known to be based in Universal City, California (although this is not specified on the DVD). The distributor, Buena Vista, is based in South Yarra, in the state of Victoria (Australia). Additional information provided in the credits: edited by Michael Kahn, Janusz Kaminski is director of photography, Rick Carter is production designer, Joanna Johnston is costume designer, music is by John Williams.

25. Conference on USB

22nd Australian Earth Sciences Convention, held on 7–10 July at the Newcastle City Hall and Civic Theatre, Newcastle, NSW, Australia

The conference was organized by the Geological Society of Australia, which published this resource.

The scientific program and abstracts are on 1 USB (5 x 9 cm). The resource includes color illustrations, maps and bibliographic references.

ANSWERS

EXERCISE 1.1

	Southside Elementary School Library	Institute of Criminology Library
Describe a typical user	*Student, early school years*	*Researcher or academic*
What information do they need in the description of the item?	*Simple, basic information: Main author, title, date, color, illustrations, audience level, basic subject(s)*	*Detailed information: All authors and creators, title, subtitle and other title information, publishing details and dates, content notes or summaries, ISBN/ISSN, detailed subjects*
What kinds of access points do they need— i.e., what do they want to be able to look up in the catalog?	*Author* *Title* *Subject*	*Author(s)* *Title(s)* *Publisher(s)* *Subjects*
List other types of libraries with the same or similar kinds of users	*Public libraries* *Middle / junior school libraries* *Secondary / High school libraries*	*Research libraries* *Special libraries* *Government libraries* *Academic libraries*

REVISION QUIZ 2.1

1. Define: descriptive cataloging, subject cataloging, classification.
   ***Descriptive cataloging** describes a resource, identifies access points and indicates relationships.*
   ***Subject cataloging** determines subject headings for a resource.*
   ***Classification** determines a classification number for a resource. The classification number also provides a shelving location for a resource in a physical collection.*

2. What are the advantages of adopting cataloging standards?
   Cataloging standards provide consistency within a single library, and between libraries.
   They reduce the time involved in cataloging.
   They provide ease of access for patrons who use more than one library.
   They ensure the purposes of the catalog are achieved.

3. Name three cataloging standards.

    RDA **(Resource Description and Access)** and AACR2 **(Anglo-American Cataloguing Rules**, 2nd edition) are descriptive cataloging standards.

    LCSH **(Library of Congress Subject Headings)** is a subject cataloging standard.

    DDC **(Dewey Decimal Classification)** and LCC **(Library of Congress Classification)** are classification standards.

4. What type of data would be useful to include in a catalog record for a book? What different data would be useful for a television series on DVD?

    Data in a catalog record for a book could include: title; authors or editors; publisher, place and date of publication; size (either physical e.g., centimeters; or electronic e.g., bytes) and number of pages; whether the book contains illustrations, a summary, references or a bibliography; whether it is a second or third etc. edition, or a revised edition; and whether it is part of a series, and its number in that series.

    Data in a catalog record for a TV series on DVD could include: series title; number of episodes and their titles; summaries and playing time of episodes, principal actors, director and producer; copyright statement/s for series and/or DVD; publisher and/or distributor of DVD version; number of DVD discs; packaging (e.g., a boxed set).

5. Name two access points that can be recorded in a descriptive catalog record.

    Any of the following can be access points in a catalog record: title, variant title/s, series title, creator/s, editors, illustrators, compilers, other people or organizations associated with the resource. Subject headings and classification numbers are also access points.

6. What three steps do catalogers follow when creating a catalog record?
    1. Examine the resource in hand.
    2. Identify key elements of the resource, using appropriate chapters of RDA.
    3. Record the information into the library's preferred cataloging format.

EXERCISE 2.2

Access points have been highlighted in **bold face**. Note: some systems also consider call numbers and ISBNs searchable access points.

a.

CALL NUMBER	JQ 24 C48 2015
TITLE	**Comparing Asian politics : India, China, and Japan / Sue Ellen M. Charlton**
EDITION	Fourth edition
PUBLISHER	Boulder, Colo. : Westview Press, 2014.
PHYSICAL DESCRIPT'N	xv, 380 pages ; 23 cm.
CREATOR	**Charlton, Sue Ellen M.**
SUBJECTS	**1. Asia – Politics and government – Case studies.**
	2. India – Politics and government.
	3. China – Politics and government.
	4. Japan – Politics and government.

b.

CALL NUMBER	709.04
TITLE	**History of modern art : painting, sculpture, architecture, photography / H.H. Arnason, Elizabeth C. Mansfield, National Humanities Center.**
EDITION	Seventh Edition
PUBLISHER	Boston : Pearson, [2013]
ISBN/ISSN	9780205259472 (paperback)
PHYSICAL DESCRIPT'N	xvi, 816 pages : illustrations ; 30 cm.
CREATOR(S)	**Arnason, H. Harvard, author.**
	Mansfield, Elizabeth, 1965– , author.
SUBJECTS	**Art, Modern – 20th century.**
	Art, Modern.
NOTES	Includes bibliographical references (pages 763–789) and index.

c.

CALL NUMBER	ND 497.Y46 M66 2013
TITLE	**The many faces of Jonathan Yeo / texts by Martin Gayford, Giles Coren, Tim Marlow and Sarah Howgate.**
PUBLISHER	London : Art Books Publishing Ltd, [2013?]
COPYRIGHT DATE	©2013
ISBN/ISSN	9781908970091
PHYSICAL DESCRIPT'N	240 pages : illustrations (some colour) ; 27 cm.
CREATOR(S)	**Yeo, Jonathan, 1970– , artist**
	Gayford, Martin, 1952– , author
	Coren, Giles, author
	Marlow, Tim, 1963– , author
	Howgate, Sarah, author
	National Portrait Gallery (Great Britain), sponsoring body
SUBJECTS	**Yeo, Jonathan – Exhibitions.**
	Yeo, Jonathan, 1970–
	Portrait painters – Great Britain.
	Celebrities – Portraits.
	Portrait painters – England – Exhibitions.
	Painters – Great Britain – Exhibitions.
	Portrait painting – Great Britain – Exhibitions.
NOTES	Published to coincide with the exhibition "Jonathan Yeo portraits" at the National Portrait Gallery, London, 11 September 2013 – 4 January 2014.
	Includes bibliographical references and index.

EXERCISE 2.3

1. Joseph Smith, middle name Edward
   Joseph Edward Smith, Joseph E. Smith, Joe Smith, Joe E. Smith

2. International Business Machines
   IBM

3. Books
   monographs, texts, volumes, publications, tomes

4. Charles Wentworth Jones
   Charles Jones, Charles W. Jones, Charlie Wentworth Jones, Charlie Jones, Charlie W. Jones, Chuck Wentworth Jones, Chuck Jones, Chuck W. Jones

5. Alicia Mary Peyton
   Alicia Peyton, Alicia M. Peyton, A.M. Peyton

6. Sadness
   unhappiness, dejection, glumness, gloominess, cheerlessness, desolation, joylessness, melancholy, misery, tristitia

7. Organisation for Economic Co-operation and Development, formerly called Organisation for European Economic Cooperation
   OECD, Organization for Economic Co-operation and Development, Organisation for Economic Cooperation and Development, Organization for Economic Cooperation and Development, OEEC, Organisation for European Economic Cooperation, Organisation for European Economic Co-operation, Organization for European Economic Cooperation, Organization for European Economic Co-operation

8. Dogs
   canines, mongrels, curs, mutts, pooches, hounds, doggies, pups, puppies, bow-wows

9. Samuel Clements, also known as Mark Twain
   Sam Clements, Mark Twain

10. James Robert Ewing
    J.R. Ewing, James R. Ewing, Jim Robert Ewing, Jim R. Ewing, James Bob Ewing, Jim Bob Ewing

11. Elton John, who changed his name from Reginald Kenneth Dwight
    Reginald Kenneth Dwight, Reginald K. Dwight, Reggie Kenneth Dwight, Reggie K. Dwight, Reggie Dwight, R.K. Dwight

12. Elizabeth K. Inchley
    Elizaabeth Inchley,, Bess Inchley, Bess K. Inchley, Betty Inchley, Betty K. Inchley, Beth Inchley, Beth K. Inchley, Liz Inchley, Liz K. Inchley, Lizzie Inchley, Lizzie K. Inchley, Liza Inchley, Liza K. Inchley

ANSWERS 215

REVISION QUIZ 3.1

1. What does RDA stand for?
   RDA stands for Resource Description and Access, the new cataloging standard introduced in 2009.

2. Why was a new cataloging scheme needed?
   The previous cataloging standard, AACR2, was too print-based and did not cope well with the digital environment.

3. What is RDA based on?
   RDA's conceptual basis is FRBR – Functional Requirements for Bibliographic Records, and FRAD – Functional Requirements for Authority Data.

4. What is meant when we say that RDA is a content standard?
   *RDA focuses on **content** (what information to record), not on **encoding** (how to code, present or display the data).*

5. Name three new terms that RDA uses, and their AACR2 equivalents.
   See the table 'RDA Terminology', page 21

EXERCISE 4.1

1. The FRBR term for the various elements that are the basis for bibliographic description is ___*entity*___. FRBR identifies three Groups of these.

2. A ___*Manifestation*___ is the physical embodiment of a resource. In a ___*Manifestation*___, all the physical objects bear the same characteristics or are produced together at the same time.

3. Two of the Group One entities are conceptual rather than physical. These are the ___*Work*___ and ___*Expression*___ entities.

4. The initial intellectual creation of a resource is known in FRBR as the ___*Work*___.

5. A single object with particular characteristics that differentiate it from the rest of the collection is called the ___*Item*___.

6. The realization of a Work is referred to as the ___*Expression*___. The textual play 'Romeo and Juliet' written in English is one ___*Expression*___ of Shakespeare's work.

EXERCISE 4.2

German translation	*Expression*
ISBN	*Manifestation*
Electronic version of *Cloudstreet*	*Expression*
Resource to be read in library only	*Item*

Movie of C.S. Lewis' *The lion, the witch and the wardrobe*	**Work**
Library barcode	**Item**
Shakespeare's *Romeo & Juliet*	**Work**
Fifth edition	**Manifestation**

EXERCISE 4.3

	Resource	**Attribute**	**WEMI Entity**
1.	**Author's inscription** on title page	Marks or inscriptions	Item
2.	Version of Harry Potter **with colored illustrations**	Illustrative content	Expression
3.	**Italian translation** of *Going solo* by Roald Dahl	Language of Expression	Expression
4.	**Parliamentary Papers series; no. 16 of 2014**	Series statement	Manifestation
5.	Tolkien's **The Hobbit**	Preferred Title for the Work	Work
6.	Shakespeare's First Folio, **owned by the British Museum**	Provenance	Item
7.	**Spoken version** of *Wild Swans: three daughters of China* by Jung Chang	Form of Expression (audio)	Expression
8.	Sculpture **manufactured by** Morris and Company **in 1975**	Manufacture statement	Manifestation
9.	A library copy of a DVD with **barcode number 23456**	Item identifier	Item
10.	**Random House publication** of *The narrow road to the deep north*	Publication statement	Manifestation
11.	**Braille version** of David Attenborough's book, *Life on earth*	Form of Expression (Braille)	Expression
12.	Map **80 x 40 cm**	Dimensions	Manifestation
13.	*New York Times* on **microfiche**	Type of carrier	Manifestation

	Resource	Attribute	WEMI Entity
14.	Sketchbook with original drawings **not available for loan**	Access restrictions on the Item	Item
15.	**TV series**, *60 minutes*	Form of the Work (TV series)	Work

EXERCISE 4.4

1. What Group Two attributes of a corporate body can you identify in this history?

    The UK Film Council (UKFC) was set up in London in 2000 by the Labour Government to develop and promote the film industry in the UK. John Woodward was the Chief Executive Officer of the UKFC. As at 30 June 2008, the company had 90 full-time members of staff. UKFC closed on 31 March 2011, with many of its functions passing to the British Film Institute.

    Name of corporate body
    Dates associated with the body
    Place associated with the body
    Field of activity
    History of corporate body

2. Here is an access point for a family. In each case identify the underlined attribute.

    Austen (Family : <u>Austen, Jane</u>, 1775 – 1817)   *Prominent member of the family*

    <u>Austen</u> (Family : Austen, Jane, 1775 – 1817)   *Name of the family*

    Austen (<u>Family</u> : Austen, Jane, 1775 – 1817)   *Type of family*

EXERCISE 5.1

a. After Everest : inside the private world of Edmund Hillary / Paul Little with Carolyne Meng-Yee. – Auckland [N.Z.] : Allen & Unwin, 2012. – xiii, 250 pages : illustrations (some color) ; 24 cm.
ISBN 9781877505201.

b. Guardianship : consultation paper / Victorian Law Reform Commission. – Melbourne, Vic. : Victorian Law Reform Commission, 2011. – 458 pages ; 30 cm. – (Consultation paper / Victorian Law Reform Commission ; number 10)
ISBN 9 78098 079 159 4.

c. Fishing tips & tricks / by C. Boyd Pfieffer. – Abridged edition. – Minneapolis, Minn. : Creative Publishers, 2008. – 175 pages, 16 unnumbered leaves of colored plates : illustrations ; 28 cm. – (Freshwater angler series)
Includes index.
ISBN 9781589234086.

d. Shells on a desert shore : mollusks in the Seri world / Cathy Moser Marlett ; foreword by Richard S. Felger. – Tucson, Ariz. : The University of Arizona Press, 2014. – xx, 281 pages : illustrations (some color), maps ; 29 cm. – (The Southwest Center series)
Maps on lining papers.
Includes bibliographical references (pages 269–272) and index.
ISBN 9780816530687.

EXERCISE 5.2

*For questions (a) and (b), correct punctuation is **underlined and in bold face.***

a.
BALZER, Julie Fei-Fan**.**
Carve, stamp, play **:** designing and creating custom stamps **/** Julie Fei-Fan Balzer. – Loveland, Colorado **:** Interweave **,** 2013. – 143 pages **:** color illustrations **;** 26 cm.
Includes index.
ISBN 9781596688865 (paperback)**.**

b.
NEW ZEALAND. Office of the Auditor-General**.**
Earthquake Commission **:** managing the Canterbury Home Repair Programme **/** Controller and Auditor General. **–** Wellington **:** Office of the Auditor-General **,** 2013. **–** 94 pages **:** colour illustrations **;** 30 cm. **–** (Parliamentary paper **;** B.29**)**
Includes bibliographical references**.**
Title from cover**.**
Online version available**.**
ISBN 9780478410372**.**

c.

Floortje Bellefleur vindt een poes	*title proper*
Cok Grashoff	*first statement of responsibility*
ill. door Lies Veenhoven	*second statement of responsibility*
9e dr.	*edition statement*
Alkmaar	*place of publication*
Kluitman	*publisher*
2011	*date of publication*
92 pages	*pagination*
illustrations	*illustration*
20 cm.	*dimensions*
Ons genoegen	*series*
Leeftijd tot 9 jaar	*note*
ISBN 90–206–7061–1	*ISBN*
geb : f.4.40	*terms of availability*

d.

illustrations	*illustration*
Cover title	*note*
autor svih stihova u ovoj knjizi, pjesama, crteza i fotografija je isto umjetnica Depcinski Veronika	*first statement of responsibility*
Prvo izdanje	*edition statement*
Sydney	*place of publication*
2013	*date of publication*
Pjesme kroz zivot i bajke za djecu	*title proper*
15 pages	*pagination*
Depcinski	*publisher*
25 cm.	*dimensions*
ISBN 0 9588754 0 5	*ISBN*
$6.50 Aust.	*terms of availability*

EXERCISE 6.1

1. In the example: **700 1# $aSawer, Marian,$d1946—**

   a. What MARC field is used and what does that field represent?
      Field 700—Added Entry for a Personal Name

   b. What does (R) in the heading for the MARC field mean?
      The field is repeatable—you can have a number of 700s in the catalog record.

   c. What does the first indicator '1' mean?
      The name is written with the surname first.

   d. What does the subfield code $d indicate?
      Dates associated with this name, in this case, date of birth.

2. In the example: **110 2# $aBritish Library. $bLending Division. $bResearch Section**

   a. What MARC field is used and what does that field represent?
      Field 110—Main Entry for a Corporate Name

   b. What does the subfield code $b mean? Can you have two subfield 'b' codes in this example? Why or why not?
      The information in the subfield is a subordinate unit to the main heading. In this case, the Research Section is a part of the Lending Division, which is a part of the British Library. You can have two subfield b codes, because the subfield is repeatable in the 110 field—this is indicated by a (R) after the subfield code.

   c. What does the first indicator '2' mean?
      The name of this organization is written without inverting it—in 'direct' order. Many corporate bodies names are written in direct order in the 110 and 710 fields; this differs from personal names in the 100 and 700 fields, which are often written in inverted order, with the surname first.

3. In the example: **082 04 $a388.0919$223**
   a. What MARC field is used and what does that field represent?
      Field 082—Dewey Decimal Classification Number
   b. What information is provided in the indicators and subfields?
      The indicators tell us the full edition of DDC was used, and the number was assigned by an agency other than the Library of Congress (for example, the library that originally cataloged the resource). The subfield codes tell us the classification number is 388.0919 and it was devised using Edition 23 of the Dewey Decimal Classification scheme.

EXERCISE 6.2

651 #0 $aRussia $xHistory $y18th century $vMaps

1. The sample line represents one ___*field*___.
2. The number 651 is its ___*tag*___.
3. There is one blank in the ___*indicator*___ position.
4. What we see on the sample line is a ___*field*___ that is made up of four ___*subfields*___.
5. The characters $a, $x, $y and $v are four examples of ___*subfield codes*___.
6. The symbols $ are examples of ___*delimiters*___.
7. In this sample line, the first ___*indicator*___ has no assigned meaning. In other words, the first ___*indicator*___ is undefined.
8. In MARC 21 records, there are 3 types of content designators: ___*tags*___, ___*indicators*___, and ___*subfield codes*___.
9. The 651 ___*tag*___ identifies this as the 'Subject Added Entry—Geographic Name' ___*field*___.
10. There are four ___*subfields*___: Geographic name, General subdivision, Chronological subdivision, and Form subdivision.

EXERCISE 6.3

1. A record entered on March 4, 2000

0	0	0	3	0	4
00	01	02	03	04	05

2. A work with the single publication date of 2014

s	2	0	1	4
06	07	08	09	10

3. A serial that began in 1990 and ceased in 2005

d	1	9	9	0	2	0	0	5
06	07	08	09	10	11	12	13	14

4. A serial that began in 1972 and is still being published

c	1	9	7	2	9	9	9	9
06	07	08	09	10	11	12	13	14

5. Published in the Czech Republic

x	r	#
15	16	17

6. Book illustrations including genealogical tables and plans

a	e	j	#
18	19	20	21

   (Note: record these codes in alphabetical order)

7. A publication intended for preschool children

a
22

8. A bibliography published by a state government

b	#	#	#	s
24	25	26	27	28

9. A book of plays in Hindi with an index

1	#	d	#	h	i	n
31	32	33	34	35	36	37

EXERCISE 6.4

*In the MARC record below, the supplied MARC tags, indicators and subfield codes are **underlined and in bold face**.*

PERSONAL NAME	Murawski, Darlyne, author.
MAIN TITLE	Ultimate bug-opedia : the most complete bug reference ever / by Darlyne Murawski & Nancy Honovich.
PUBLISHED	Washington, D.C. : National Geographic, [2013]
DESCRIPTION	271 pages : color illustrations ; 28 cm
ISBN	9781426313769 (hardcover)
LC CLASSIFICATION	QL462.3 .M87 2013
VARIANT TITLE	National Geographic kids ultimate bug-opedia
RELATED NAMES	Honovich, Nancy, author.
SUBJECTS	Insects – Encyclopedias, Juvenile.
NOTES	At head of title: National Geographic kids.
	Includes bibliographical references (pages 264–265) and index.
DEWEY CLASS NO.	595.703
CONTENT TYPE	text
	still image
MEDIA TYPE	unmediated
CARRIER TYPE	volume

000 02525cam a22004337i 4500

001 18082551

008 140326s2013 dcua j be 001 0 eng d

020 ## $a 9781426313769 (hardcover)

040 ## $a UKMGB $b eng $c UKMGB $**e** rda $d OCLCO $d DLC

050 00 $a QL462.3 $b .M87 2013

082 04 $a 595.703 $2 23

100 1# $a Murawski, Darlyne, $**e** author.

245 10 $**a** Ultimate bug-opedia : $**b** the most complete bug reference ever $**c** by Darlyne Murawski & Nancy Honovich.

246 3# $a National Geographic kids ultimate bug-opedia

264 #1 $**a** Washington, D.C. : $**b** National Geographic, $**c** [2013]

300 ## $a 271 pages : $b color illustrations ; $c 28 cm

336 ## $a text $2 rdacontent

336 ## $a still image $2 rdacontent

337 ## $a unmediated $2 rdamedia

338 ## $a volume $2 rdacarrier

500 ## $a At head of title: National Geographic kids.

504 ## $a Includes bibliographical references (pages 264–265) and index.

650 #0 $**a** Insects $v Encyclopedias, Juvenile.

700 1# $a Honovich, Nancy, $**e** author.

ANSWERS 223

EXERCISE 7.1

1. Which section contains instruction number 7.4?
   Section 2

2. Which section contains instruction number 1.7.2?
   Section 1

3. What is instruction number 2.4.3?
   Parallel statement of responsibility relating to title proper

4. What information do you find at instruction number 29.1?
   Terminology for persons, families and corporate bodies; related persons, families and corporate bodies, access points, and relationship designators

5. What does RDA Chapter 33 cover?
   General guidelines on recording relationships between Concepts, Objects, Events and Places—but note there is no information here, these guidelines are to be developed in the future

6. What is instruction number 3.5.1.4.14?
   Instructions about recording the dimensions of volumes (e.g., texts).

EXERCISE 7.2

1. Where in the Toolkit will you find information on abbreviations?
   Appendix B

2. Which sections of RDA deal with recording attributes?
   Sections 1–4

3. Which sections of RDA deal with recording relationships?
   Sections 5–10

4. Are the RDA to MARC mappings for bibliographic data and authority data in the same file?
   No—there are separate lists for:
   RDA to MARC Bibliographic Mapping
   MARC Bibliographic to RDA Mapping
   RDA to MARC Authority Mapping
   MARC Authority to RDA Mapping

5. Where do you find the link to the MARC Standards in the RDA Toolkit?
   Resources tab > Other Resources > Element Sets & Encoding Standards > MARC Standards

EXERCISE 7.3

1. Where in RDA Chapter 2 are instructions for recording copyright date?
    RDA 2.11

2. Is 9.2 a core element?
    Yes. Name of the Person (core element)

3. Where do you find information about color illustrations? [Hint: navigate to the page if you know the chapter to look for, otherwise do a quick search]
    RDA 7.15 and RDA 7.17

4. Where would you look for instructions on a prominent member of the family?
    RDA 10.6 and its subsections

5. Where would you find the definition for a 'sheet'?
    In the Glossary, under 'S'

EXERCISE 8.1

1. *Folk music journal.* London : The English Folk Dance and Song Society 1965–
    a) *serial*
    b) *comprehensive*

2. *Bollywood and beyond* / edited by Rachel Dwyer. [Volume 1 of 4 volume set titled *Bollywood : critical concepts in media and cultural studies* / edited by Rachel Dwyer.] Milton, Abingdon, Oxon : Routledge, 2015.
    a) *multipart monograph*
    b) *analytical*

3. *A Guide to the labeling of soft drink products* / prepared by the National Soft Drink Association. Washington, D.C. : National Soft Drink Association., 1982. 1 volume (loose-leaf) ; 28 cm
    a) *integrating resource*
    b) *comprehensive*

4. *The Hunger Games.* West Hollywood, Cal : Color Force, 2012. (This is a DVD)
    a) *single unit*
    b) *comprehensive*

5. Willingham, Bill. *March of the wooden soldiers.* New York : DC Comics, 2004.
    a) *single unit*
    b) *comprehensive*

6. *The official Bruce Springsteen website.* [Colts Neck, NJ] : Thrill Hill Productions, Inc, ©2014. Title from title screen (viewed on 24 October 2014). Mode of access: Internet via World Wide Web. At: http://brucespringsteen.net/.
    a) *integrating resource*
    b) *comprehensive*

7. *Biodiversity in Aotearoa : walking the talk* / Anne Nicolson and Greenpeace. Auckland : Greenpeace New Zealand, 1997. 1 videocassette (35 minutes) + 1 computer disk (3 ¾ inches) + 1 booklet (42 leaves : illustrations, maps ; 30 cm) ; in container.
   a) *multipart monograph*
   b) *comprehensive*

EXERCISE 8.2

Topic	Instruction Number	Transcribe or record?
1. Edition statement	2.5.1.4	*Transcribe*
2. Inaccuracies	1.7.9	*Transcribe unless a specific element gives other instructions*
3. Terms of availability	4.2.1.3	*Record*
4. Production statement	2.7.1.4	*Transcribe place of publication and producer; record date of production*
5. Title proper	2.3.2.7 & 2.3.1.4	*Transcribe (as per 2.3.1.4)*
6. Numbering within series	2.12.9.3	*Record*
7. Numbering of serials	2.6.1.4	*Record numbers; transcribe other words*
8. Title proper of subseries	2.12.10.3, 2.12.2.3 & 2.3.1.4	*Transcribe (as per 3.2.1.4)*
9. Punctuation	1.7.3	*Transcribe*
10. Chronograms	2.7.6.4, 2.8.6.4, 2.9.6.4 & 2.10.6.4	*Transcribe*

EXERCISE 9.1

a. Title proper: *Benchmarking eventually consistent distributed storage systems*
   Statement of responsibility: *David Bermbach*

b. Title proper: *Growing up social*
   Statement of responsibility: *Gary Chapman, Arlene Pellicane*

c. Title proper: *Tasting India*
   Statement of responsibility: *Christine Manfield*
   OR
   Statement of responsibility: *Christine Manfield; photography by Anson Smart*
   COMMENT: IN RDA, ONLY FIRST STATEMENT OF RESPONSIBILITY IS CORE, OTHERS ARE OPTIONAL

d. Title proper: *Grain brain*
   Statement of responsibility: *Dr David Perlmutter with Kristin Loberg*
   OR
   Statement of responsibility: *Dr David Perlmutter [and 1 other]*

e. Title proper: *Schrijverschap in de Belgische belle époque*
   Statement of responsibility: *Christophe Verbruggen*

f. Title proper: *Decision making in health and medicine*
   Statement of responsibility: *Myrlam Hunink [and six others]*
   OR
   Statement of responsibility: *Myrlam Hunink and Paul Glasziou, Joanna Siegel, Jane Weeks, Joseph Pliskin, Arthur Elstein, Milton Weinstein*

g. Title proper: *20,000 leagues under the sea*
   Statement of responsibility: *Jules Verne; read by John Carlisle*
   OR
   Statement of Responsibility: *Jules Verne*

h. Title proper: *Mandell, Douglas, and Bennett's principles and practice of infectious diseases*
   OR
   Title proper: *Principles and practice of infectious diseases*
   Statement of responsibility: *Gerald L. Mandell, John E. Bennett, Raphael Dolin*
   OR
   Statement of responsibility: *Gerald L. Mandell [and 2 others]*

EXERCISE 9.2

1. *Cultural diversity : A primer for the human services.* Fifth edition

   Fifth edition
   _____

2. Updated 8th ed. of *Physical geology* by Charles C. Plummer, David McGeary and Diane H. Carlson

   Updated 8th ed.
   _____

3. McCance and Widdowson's *The composition of foods* 6th ed

   _6th ed_
   _____

4. *World music : a global journey* by Terry E. Miller and Andrew Shahriari. Concise edition

   Concise edition
   _____

5. *M.Y.O.B. Accounting : user guide* Version 19.1

   Version 19.1
   _____

6. *Introduction to Econometrics* 2nd Revised International Edition

   2nd Revised International Edition
   _____

EXERCISE 9.3

*(Note: answers are in **bold face**):*

1. Book

245 field (Title and statement of responsibility)

    245 00 $a Soil fertility and fertilizers : $b an introduction to nutrient management / $c John L. Havlin ... [et al.].
        COMMENT: DON'T USE LATIN ABBREVIATIONS—EITHER LIST ALL AUTHORS OR USE [AND X OTHERS]

    245 10 $a Soil fertility and fertilizers : $b an introduction to nutrient management / $c John L. Havlin, Samuel L. Tisdale, Werner L. Nelson, James D. Beaton.

    245 00 $a Soil fertility and fertilizers ... / $c John L. Havlin [and others].
        COMMENT: WHEN NOT LISTING ALL AUTHORS, SPECIFY THE NUMBER OF AUTHORS, E.G., [AND THREE OTHERS]

250 field (Edition)

    250 ## $a 8th edition.

    250 ## $a Eighth ed.

    250 ## $a Eighth edition

    250 ## $a 8th ed.
        COMMENT: RECORD EDITION STATEMENT AS IT APPEARS ON THE RESOURCE

264 field (Publication, distribution)

    264 #1 $a Upper Saddle River, N.J. : $b Pearson, $c 2014.

    264 #1 $a Upper Saddle, New Jersey : $b Pearson, $c 2014.
        COMMENT: RECORD PLACE OF PUBLICATION AS IT APPEARS ON THE RESOURCE

    264 #1 $a New Jersey : $b Pearson Publishers, $c 2014.
        COMMENT: RECORD PLACE OF PUBLICATION AND PUBLISHER AS THEY APPEAR ON THE RESOURCE

2. Sound Recording on CD

245 field (Title and statement of responsibility)

    245 10 $a The magic faraway tree $h [sound recording] / $c Enid Blyton ; read by Kate Winslet.
        COMMENT: DO NOT INCLUDE GMD (GENERAL MATERIAL DESIGNATION)

    245 10 $a The magic faraway tree / $c Enid Blyton ; read by Kate Winslet.
        COMMENT: AS PER RDA 2.3.1.6

    245 10 $a The magic faraway tree / $c Kate Winslet.
        COMMENT: TRANSCRIBE STATEMENT OF RESPONSIBILITY AS IT APPEARS; ALSO, NEED TO INDICATE THE ORIGINAL CREATOR

    245 10 $a Blyton's The magic faraway tree / $c Enid Blyton ; read by Kate Winslet.
        COMMENT: AS PER OPTIONAL ADDITION FOR RDA 2.3.1.6

264 field (Publication, distribution)

    264 #1 $a Ultimo, N.S.W. : $b Australian Broadcasting Commission, $c 2012.
        COMMENT: PLACE OF PUBLICATION DOES NOT APPEAR ON ITEM, SHOULD BE IN SQUARE BRACKETS; RECORD PUBLISHER AS IT APPEARS ON THE ITEM; DATE IS INCORRECT

264 #2 $a Tullamarine, Vic. : $b Bolinda Audio, $c ℗ 2004.
COMMENT: USE PUBLISHER DETAILS IN PREFERENCE TO DISTRIBUTION DETAILS IF BOTH ARE AVAILABLE; PHONOGRAM COPYRIGHT STATEMENT SHOULD BE IN A SEPARATE 264 #4 FIELD

264 #1 $a Ultimo, N.S.W. : $b ABC Audio, $c 2004.

264 #1 $a [Place of publication not identified] : $b Hodder and Stoughton, $c 2012
COMMENT: THESE ARE THE COPYRIGHT DETAILS FOR BLYTON'S TEXT, NOT FOR THE SOUND RECORDING BEING CATALOGED

3. Poster

245 field (Title and statement of responsibility)

245 00 $a Crowns and ducats $h [picture] : $b Shakespeare's money and medals.
COMMENT: DO NOT INCLUDE GMD (GENERAL MATERIAL DESIGNATION)

245 00 $a Crowns and ducats : $b Shakespeare's money and medals.

245 00 $a Crowns and ducats : $b Shakespeare's money and medals: $b this display looks at the role of coins and medals in Shakespeare's works and his world.
COMMENT: $B INFORMATION WOULD BE BETTER LISTED IN A 'NOTE' FIELD RATHER THAN AS THE SUBTITLE; ALSO, $B IS NOT REPEATABLE—ALL INFORMATION SHOULD BE IN ONE $B

264 field (Publication, distribution)

264 #1 $a [London? : $b s.n., $c 2012?]
COMMENT: DON'T USE LATIN ABBREVIATIONS

264 #1 $a [London] : $b British Museum, $c 2012
COMMENT: NO INDICATION THAT THE BRITISH MUSEUM PUBLISHED THE POSTER

264 #1 $a [London : $b publisher unknown, $c 2012?]
COMMENT: USE [ ] FOR EACH SUBFIELD—DO NOT GROUP THEM ALL TOGETHER IN ONE SET OF [ ]; WHEN PUBLISHER IS NOT KNOWN, USE THE TERMINOLOGY 'PUBLISHER NOT IDENTIFIED'

264 #1 $a [London?] : $b [publisher not identified] , $c [2012?]

REVISION QUIZ 9.4

1. What is a core element? Name two core elements at the Manifestation level.
   Core elements are those attributes that must be included in a record, if they are applicable to the resource being cataloged, to make it RDA–compliant.
   Core elements at the Manifestation level are: title proper, statement of responsibility, edition, numbering of serials, publication statement, copyright date (core if necessary), identifier, carrier type, extent, dimensions.

2. What type of publication statement would you use for each of the following resources?
   a) a music CD distributed by EMI – *distribution statement*
   b) an unpublished manuscript – *production statement*
   c) a painting created by an artist – *manufacture statement*
   d) a book of poems published in 2013 – *publication statement*
   e) an electronic version of a printed screenplay – *publication statement*
   f) an oral history recorded by the speaker at home, no additional copies were made or distributed – *production statement*

3. Should you use a URL as an Identifier for an online Manifestation? Why or why not?
   No. A URL is not considered stable enough to be used as an Identifier, since they can change if a Web address is altered. URNs or PURLs are preferred.

EXERCISE 10.1

1. *The Chronicles of Narnia* by C. S. Lewis : read by an all-star cast of England's brightest talent from the stage and screen. Audio book on CD.
    337   $a *audio* $2 *rdamedia*
    338   $a *audio disc* $2 *rdacarrier*

2. Hard copy aerial photograph of Franjo Tudjman Bridge, Dubrovnik, Croatia
    337   $a *unmediated* $2 *rdamedia*
    338   $a *sheet* $2 *rdacarrier*   **OR**
    338   $a *card* $2 *rdacarrier*
    (CARRIER TYPE WOULD DEPEND ON SEEING THE ITEM—THE PHOTO MAY BE PRINTED ON A NORMAL SHEET OF PAPER, OR MOUNTED ON A HARDER SHEET OR CARD)

3. Hard copy map of Petrogradsky Island, St Petersburg, Russia
    337   $a *unmediated* $2 *rdamedia*
    338   $a *sheet* $2 *rdacarrier*

4. Hard copy sheet music for the song *Hiawatha (His Song to Minnehaha)* words by James O'Dea and music by Neil Moret. Detroit : Whitney-Warner Publishing Company, 1903.
    337   $a *unmediated* $2 *rdamedia*
    338   $a *volume* $2 *rdacarrier*   **OR**
    338   $a *sheet* $2 *rdacarrier*
    (CARRIER TYPE WOULD DEPEND ON WHETHER THE MUSIC WAS PRINTED ON A NUMBER OF PAGES, I.E., A VOLUME, OR A SINGLE PAGE, I.E., A SHEET)

5. *The Guardian* Charlottetown newspaper—copy on microfiche
    337   $a *microform* $2 *rdamedia*
    338   $a *microfiche* $2 *rdacarrier*

6. *The Guardian* Charlottetown newspaper—paper copy
    337   $a *unmediated* $2 *rdamedia*
    338   $a *volume* $2 *rdacarrier*

7. *The Guardian* Charlottetown online newspaper
    337   $a *computer* $2 *rdamedia*
    338   $a *online resource* $2 *rdacarrier*

8. The David Vases (Yuan dynasty, 1351 AD) in Room 95, Chinese ceramics, British Museum (physical object)
    337   $a *unmediated* $2 *rdamedia*
    338   $a *object* $2 *rdacarrier*

EXERCISE 10.2

*(Note: answers are in **bold face**):*

245 field

    245 $a Grande transformation du capitalisme japonais (1980–2010).
        COMMENT: TITLE DOES NOT REFLECT THE RESOURCE BEING CATALOGED; WE ARE NOT CATALOGING THE ORIGINAL FRENCH TEXT

    245 $a The great transformation of Japanese capitalism / $c edited by Sébastien Lechevalier ; translated by J. A. A. Stockwin.
        COMMENT: SECOND STATEMENT OF RESPONSIBILITY NOT REQUIRED

    245 $a The Great Transformation of Japanese Capitalism / $c edited by Sébastien Lechevalier.
        COMMENT: CAPITALIZATION DOES NOT FOLLOW THE INSTRUCTIONS IN RDA 2.3.1.4, RDA 1.7.2 AND APPENDIX A.4

    245 $a The great transformation of Japanese capitalism / $c edited by Sébastien Lechevalier.

264 field

    264 #1 $a [Paris] : $b Presses de Sciences Po., $c 2011.
        COMMENT: DETAILS DO NOT REFLECT THE RESOURCE BEING CATALOGED; WE ARE NOT CATALOGING THE ORIGINAL FRENCH TEXT

    264 #1 $a New York : $b Routledge, $c 2014.
        COMMENT: ONLY FIRST-NAMED PLACE OF PUBLICATION IS CORE

    264 #1 $a Abingdon : $b Routledge, $c 2014.

    two 264 fields:
        264 #1 $a Abingdon : $b Routledge, $c 2014.
        264 #4 $c copyright 2014.
        COMMENT: ACCEPTABLE BUT NOT REQUIRED

300 field

    300 $a 198 p. ; $c 25 cm.
        COMMENT: SPELL OUT ABBREVIATION

    300 $a xxxv, 198 pages ; $c 25 cm.

    300 $a xxxv, 198 pages ; $c 24½ cm.
        COMMENT: RECORD DIMENSIONS ROUNDED UP TO WHOLE CENTIMETER

    300 $a pages ; $c cm.
        COMMENT: NO DETAILS HAVE BEEN GIVEN (THIS OFTEN OCCURS IN CATALOGING-IN-PUBLICATION RECORDS)

EXERCISE 10.3

RDA number	RDA element	MARC field	Data Recorded	Notes
1.7 2.3.1.4 &2.3.2	General guidelines Recording titles, title proper	245 00 $a	*Browsing Canberra's bookshops*	Check general guidelines for transcribing titles
2.3.4	Other title information	245 $b	*a guide to book sources in the Canberra region*	
2.4.2	Statement of responsibility	245 $c	*Datascape Information*	Taken from foreword
2.5	Edition	250 $a		
2.8.1.4, 2.8.2.3	Place of publication	264 01 $a	*Canberra*	
2.8.4	Publisher	264 $b	*Datascape Information Pty Ltd*	Taken from title page
2.8.6	Date of publication	264 $c	*1994*	Taken from title page
2.11	Copyright date	264 04 $c	*© 1994* or *copyright 1994*	Not a core element, but core at LC and many other libraries
2.15	Identifier	020 $a	*0646218336*	ISBN
3.2	Media type	337 $a $2	*unmediated* *rdamedia*	No capitals to start this field
3.3	Carrier type	338 $a $2	*volume* *rdacarrier*	No capitals to start this field
3.4.5	Extent	300 $a	*viii, 140 pages*	
3.5	Dimensions	300 $c	*21 cm.*	

EXERCISE 11.1

1. The Chronicles of Narnia by C. S. Lewis : read by an all-star cast of England's brightest talent from the stage and screen. Audio book on CD.
    336 ## $a *spoken word* $2 *rdacontent*
    337 ## $a audio $2 rdamedia
    338 ## $a audio disc $2 rdacarrier

2. Aerial photograph of Franjo Tudjman Bridge, Dubrovnik, Croatia
    336 ## $a *still image* $2 *rdacontent*
    337 ## $a unmediated $2 rdamedia
    338 ## $a sheet $2 rdacarrier

3. Hard copy map of Petrogradsky Island, St Petersburg, Russia
    336 ## $a *cartographic image* $2 *rdacontent*
    337 ## $a unmediated $2 rdamedia
    338 ## $a sheet $2 rdacarrier

4. Hard copy sheet music for the song Hiawatha (His Song to Minnehaha) words by James O'Dea and music by Neil Moret. Detroit : Whitney-Warner Publishing Company, 1903.
    336 ## $a *notated music* $2 *rdacontent*
    337 ## $a unmediated $2 rdamedia
    338 ## $a volume $2 rdacarrier

5. *The Guardian* Charlottetown newspaper—copy on microfiche
    336 ## $a *text* $2 *rdacontent*
    336 ## $a *still image* $2 *rdacontent*
    337##$a microform $2 rdamedia
    338##$a microfiche $2 rdacarrier

6. *The Guardian* Charlottetown newspaper—paper copy
    336 ## $a *text* $2 *rdacontent*
    336 ## $a *still image* $2 *rdacontent*
    337##$a unmediated $2 rdamedia
    338##$a volume $2 rdacarrier

7. *The Guardian* Charlottetown online newspaper
    336 ## $a *text* $2 *rdacontent*
    336 ## $a *still image* $2 *rdacontent*
    337##$a computer $2 rdamedia
    338##$a online resource $2 rdacarrier

8. The David Vases (Yuan dynasty, 1351 AD) in Room 95, Chinese ceramics, British Museum (physical object)
    336 ## $a *three-dimensional form* $2 *rdacontent*
    337 ## $a unmediated $2 rdamedia
    338 ## $a object $2 rdacarrier

ANSWERS 233

EXERCISE 11.2
1. A book is 20.5 centimeters high and 14.6 centimeters wide and has 287 pages and 163 illustrations, including 55 in full color.
   300 ## $a 287 pages :$b 163 illustrations (55 color) ;$c 21 cm.

2. A continuing serial is 20.3 centimeters wide and 24.6 centimeters high, the latest issue has 108 pages and a picture on the cover.
   300 ## $a   volumes ;$c 25 cm.
   COMMENT: RDA 7.15.1.3 SAYS 'DISREGARD ILLUSTRATED TITLE PAGES, ETC., AND MINOR ILLUSTRATIONS'.

3. A computer program has six 12 centimeter computer disks, a large reference manual and a quick reference card, contains color animations and sound.
   300 ## $a 6 computer disks :$b sound, color animations ;$c 12 cm. +$e reference manual and 1 quick reference card.

4. A set of 3 digitally recorded stereo compact discs and a booklet in a cardboard box. The discs are 4 and ¾ inches in diameter, and play for 56 minutes, 58 minutes and 65 minutes.
   300 ## $a 3 CDs (56 min.; 58 min.; 55 min.) :$b digital, stereo ;$c 4 ¾ inch +$e 1 booklet.
   COMMENT: DIGITAL AND STEREO CHARACTERISTICS CAN ALSO BE RECORDED IN THE MARC 344 FIELD.

REVISION QUIZ 11.3
1. What are the core elements for Works?
   Preferred Title for the Work, and Identifier for the Work.

2. Name the core elements at the Expression level.
   Content Type and Identifier for the Expression.

3. When would you use 'core if necessary' elements at the Work level?
   To differentiate between two Works with the same title.

4. When would you use 'core if necessary' elements at the Expression level?
   To differentiate an Expression from another Expression of the same Work.

5. What are six attributes, described in RDA Chapter 7, that you could use to describe the content of a resource? Are any of these core elements?
   RDA 7.2 to RDA7.28 list all the attributes that can describe content. None are core.

EXERCISE 12.1
a. A journal with the title proper *Trends in evolutionary biology*
   Access point: *Trends in evolutionary biology*
   MARC coding: *245 00 $a Trends in evolutionary biology*

b. Another journal with the title *Trends in evolutionary biology* that is published in Los Angeles
   Access point: *Trends in evolutionary biology (Los Angeles, Calif.)*
   MARC coding: *130 0# $a Trends in evolutionary biology (Los Angeles, Calif.)*
   245 00 $a Trends in evolutionary biology

c. A book by Peter Williams with the title *Cooking for fun*
   Access point: *Williams, Peter. Cooking for fun*
   MARC coding: *100 1# $a Williams, Peter*
   245 10 $a Cooking for fun

d. A book with no known authors with the title *Cooking for fun,* published in 2012 by Culinary Press
   Access point: *Cooking for fun*
   MARC coding: *245 00 $a Cooking for fun*

e. Another book with no known authors with the title *Cooking for fun,* published in 2014 by Household Press
   Access point: *Cooking for fun (2014)*
   MARC coding: *130 0# $a Cooking for fun (2014)*
   245 00 $a Cooking for fun

   OR

   Access point: *Cooking for fun (Household Press)*
   MARC coding: *130 0# $a Cooking for fun (Household Press)*
   245 00 $a Cooking for fun

f. A compilation of works by different authors with the title *Selected folk tales,* published in Tokyo in 2013
   Access point: *Selected folk tales*
   MARC coding: *245 00 $a Selected folk tales*

g. Another compilation of works by different authors with the title *Selected folk tales,* published in Bangkok in 2014
   Access point: *Selected folk tales (2014)*
   MARC coding: *130 0# $a Selected folk tales (2014)*
   245 00 $a Selected folk tales

   OR

   Access point: *Selected folk tales (Bangkok)*
   MARC coding: *130 0# $a Selected folk tales (Bangkok)*
   245 00 $a Selected folk tales

h. A newly-discovered sonnet by Shakespeare, *As you like it* (not to be confused with the better-known play of the same title that your library holds)
   Access point: *Shakespeare, William, 1564–1616. As you like it (Sonnet)*
   MARC coding: *100 1# $a Shakespeare, William, $d 1564–1616*
   240 10 $a As you like it. $k Sonnet
   245 10 $a As you like it

EXERCISE 12.2

a. *Tren dalam biologi evolusi,* an Indonesian translation of the work in Exercise 12.1a (a journal with the title proper *Trends in evolutionary biology*)
   Access point: *Trends in evolutionary biology. Indonesian*
   MARC coding: *130 0# $a Trends in evolutionary biology. $l Indonesian*
   245 00 $a Tren dalam biologi evolusi

b. An audio version of the work in Exercise 12.1c (a book by Peter Williams with the title *Cooking for fun*)
   Access point: *Williams, Peter. Cooking for fun. Spoken word.*
   MARC coding: *100 1# $a Williams, Peter*
   240 10 $a Cooking for fun. $k Spoken word
   245 10 $a Cooking for fun

c. *Cucinare per divertimento,* an Italian translation of the work in Exercise 12.1d (a book with no known authors with the title *Cooking for fun* published in 2012 by Culinary Press)
   Access point: *Cooking for fun. Italian*
   MARC coding: *130 0# $a Cooking for fun. $l Italian*
   245 00 $a Cucinare per divertimento

d. *Cucinare per divertimento,* an Italian translation of the work in Exercise 12.1e (another book with no known authors with the title *Cooking for fun* published in 2014 by Household Press)
   Access point: *Cooking for fun (2014). Italian*
   MARC coding: *130 0# $a Cooking for fun (2014). $l Italian*
   245 00 $a Cucinare per divertimento
   OR
   Access point: *Cooking for fun (Household Press). Italian*
   MARC coding: *130 0# $a Cooking for fun (Household Press). $l Italian*
   245 00 $a Cucinare per divertimento

EXERCISE 13.1

1. Ian Harrison – RDA 9.2.2.9
   Harrison, Ian

2. Stevan Eldred-Grigg – RDA 9.2.2.10
   Eldred-Grigg, Stevan

3. Tomie de Paola, an American writer of Italian descent – RDA 9.2.2.9 + 9.2.2.11.1 or 9.2.2.10.2
   De Paola, Tomie

4. Maurice Gough Gee who prefers not to use his middle name – RDA 9.2.2
   Gee, Maurice

5. Mao Zedong (Mao is the surname) – RDA 9.2.2.9
   Mao, Zedong

6. Pelham Grenville Wodehouse's name appears on his title pages as P.G. Wodehouse. He is commonly known by his initials. – RDA 9.5
   Wodehouse, P. G. (Pelham Grenville)

7. Michael O'Leary who wrote on risk management. His middle name Peter distinguishes him from other creators called Michael O'Leary – RDA 9.5.1
   O'Leary, Michael (Michael Peter)

8. Michael O'Leary who wrote on rail travel. His middle initial "D" distinguishes him from other creators called Michael O'Leary – RDA 9.5.1
   O'Leary, Michael (Michael D.)

9. Kathleen Mansfield Beauchamp married John Murray and always wrote under the pseudonym Katherine Mansfield – RDA 9.2.2.8
   Mansfield, Katherine

10. José Maria Escrivá de Balaguer (Escrivá de Balaguer is a Spanish compound surname); born 1902, died 1975. – RDA 9.2.2.10
    Escrivá de Balaguer, José Maria, 1902–1975

EXERCISE 13.2

MARC code	RDA instruction number	MARC field and subfield name
010	9.18	Library of Congress Control Number
035	9.18	System control number
040	---	Cataloging source
046	9.3.2 + 9.3.3	$f Birth date
100	9.2.2 + 9.3	Heading – personal name (Creator)
372	9.15	Field of activity
373	9.13.1.3	Affiliation
374	9.16.1.3	Occupation
375	9.7.1.3	Gender
377	9.14.1.3	Associated language
400	9.2.3	Personal name (Variant name for the person)
670	8.12	Source data found : $a source citation $b information found

EXERCISE 13.3

Note: there are no absolute right or wrong answers for this exercise. Here is one possible solution:

RDA Element	Data Recorded
10.2.2 Preferred name for the family	*Barrymore*
10.3 Type of family	*Family*
10.4 Date associated with the family	*1875—*
10.5 Place associated with the family	*United States of America*
10.6 Prominent member/s of the family	*Maurice Barrymore, Lionel Barrymore, Ethel Barrymore, John Drew Barrymore, Drew Blythe Barrymore*
10.8 Language of the family	*English*
10.9 Family history	*The Barrymore family is notable for their success in the acting world, both on stage and on the screen. The Barrymore family has been called a multi-generation theatrical dynasty, beginning with Maurice's acting debut in 1875 and continuing to Drew Barrymore who is still active today.*
10.10 Identifier for the family	
10.11 Authorized Access point	*Barrymore (Family)*
10.11.2 Variant access point/s	*Barrymore (Family : 1875—)* *Barrymore (Family : United States)* *Barrymore (Family : Barrymore, Maurice, 1849–1905)* *Barrymore (Family : Barrymore, Lionel, 1878–1954)* *Barrymore (Family : Barrymore, Ethel, 1879–1959)* *Barrymore (Family : Barrymore, Drew)* (and/or any of the other family members)
8.12 Source/s consulted	*Encyclopedia Brittanica website, http://www.britannica.com/EBchecked/topic/1365389/Barrymore-family, viewed 25 Oct 2014*

EXERCISE 13.4

*(Note: answers are in **bold face**):*

1. Colonial Sugar Refinery Limited, usually known by its initials, CSR Limited
    Colonial Sugar Refinery
    CSR Limited
    CSR Ltd.
    CSR
    Colonial Sugar Refinery Limited

2. The Lao People's Democratic Republic
    Lao People's Democratic Republic
    The Lao Democratic Republic
    Laos
    Lao Republic

3. Tourism Industry Association of Canada, formerly the Canadian Tourist Association
    Tourist Association of Canada
    Tourism Industry Association of Canada
    Canadian Tourist Association
    CTA
    TIAC

4. United Nations Educational, Scientific and Cultural Organization, or UNESCO (Unesco is the formally presented version on most publications)
    UNESCO
    United Nations Educational, Scientific and Cultural Organisation
    United Nations Educational, Scientific and Cultural Organization
    Unesco

5. One for All, a jazz group
    One for All
    1 for All
    One for All (Musical group)
    1 for All (Musical group)

6. Canadian Federation of Musicians (CFM), formerly referred to as AFM Canada
    AFM Canada
    Canadian Federation of Musicians
    Canada. Federation of Musicians
    CFM

EXERCISE 13.5

1. The Committee on Manpower Resources for Science and Technology of the Department of Education and Science of the United States government

   United States. Department of Education and Science. Committee on Manpower Resources for Science and Technology

2. The Australian Nuclear Science and Technology Organisation (ANSTO) of the Department of Industry of the Australian government.

   Australian Nuclear Science and Technology Organisation

3. The Agricultural Division of Imperial Chemical Industries

   Imperial Chemical Industries. Agricultural Division

4. Faculté de Médicine Saint-Antoine (part of the Université Pierre et Marie Curie)

   Université Pierre et Marie Curie. Faculté de Médicine Saint-Antoine

5. The United Nations Children's Fund, most commonly referred to as UNICEF

   UNICEF

6. The Federal Aviation Administration, an agency of the U.S. Department of Transportation

   United States. Federal Aviation Administration

7. Ministry of Agriculture, Fisheries and Food (located in Britain)

   Great Britain. Ministry of Agriculture, Fisheries and Food

8. University of the South Pacific, in Suva, Fiji

   University of the South Pacific

9. The United Nations Department of Public Information's Education Information Programmes

   United Nations. Education Information Programmes

10. Facebook, the company founded by Mark Zuckerberg

    Facebook (Firm)

EXERCISE 13.6

RDA Element	MARC tag and subfields	Data Recorded
11.2.2 Preferred name for the corporate body	*110 2# $a*	Red Hot Chili Peppers
11.2.3 Variant name	*410 2# $a* *410 2# $a* *410 2# $a*	Red Hot Chilli Peppers Chili Peppers RHCP
11.3 Place	*370 ## $e*	Los Angeles, USA
11.4.3 Date of establishment	*046 ## $s*	1983
11.4.4 Date of termination	*046 ## $t*	
11.7 Other designation	*110 ## $g* *410 ## $g*	Musical group
11.8 Language	*377 ## $a*	English
11.10 Field of activity	*372 ## $a*	Music
8.12 Source consulted	*670 ##$a* *$b* *$u*	Wikipedia entry, viewed 25 February 2014. (Red Hot Chili Peppers (also known as "Chili Peppers" or "RHCP") are an American funk rock band formed in Los Angeles in 1983. Currently, the band consists of founding members Anthony Kiedis (vocals) and Michael "Flea" Balzary (bass), longtime drummer Chad Smith, and guitarist Josh Klinghoffer, who joined in late 2009, following the departure of John Frusciante. Red Hot Chili Peppers have won seven Grammy Awards, and have become one of the best-selling bands of all time, selling over 80 million records worldwide. In 2012, they were inducted into the Rock and Roll Hall of Fame. The band's original line-up featured guitarist Hillel Slovak and drummer Jack Irons, alongside Kiedis and Flea.) http://en.wikipedia.org/wiki/Red_Hot_Chili_Peppers
11.13.1 Access point	*110 2# $a* *$g*	**Red Hot Chili Peppers** ***Musical group***
11.13.2 Variant access point	*410 2# $a* *$g*	**Red Hot Chilli Peppers** ***Musical group***
11.13.2 Variant access point	*410 2# $a* *$g*	***Chili Peppers*** ***Musical group***
11.13.2 Variant access point	*410 2# $a* *$g*	***RHCP*** ***Musical group***
(Note: if not coding in MARC, the Access point fields would include brackets, e.g., Red Hot Chili Peppers (Musical group), Chili Peppers (Musical group), etc.		

ANSWERS 241

EXERCISE 13.7

1. World Library and Information Congress (2013 : Singapore)
   111 2# $aWorld Library and Information Congress $d(2013 :$cSingapore)

2. American Anthropological Association. Annual Meeting (113th : 2014 : Washington, D.C.)
   111 2# $aAmerican Anthropological Association.$eAnnual Meeting $n(113th :$d2014 :$cWashington, D.C.)

3. International Conference on Sport Medicine and Sport Science (12th : 2014 : Cape Town, South Africa)
   111 2# $aInternational Conference on Sport Medicine and Sport Science $n(12th :$d2014 :$cCape Town, South Africa)

4. International Conference on Secure Knowledge Management (2014 : Dubai, United Arab Emirates)
   111 2# $aInternational Conference on Secure Knowledge Management $d(2014 :$cDubai, United Arab Emirates)

5. Annual Green Building Convention (7th : 2014 : Cape Town, South Africa)
   111 2# $aAnnual Green Building Convention $n(7th :$d2014 :$cCape Town, South Africa)

6. International Conference on Software Engineering (36th : 2014 : Hyderabad, India)
   111 2# $aInternational Conference on Software Engineering $n(36th :$d2014 :$cHyderabad, India)

7. International Congress of Aerobiology. General Assembly Meeting (10th : 2014 : University of Western Sydney. School of Medicine)
   111 2# $aInternational Congress of Aerobiology.$eGeneral Assembly Meeting $n(10th :$d2014 :$c University of Western Sydney. School of Medicine)
   OR
   International Congress of Aerobiology. General Assembly Meeting (10th : 2014 : Campbelltown N.S.W.)
   111 2# $aInternational Congress of Aerobiology.$eGeneral Assembly Meeting $n(10th :$d2014 :$cCampbelltown, N.S.W.)

EXERCISE 13.8

040	##	*$a ABCD $b eng $e rda $c ABCD*
046	##	*$s 20140228 $t 20140302*
111	2#	*$a Annual Illustration, Comics and Animation Conference $n(2nd : $d 2014 : $c Hanover, N.H.)*
368	##	*$a Conference.*
370	##	*$e Hanover, N.H.*
377	## OR ##	*$a eng* OR *$a eng $l English*
670	##	*$a Illustration, Comics, and Animation Conference at Dartmouth website, viewed 11/14/14 $u https://sites.dartmouth.edu/illustrationcomicsanimationconference/*

EXERCISE 14.1

1. Washington, D.C.
   Washington (D.C.)

2. Washington State
   Washington (State)

3. Milan (city in Italy)
   Milan (Italy)

4. Vancouver Island, British Columbia, Canada
   Vancouver Island (B.C.)

5. Antarctic regions
   Antarctica

6. Addis Ababa
   Addis Ababa (Ethiopia)

7. Mount Isa (western Queensland)
   (Mount Isa (Qld.)

8. Kiev in the Ukraine
   Kiev (Ukraine)

9. Ayrshire, a county in Scotland
   Ayrshire (Scotland)

10. Southern Ocean
    Antarctic Ocean

EXERCISE 15.2

1. French translation of *Wind in the Willows*
   100 1# $a Grahame, Kenneth,$d1859–1932,$e **author**
   700 1# $a Parsons, Jacques,$e **translator**
   700 1# $a Shepard, Ernest H,$e **illustrator**

2. Book published by the Australian War Memorial
   700 1# $a Heywood, Warwick,$e **organizer**
   700 1# $a Nelson, Brendan,$d1958–   ,$e **writer of introduction**
   710 2# $a Australian War Memorial,$e **host institution**

3. CD of Clara Schumann's Piano Concerto
   100 1# $a Schumann, Clara,$d1819–1896,$e **composer**
   700 1# $a Jochum, Veronica,$e **instrumentalist**
   700 1# $a Silverstein, Joseph, 1932–   ,$e **instrumentalist**
   700 1# $a Silverstein, Joseph, 1932–   ,$e **conductor**

EXERCISE 16.1

1. Membership directory of the American Bar Association
   Authorized access point: *American Bar Association*
   Creator? *Yes*

2. The annual report of the Trinidad Netball Association
   Authorized access point: *Trinidad Netball Association*
   Creator? *Yes*

3. The Anarchist Federation Program in London / by the London Section of the Anarchist Federation
   Authorized access point: *Anarchist Federation. London Section*
   Creator? *Yes*

4. Standards for air quality developed by the Standards Committee of the American Antipollution Society
   Authorized access point: *American Antipollution Society. Standards Committee*
   Creator? *Yes*

5. The National Advisory Council on Ageing's discussion paper 'Euthanasia: an issue for your consideration'. (Note: the Council is in Canada)
   Authorized access point: *National Advisory Council on Ageing (Canada)*
   Creator? *No*

6. A room-by-room guide to the Cleveland Museum of Art by Melissa Cranshaw
   Authorized access point: *Cleveland Museum of Art*
   Creator? *Yes* (COMMENT: SEE EXAMPLES, RDA 19.2.1.3)

EXERCISE 16.2

1. Jim Fern   *artist*
2. Adam Hughes   *artist*
3. Lovern Kindzierski   *illustrator*
4. Todd Klein   *letterer*
5. Joao Ruas   *illustrator*
6. Bill Willingham   *author*

EXERCISE 17.1

Explanation	Relationship designator	Type of relationship
An expression of a larger work of which the expression is a discrete component.	Contained in (expression)	Whole-Part Expression Relationships
An item that exemplifies a manifestation that embodies the same expression of a work.	Equivalent (item)	Equivalent Item Relationships
A work that enlarges upon the content of the source work.	Expanded as (work)	Derivative Work Relationship
An expression of a work that came together with one or more expressions to form the new expression.	Merger of (expression)	Sequential Expression Relationships
An item that is contained on the same microform with the item being described.	Filmed with (item)	Accompanying Item Relationships
An expression of a work that has been updated, corrected, or expanded.	Revised as	Derivative Expression Relationships
A work that split into two or more separate works with new titles. Apply generally to serials.	Continuation in part of (work)	Sequential Work Relationships
A manifestation that reproduces another manifestation.	Reproduced as (manifestation)	Equivalent Manifestation Relationships
A work that contains a critical evaluation of the described work.	Critiqued in (work)	Descriptive Work Relationships
A serial or newspaper containing a single issue or a supplementary section devoted to a special subject, with or without serial numbering, such as an anniversary number of a periodical or newspaper.	Special issue of	Whole-Part Manifestation Relationships

EXERCISE 17.2

The journal Coin News was published in 1954 in Kingston, Jamaica. In 1989 it changed its name to Numismatics Jamaica. In 1991 the journal Jamaican Coins Monthly was incorporated into it. This journal, incorporating Jamaican Coins Monthly, was published with a new title Coin News Jamaica in 1995. In 2003 the journal moved to Montego Bay and expanded its coverage, changing its name to Caribbean Coin News.

Relationship designators that show the linkages between these titles:

Coin News (1954–1989)
    Continued by (work): *Numismatics Jamaica*

Numismatics Jamaica (1989–1995)
    Continuation of (work): *Coin News*
    Absorption of (work): *Jamaican Coins Monthly*
    Continued by (work): *Coin News Jamaica*

Jamaican Coins Monthly (1930–1991)
    Absorbed by (work): *Numismatics Jamaica*

Coin News Jamaica (1995–2003)
    Continuation of (work): *Numismatics Jamaica*
    Continued by (work): *Caribbean Coin News*

Caribbean Coin News (2003—   )
    Continuation of (work): *Coin News Jamaica*

EXERCISE 18.1

1. Work record

RDA Reference	RDA Element	Data Recorded
6.2.1	Preferred title for Work	*Learn cataloging the RDA way*
6.2.3	Variant title	*Cataloging the RDA way*
6.4.1	Date of Work	*2015*
19.2.1.3 Appendix I	Creator associated with the Work	*Lynn Farkas* *Helen Rowe*
6.27	Authorized access point for the Work	*Farkas, Lynn, 1951– . Learn cataloging the RDA way*
7.7	Intended audience	*For tertiary students*

2. Expression record

RDA Reference	RDA Element	Data Recorded
6.9	Content type	*text*
6.10	Date of Expression	*2015*
6.11	Language of Expression	*English*
7.10	Summarization of content	*A practical study guide for learning descriptive cataloging using Resource Description and Access (RDA) and MARC*
7.15	Illustrative content	*Illustrations*
7.16	Supplementary content	*Bibliography, page 279* *Includes index*
7.17	Colour content	*black and white*

3. Manifestation record

RDA Reference	RDA Element	Data Recorded
2.3	Title proper of manifestation	*Learn cataloging the RDA way*
2.3.6	Variant title of manifestation	*Cataloging the RDA way*
2.4.2	Statement of responsibility	*Lynn Farkas and Helen Rowe*
2.5	Edition statement	*International edition*
2.8.2	Place of publication	*Friendswood, Texas*
2.8.4	Name of publisher	*TotalRecall Publications, Inc.*
2.8.6	Date of publication	*2015*
2.11	Copyright date	*© 2015*
2.12	Series	*Learn Library Skills series*
2.13	Mode of issuance	*Single unit*
2.15	Identifier for the manifestation	*ISBN 9781590954355*
3.2	Media type	*unmediated*
3.3	Carrier type	*volume*
3.4.5	Extent	*vi, 282 pages*
3.5	Dimensions	*30 cm.*

4. **MARC bibliographic record**

MARC field	Subfield	Data Recorded	Template Used (W, E, or M)
020	$a	9781590954355	M
040	$e	$a ABCD $b eng $c ABCD $e rda	
100	$a 1# $d $e	Farkas, Lynn, 1951— , author.	W
245	$a 10 $b $c	Learn cataloging the RDA way / Lynn Farkas, Helen Rowe.	M
250	$a	International edition.	M
264 01	$a $b $c	Friendswood, Tx. : TotalRecall Publications, Inc., 2015.	M
264 04	$c	© 2015	M
300	$a $b $c	vi, 282 pages : black and white illustrations ; 30 cm.	M E M
336	$a $2	text rdacontent	E
337	$a $2	unmediated rdamedia	M
338	$a $2	volume rdacarrier	M
490	$a	Learn library skills series	M
500	$a	Includes index.	E
504	$a	Bibliography: page 279.	E
520	$a	A practical study guide for learning descriptive cataloging using Resource Description and Access (RDA) and MARC	E
7XX	$a $e	Rowe, Helen, author	W

5. Authority record for author #1

RDA No.	RDA Element	Data Recorded	MARC
9.2	Name of the person	Lynn Farkas	100
9.3	Dates associated with a person	1951—	100 $d 046 $f
9.7	Gender	Female	375
9.10	Country associated with a person	Australia	370 $c
9.11	Place of residence	Canberra	370 $e
9.13	Affiliation	Lynn Farkas Information Services Pty Ltd	373
9.14	Language	English	377
9.15	Field of activity	Librarianship, Knowledge management	372
9.16	Profession or occupation	Librarian, Educator, Company Director	374
9.17	Biographical information	Lynn Farkas is a library trainer and director of an Australian information services consulting company. Her expertise includes subject analysis, thesaurus development, knowledge management applications, and database indexing.	678
9.19	Authorized access point	Farkas, Lynn, 1951—	100
8.12	Sources consulted	Learn cataloging the RDA way, back cover	670

Authority record for author #2

RDA No.	RDA Element	Data Recorded	MARC
9.2	Name of the person	Helen Rowe	100
9.7	Gender	Female	375
9.10	Country associated with a person	Australia	370 $c
9.11	Place of residence	Canberra	370 $e
9.13	Affiliation	Lynn Farkas Information Services Pty Ltd; Libraries Australia	373
9.14	Language	English	377
9.15	Field of activity	Librarianship	372
9.16	Profession or occupation	Cataloger, Librarian, Educator	374
9.17	Biographical information	Helen Rowe is a cataloger and accredited trainer for Libraries Australia and for Lynn Farkas Information Services Pty. Ltd.	678
9.19	Authorized access point	Rowe, Helen	100
8.12	Sources consulted	Learn Cataloging the RDA way, back cover	670

EXERCISE 19.1

1. Book
050 field: Second $a should be a $b
082 field: Second $a should be a $2
Note: 260 field is acceptable, since this is an AACR2 record. However, if upgrading to make it RDA–compliant, this should be changed to a 264 field, second indicator '1', $c changed to '$c2014'; and a second indicator '264 #4 $c © 2014' should be added. Changes would also be needed in the 040 field (add $e rda), the 245 field (change '[et al.]'), and the 504 field (spell out 'pages'). In addition, the 336, 337 and 338 fields would have to be added.
300 field is missing
500 field: Gallery name is spelled 'Sacler', should be 'Sackler'
Final 650 field: 'Poetry, Chinese' should be 'Pottery, Chinese', since this work is about an exhibition of teapots.

2. Map
100 field: Should be 110 field 'Main Entry—Corporate Name'
245 field: Incorrect spelling of 'deposits'
Second 264 field: should have second indicator '4', not '1' – to indicate it is a copyright statement
336 field is missing
Second 500 field: Incorrect spelling of 'currency'
650 field: $a Should be 'Iron mines and mining'
710 field should include a '$e issuing body' after corporate body name

3. Conference
111 field: Subfield $n is incorrectly positioned, should be outside the parentheses
Missing a 264 #1 field, for publication statement
300 field: Abbreviations should not be used—spell out 'pages' and 'illustration/s'
520 field: Incorrect field tag used, should be a 504 'Bibliography, etc Note' (520 is used for summaries of the content)
700 field: one of the editors, 'Krisantini', has been omitted, should have a 700 entry like the others
Second 710 field: Incorrect capitalization of the proper nouns in $a and $b

4. Serial
245 field: Incorrect spelling of 'Society'
264 field: No ISBD punctuation; field should read '$a London :$b Huguenot Society of Great Britain and Ireland, $c 2013— '
300 field: 'volume' should be spelled out in an RDA compliant record
Second 336 field: Incorrect field tag used, should be 337
Second 650 field: Incorrect spelling of 'Huguenots'

EXERCISE 19.2

1.
008 *yymmdd*s2014   txu   d   000 0 eng d
020 __ $a 9781590954546
040 __ $a ABCD $b eng $c ABCD $e rda
050 _4 $a Z1006 $b .L5 2014
082 04 $a 020.3 $2 23
100 1_ $a Farkas, Lynn $d 1951– ,$e compiler.
245 10 $a LibrarySpeak :$b a glossary of terms in librarianship and information management /$c compiled by Lynn Farkas.
246 14 $a Library speak :$b a glossary of terms in librarianship and information management.
246 30 $a Glossary of terms in librarianship and information management.
250 __ $a First international edition.
264 _1 $a Friendswood, Texas :$b TotalRecall Publications, Inc., $c 2014.
264 _4 $c© 2014.
300 __ $a v, 187 pages, 4 unnumbered pages ;$c 21 cm.
336 __ $a text $2 rdacontent
337 __ $a unmediated $2 rdamedia
338 __ $a volume $2 rdacarrier
504 __ $a Includes bibliographical references (page 186).
650 _0 $a Library science $v Dictionaries.
650 _0 $a Library science $v Terminology.
650 _0 $a Information science $v Dictionaries.
650 _0 $a Information science $v Terminology.

2.
007 sd |sngnnmmned
008 *yymmdd*s2013   vrannnnjq   f n eng d
020 __ $a 9781743178539.
020 __ $a 1743178530
040 __ $a ABCD $b eng $c ABCD $e rda
082 04 $a A823.4 $2 23
100 1_ $a Griffiths, Andy, $d 1961– , $e author.
245 14 $a The 39-storey treehouse /$c Andy Griffiths ; read by Stig Wemyss ; illustrated by Terry Denton.
246 3_ $a Thirty-nine storey treehouse
246 3_ $a Thirty-nine storey tree house
246 3_ $a 39 storey tree house
250 __ $a Unabridged.
264 _1 $a Tullamarine, Victoria :$b Bolinda Audio, $c 2013.
264 _4 $c ℗2013.
300 __ $a 2 audio discs (2 hr., 7 min.) :$b digital, stereo ;$c 12 cm.
336 __ $a spoken word $2 rdacontent
337 __ $a audio $2 rdamedia
338 __ $a audio disc $2 rdacarrier
500 __ $a Book edition illustrated by Terry Denton.

ANSWERS   251

```
511  0_  $a Read by Stig Wemyss.
520  __  $a Join Andy and Terry in their newly expanded 39-storey treehouse, featuring 13
             brand-new, surprising, crazy and fun-packed storeys!
650  _0  $a Tree houses $v Juvenile fiction.
650  _0  $a Australian fiction.
655  _0  $a Short stories
700  1_  $a Denton, Terry, $d 1950–   ,$e illustrator.
700  1_  $a Wemyss, Stig,$e narrator.
```

3.
```
008  yymmdds2015   txu    f    001 0 eng d
020  ##  $a 9781590954393
040  ##  $a ABCD $b eng $c ABCD $e rda
082  04  $a 025.47076 $2 23
100  1#  $a Farkas, Lynn $d 1951—   ,$e author
245  10  $a Learn Library of Congress subject access /$c by Lynn Farkas.
250  ##  $a International edition.
264  #1  $a Friendswood, Texas :$b TotalRecall Publications, Inc., $c 2015.
300  ##  $a 116 pages :$b illustrations, 1 chart ;$c 30 cm.
336  ##  $a text $2 rdacontent
337  ##  $a unmediated $2 rdamedia
338  ##  $a volume $2 rdacarrier
490  1#  $a Learn library skills series
500  ##  $a Includes index.
504  ##  $a Bibliography: page 113.
650  #0  $a Subject cataloging.
650  #0  $a Subject cataloging $v Problems, exercises, etc.
650  #0  $a Subject headings, Library of Congress.
650  #0  $a Subject headings, Library of Congress $v Problems, exercises, etc.
```

REVISION QUIZ 19.3

1. Name three sources of copy cataloging.

   There are a number of options for obtaining copy cataloging records, including:
   - *manual copy cataloging by finding a record in another catalog. Once found, these records can be downloaded, or copied and pasted into your library's catalog*
   - *using Cataloging-in-Publication (CIP) records*
   - *using catalog subscription services that find or create records and sell them to libraries. These services are provided on a commercial basis, offering original and copy cataloging*
   - *purchasing MARC records when you purchase resources from suppliers*
   - *copying a record from a network or consortium that your library belongs to, like OCLC, Libraries Australia, etc.*
   - *'triggering' an automatic download by adding your holdings to a record.*

2. Define cloning. How does it differ from copy cataloging?
   Cloning involves creating a new catalog record based on a record for a similar resource (e.g., the spoken word version of a monograph, or a new edition of the monograph) by copying the original record and making appropriate changes.
   Copy cataloging uses a catalog record that another library has created for the resource in hand, and this avoids preparing another original catalog record for the resource.
   The difference between them is that copy cataloging finds an existing record for the same resource and simply adds it to its own catalog; cloning uses a record for a related resource and changes it to create a new record for a different resource.

3. What are the advantages of upgrading an AACR2 copy catalogued record to make it RDA–compliant? What are the disadvantages?
   Advantages: Upgrading AACR2 records will result in a more consistent catalog. It is a better use of cataloging time, since cataloging staff do not need to use two sets of rules and guidelines. This may be more efficient and cost-effective in the long run. Upgrading records can add value to the catalog and make it a more effective tool for users.
   Disadvantages: It takes more time to upgrade a record than to accept the AACR2 record provided, so it may seem easier to accept the AACR2 copy as it is. However it does require the cataloger to know the AACR2 rules in order to ensure the information is correctly presented, and it results in a catalog that presents information to the user in different and sometimes conflicting formats.

EXERCISE 20.1

1. Book

```
008  yymmdds1983    dcua    b    000 0 eng
020  __  $a 094318200X
020  __  $a 0943182018 (paperback)
040  __  $a ABCD $b eng $c ABCD $e rda
050  00  $a DS63.2.U5 $b S64 1983
082  00  $a 305.8927 $2 19
245  00  $a Split vision :$b the portrayal of Arabs in the American media /$c edited by
             Edmund Ghareeb.
250  __  $a Revised and expanded edition.
264  _1  $a Washington, D.C. :$b American-Arab Affairs Council, $c 1983.
300  __  $a xvii, 402 pages :$b illustrations ;$c 24 cm.
336  __  $a text $2 rdacontent
337  __  $a unmediated $2 rdamedia
338  __  $a volume $2 rdacarrier
500  __  $a Includes index.
504  __  $a Includes bibliographical references.
650  _0  $a Public opinion $z United States.
650  _0  $a Mass media $z United States.
651  _0  $a Arab countries $x In mass media.
651  _0  $a Arab countries $x Foreign public opinion, American.
700  1_  $a Ghareeb, Edmund,$e editor.
710  2_  $a American-Arab Affairs Council.
```

2. Audiobook

```
007    sd fungnnmmnzd
008    yymmdds2013    miu    q    000 0 eng d
020 __  $a 9781480554030
040 __  $a ABCD $b eng $c ABCD $e rda
050 14  $a HD57.7 $b .M3937 2013
082 04  $a 658.4/092 $2 23
100 1_  $a Maxwell, John C., $d 1947–   ,$e author,$e narrator.
245 14  $a The 21 irrefutable laws of leadership :$b follow them and people will follow you
        /$c John C. Maxwell ; foreword by Stephen R. Covey ; read by John C. Maxwell.
246 3_  $a Twenty-one irrefutable laws of leadership
250 __  $a Abridged, revised & updated 10th anniversary edition.
264 _1  $a [Grand Haven, Mich.] :$b Brilliance Audio, Inc., $c 2013.
300 __  $a 1 audio disc (3 hr., 28 min.) ;$c 12 cm.
336 __  $a spoken word $2 rdacontent
337 __  $a audio $2 rdamedia
338 __  $a audio disc $2 rdacarrier
344 __  $a digital $2 rda
347 __  $a audio file $b CD audio $2 rda
500 __  $a Title from container.
511 0_  $a Read by the author.
520 __  $a Provides insights and observations on the laws of leadership that govern
        personal and organizational effectiveness.
650 _0  $a Leadership.
650 _0  $a Industrial management.
700 1_  $a Covey, Stephen R.,$e writer of introduction.
```

3. Serial

```
008    yymmddd19682003enkmr p    0 a0eng
022 0_  $a 0018-2214
040 __  $a ABCD $b eng $c ABCD $e rda
050 00  $a QH613 $b .H53
082 04  $a 572 $2 22
210 0_  $a Histochem. j.
222 _0  $a Histochemical journal
245 04  $a The Histochemical journal.
264 _1  $a London :$b Chapman and Hall, $c 1968–2003.
300 __  $a 34 volumes :$b illustrations ;$c 23 cm.
310 __  $a Monthly, $b January 1983–2003
321 __  $a Quarterly, $b 1968–1972
321 __  $a Bimonthly, $b January 1973–December 1982
336 __  $a text $b txt $2 rdacontent
337 __  $a unmediated $b n $2 rdamedia
338 __  $a volume $b nc $2 rdacarrier
362 0_  $a Volume 1, number 1 (August 1968)—volume 34, number 11/12 (2002–2003)
588 __  $a Description based on: Volume one, number three (February 1969).
650 _0  $a Histochemistry $v Periodicals.
```

785 00 $t Journal of molecular histology.

4. Map
008 *yymmdd*q19801986enkcg   a   0   eng d
020 __ $a 0861450728
040 __ $a ABCD $b eng $c ABCD $e rda
043 __ $a ed----- $a e-hu---
082 04 $a 914.96 $2 21
110 2_ $a Automobile Association (Great Britain). $b Cartographic Services Department.
245 10 $a South-east Europe :$b Bulgaria, Greece, Hungary, Romania, Yugoslavia /$c produced in the United Kingdom by the Cartographic Services Department of the Automobile Association.
246 3_ $a AA south-east Europe
255 __ $a Scale 1:1,250,000.
264 _1 $a Basingstoke, Hants :$b Automobile Association, $c [not after 1986]
300 __ $a 1 map :$b color ;$c 52 x 136 cm, folded to 26 x 13 cm.
336 __ $a cartographic image $b cri $2 rdacontent
337 __ $a unmediated $b n $2 rdamedia
338 __ $a sheet $b nb $2 rdacarrier
490 1_ $a European route planning series ;$v no. 5
650 _0 $a Roads $z Balkan Peninsula $v Maps.
650 _0 $a Roads $z Hungary $v Maps.

5. Series
008 *yymmdd*s2006   nyu   000 f eng d
020 __ $a 9780061145919
020 __ $a 0061145912
040 __ $a ABCD $b eng $c ABCD $e rda
082 04 $a 823.92 $2 22
100 1_ $a George, Elizabeth, $d 1949–   ,$e author.
245 10 $a What came before he shot her /$c Elizabeth George.
250 __ $a Large print edition.
264 _1 $a New York, N.Y. :$b HarperLargePrint, $c 2006.
300 __ $a 1028 pages ;$c 20 cm.
336 __ $a text $2 rdacontent
337 __ $a unmediated $2 rdamedia
338 __ $a volume $2 rdacarrier
490 1_ $a Inspector Lynley mysteries ;$v 14
520 __ $a New York Times bestselling author Elizabeth George delivers an explosive new novel. The brutal, inexplicable death of Inspector Thomas Lynley's wife has left Scotland Yard searching for answers. Who is the twelve-year-old boy who pulled the trigger? What were the circumstances that led to his horrific act? That story begins on the other side of London, where the three mixed-race Campbell children are sent to live with their aunt. The oldest, fifteen-year-old Ness, is headed for trouble as fast as her high-heeled boots will take her. That leaves the middle child, Joel, to care for the youngest, Toby. But before long, Joel has his

own problems with a local gang. To protect his family, he makes a pact with the devil—a move that leads straight to the front doorstep of Thomas Lynley.

650	_0	$a Lynley, Thomas (Fictitious character) $v Fiction.
650	_0	$a Abandoned children $z England $z London $v Fiction.
650	_0	$a Male juvenile delinquents $z England $z London $v Fiction.
650	_0	$a Murder $v Fiction.
651	_0	$a London (England) $x Social conditions $v Fiction.

6. Book

008	*yymmdd*t20142014dcu 001 0 eng d	
020	__	$a 9780935302356
040	__	$a ABCD $b eng $c ABCD $e rda
043	__	$a n-us---
050	00	$a LB3051 $b .A693 2014
082	00	$a 371.26/0973 $2 23
110	2_	$a American Educational Research Association,$e author.
245	10	$a Standards for educational and psychological testing /$c American Educational Research Association, American Psychological Association, National Council on Measurement in Education.
264	_1	$a Washington, DC :$b American Educational Research Association, $c [2014].
264	_4	$a ©2014.
300	__	$a ix, 230 pages ;$c 26 cm.
336	__	$a text $b txt $2 rdacontent
337	__	$a unmediated $b n $2 rdamedia
338	__	$a volume $b nc $2 rdacarrier
500	__	$a "Prepared by the Joint Committee on Standards for Educational and Psychological Testing of the American Educational Research Association, American Psychological Association and National Council on Measurement in Education"—Title page verso.
500	__	$a Includes index.
650	_0	$a Educational tests and measurements $x Standards $z United States.
650	_0	$a Psychological tests $x Standards $z United States.
710	2_	$a American Psychological Association,$e author.
710	2_	$a National Council on Measurement in Education,$e author.
710	2_	$a Joint Committee on Standards for Educational and Psychological Testing (U.S.),$e author.

7. Newspaper

008	*yymmdd*c20139999enkwr n 0 a0eng	
022	1_	$a 2054–3395
040	__	$a ABCD $b eng $c ABCD $e rda
082	04	$a 072.298 $2 23
130	0_	$a Bracknell times (2013)
222	_4	$a The Bracknell times
245	14	$a The Bracknell times.
264	_1	$a Reading, Berkshire :$b Trinity Mirror, $c 2013–
300	__	$a volumes :$b illustrations (black and white, and colour) ;$c 36 cm.

310 __ $a Weekly
336 __ $a text $2 rdacontent
336 __ $a still image $2 rdacontent
337 __ $a unmediated $2 rdamedia
338 __ $a volume $2 rdacarrier
362 1_ $a Began with Thursday, October 24, 2013 issue.
588 __ $a Description based on: Thursday, October 31, 2013 issue.
651 _0 $a Bracknell (England) $v Newspapers.
651 _0 $a Berkshire (England) $v Newspapers.
780 00 $t Bracknell Forest standard $x 1758–9134

8. e-book
007 cr |n|||||||||
008 *yymmdd*s2014   miu   ob   000 0 eng d
020 __ $a 9781607853145
040 __ $a ABCD $b eng $c ABCD $e rda
050 00 $a QC903
100 1_ $a Collings, David A.
245 10 $a Stolen future, broken present :$b the human significance of climate change /$c David A. Collings.
246 1_ $a Human significance of climate change
264 _1 $a Ann Arbor, Mich. :$b Open Humanities Press, $c 2014.
264 _4 $c ©2014
300 __ $a 241 pages
336 __ $a text $2 rdacontent
337 __ $a computer $2 rdamedia
338 __ $a online resource $2 rdacarrier
347 __ $a text file $b PDF $2 rda
490 1_ $a Critical climate change
504 __ $a Bibliography: pages 229–241.
538 __ $a Mode of access: World Wide Web.
650 _0 $a Climatic changes.
710 2_ $a Open Humanities Press.
710 2_ $a University of Michigan. $b Library. $b Michigan Publishing.
856 40 $z Access to the online version: $u http://dx.doi.org/10.3998/ohp.12832550.0001.001

9. e-serial
007 cr cn ||||||||
008 *yymmdd*c20139999ch qr p|o||||| |0eng d
022 __ $a 2308-0477
024 7_ $a10.6493/SMARTSCIENCE $2doi
040 __ $a ABCD $b eng $c ABCD $e rda
050 _4 $a TA418.9.S62
130 0_ $a Smart science (Online)
222 _0 $a Smart science
245 10 $a Smart science.

264 _1 $a Nantou City, Taiwan :$b TAETI Academic Publisher, $c 2013–
310 __ $a 4 issues per year
336 __ $a text $2 rdacontent
336 __ $a still image $2 rdacontent
337 __ $a computer $2 rdamedia
338 __ $a online resource $2 rdacarrier
362 1_ $a Began with Volume 1, Number 1 (2013).
538 __ $a Mode of access: World Wide Web.
538 __ $a System requirements: Acrobat Reader.
588 __ $a Description based on: Volume 1, Number 1 (2013) (viewed September 29, 2014)
588 __ $a Latest issue consulted: Volume 2, Number 3 (2014) (viewed September 29, 2014)
650 _0 $a Smart materials $v Periodicals.
650 _0 $a Technological innovations $v Periodicals.
856 40 $u http://www.taeti.org/journal/index.php/smartsci

10. Report of a Conference
008 *yymmdd*s1981   th   i100 0 eng
040 __ $a ABCD $b eng $c ABCD $e rda
043 __ $a a------ $a p------
050 00 $a LC5257.A2 $b P76 1980
082 00 $a 374.95 $2 19
245 00 $a Prospects for adult education and development in Asia and the Pacific :$b report of a regional seminar, Bangkok, 24 November–4 December 1980.
264 _1 $a Bangkok, Thailand :$b Unesco Regional Office for Education in Asia and the Pacific, $c 1981.
300 __ $a 69 pages ;$c 27 cm.
336 __ $a text $2 rdacontent
337 __ $a unmediated $2 rdamedia
338 __ $a volume $2 rdacarrier
650 _0 $a Adult education $z Asia $x Congresses.
651 _0 $a Islands of the Pacific $x Congresses.
711 2_ $a Regional Seminar on Adult Education and Development in Asia and Oceania $d (1980 :$c Bangkok, Thailand)

11. Book on CD
007 co |g|||||||||
008 *yymmdd*s2015   enk   q |0|0 0|eng d
020 __ $a 9781107677708 (CD-ROM)
020 __ $a 110767770X (CD-ROM)
040 __ $a ABCD $b eng $c ABCD $e rda
082 04 $a 540.76 $2 23
100 1_ $a Wooster, Mike,$e author.
245 10 $a Cambridge international AS and A level chemistry :$b teacher's resource /$c Mike Wooster, Lawrie Ryan and Roger Norris.
250 __ $a Second edition, Version 1.00.
264 _1 $a Cambridge :$b Cambridge University Press, $c 2015.

300 __ $a 1 CD-ROM ;$c 12 cm.
336 __ $a text $2 rdacontent
337 __ $a computer $2 rdamedia
338 __ $a computer disc $2 rdacarrier
500 __ $a "CD-ROM for Windows and Mac OSX".
500 __ $a "Completely Cambridge".
500 __ $a "Endorsed by Cambridge International Examinations".
610 20 $a University of Cambridge. $b Local Examinations Syndicate. $b International Examinations $x Examinations.
650 _0 $a Chemistry $x Study and teaching (Secondary)
650 _0 $a Chemistry $x Study and teaching (Secondary) $v Problems, exercises, etc.
650 _0 $a Chemistry $x Examinations $v Study guides.
700 1_ $a Ryan, Lawrie,$e author.
700 1_ $a Norris, Roger, $d 1947– ,$e author.

12. Conference

008 *yymmdd*s1984   ctua   b   101 0 eng
020 __ $a 0313235244
040 __ $a ABCD $b eng $c ABCD $e rda
043 __ $a n-us---
050 00 $a ML1711 $b .C66 1981
082 04 $a 782.140973 $2 22
111 2_ $a Conference on the Musical Theatre in America $d (1981 :$c C.W. Post Center)
245 10 $a Musical theatre in America :$b papers and proceedings of the Conference on the Musical Theatre in America /$c edited by Glenn Loney ; sponsored jointly by the American Society for Theatre Research, the Sonneck Society, and the Theatre Library Association.
264 _1 $a Westport, Conn. :$b Greenwood Press, $c 1984.
300 __ $a xxi, 441 pages :$b black and white illustrations ;$c 25 cm.
336 __ $a text $b txt $2 rdacontent
337 __ $a unmediated $b n $2 rdamedia
338 __ $a volume $b nc $2 rdacarrier
490 1_ $a Contributions in drama and theatre studies, $x 0163-3821 ;$v no. 8
504 __ $a Includes bibliographical references (pages 415–420) and index.
650 _0 $a Musicals $z United States $v Congresses.
700 1_ $a Loney, Glenn Meredith, $d 1928– ,$e editor.
710 2_ $a American Society for Theatre Research,$e sponsoring body.
710 2_ $a Sonneck Society,$e sponsoring body.
710 2_ $a Theatre Library Association,$e sponsoring body.

13. Map

007 aj canzn
008 *yymmdd*s2000   rh   a 0 eng
040 __ $a ABCD $b eng $c ABCD $e rda
050 00 $a G8561.E635 2000 $b .G8
245 00 $a Map of Zimbabwe :$b accommodation, national parks, habitats, roads.
255 __ $a Scale approximately 1:2,000,000.

264	_1	$a Harare, Zimbabwe :$b Gwaai River Stuff, $c [2000?]
300	__	$a 1 map :$b color ;$c 43 x 60 cm, folded to 22 x 15 cm.
336	__	$a cartographic image $2 rdacontent
337	__	$a unmediated $2 rdamedia
338	__	$a sheet $b nb $2 rdacarrier
490	0_	$a The natural selection
500	__	$a Includes lists of tourist attractions.
500	__	$a Distance table, text, and color illustrations on verso.
651	_0	$a Zimbabwe $v Maps.
710	2_	$a Gwaai River Stuff (Firm)

14. Computer Game

007		co cga||||||||
008		*yymmdd*s2014 sz gq g eng d
024	1_	$a 5030944112403
082	04	$a 794.86334668 $2 23
040	__	$a ABCD $b eng $e rda $c ABCD
041	__	$a eng $a spa
245	00	$a 2014 FIFA World Cup Brazil.
246	30	$a FIFA World Cup Brazil
250	__	$a Xbox 360.
264	_1	$a Geneva, Switzerland :$b EA Sports, $c 2014.
300	__	$a 1 computer disc :$b DVD video, sound, colour ;$c 12 cm. + $e 1 booklet.
336	__	$a two-dimensional moving image $2 rdacontent
337	__	$a computer $2 rdamedia
338	__	$a computer disc $2 rdacarrier
500	__	$a 1–4 players ; 2 online multiplayer.
520	__	$a Lead your country to FIFA World Cup glory while experiencing all the fun, excitement and drama of soccer's greatest event.
521	__	$a Censorship classification : G.
538	__	$a System requirements: Xbox 360; 20 MB to save game ; HDTV 720p/1080i/1080p; in-game Dolby digital.
546	__	$a Game in English and Spanish.
610	20	$a World Cup (Soccer) $d (2014 : $c Brazil)
610	20	$a Fédération internationale de football association $v Computer games.
650	_0	$a Soccer $v Computer games.
650	_0	$a Xbox video games.
650	_0	$a Video games.
710	2_	$a EA Sports (Firm)
710	2_	$a Fédération internationale de football association.

15. Series

008		*yymmdd*s1987 acao b f000 0 eng d
020	__	$a 0644076445
022	__	$a 0818-8882
040	__	$a ABCD $b eng $c ABCD $e rda
043	__	$a u-at-ac

260 LEARN CATALOGING THE RDA WAY

```
082  04   $a 362.2938099471 $2 22
100  1_   $a Latukefu, Ruth A.,$e author.
245  10   $a Karralika :$b an evaluation of a therapeutic community for drug users in the
          Australian Capital Territory /$c Ruth A. Latukefu, M.A. (Syd.), Ph.D. (Columbia).
264  _1   $a Canberra :$b Australian Government Publishing Service, $c 1987.
300  __   $a vi, 166 pages :$b black and white illustrations ;$c 25 cm.
336  __   $a text $2 rdacontent
336  __   $a still image $2 rdacontent
337  __   $a unmediated $2 rdamedia
338  __   $a volume $2 rdacarrier
490  1_   $a Monograph series / National Campaign Against Drug Abuse, $x 0818–8882 ;$v
          no. 6
500  __   $a At head of title: National Campaign Against Drug Abuse.
504  __   $a Bibliography: pages 164–166.
610  20   $a Karralika Therapeutic Community.
650  _0   $a Therapeutic communities $z Australian Capital Territory $z Canberra $x
          Evaluation.
650  _0   $a Drug abuse $x Treatment $z Australian Capital Territory $z Canberra.
710  2_   $a National Campaign Against Drug Abuse (Australia)
830  _0   $a National Campaign Against Drug Abuse (Australia). Monograph series ; $v no. 6.
```

16. Music CD

```
007  sd fsngnnmmneu
008  yymmdds2014   nyurcnndqd    n eng d
028  32   $a 88843-07404-2 $b Monkey Puzzle Records
040  __   $a ABCD $b eng $c ABCD $e rda
050  _4   $aM1630.18.S53 $bA15 2014
082  04   $a 782.42166 $2 23
100  0_   $a Sia $c (Singer)
245  10   $a 1000 forms of fear / $c Sia.
246  3_   $a One thousand forms of fear
246  3_   $a Thousand forms of fear
264  _1   $a New York, NY :$b Monkey Puzzle Records, $c 2014.
264  _4   $c ©2014 $c ℗2014
300  __   $a 1 audio disc (47 min., 07 sec.) :$bdigital, stereo ;$c 12 cm.
336  __   $a performed music $b prm $2 rdacontent
337  __   $a audio $b s $2 rdamedia
338  __   $a audio disc $b sd $2 rdacarrier
344  __   $a digital $g stereo $2 rda
347  __   $a audio file $b CD audio $2 rda
505  00   $t Chandelier $g (3:36) -- $t Big girls cry $g (3:31) -- $t Burn the pages $g (4:00) -- $t
          Eye of the needle $g (4:00) -- $t Hostage $g (4:00) -- $t Straight for the knife $g
          (4:00) -- $t Fair game $g (4:00) -- $t Elastic heart $g (4:00) -- $t Free the animal
          $g (4:00) -- $t Fire meet gasoline $g (4:00) -- $t Cellophane $g (4:00) -- $t
          Dressed in black $g (4:00).
511  0_   $a Performed by Sia.
650  _0   $a Popular music $y 2011–2020.
```

650 _0 $a Electronic music.
650 _0 $a Folk-rock music.
650 _0 $a Rock music $y 2011–2020.

17. USB

007 cb cn#---auuuu
008 yymmdds2014   xnaao q   000 0 eng d
024 __ $a 9780977555321 $2 stock-number
040 __ $a ABCD $b eng $c ABCD $e rda
100 1_ $a Harden, Gwen. J. $q (Gwen Jean),$e author.
245 10 $a Rainforest plants of Australia :$b Rockhampton to Victoria /$c Gwen Harden, Hugh Nicholson, Bill McDonald, Nan Nicholson, Terry Tame and John Williams.
264 _1 $a Nambucca Heads, [New South Wales] :$b Gwen Harden Publishing, $c 2014.
300 __ $a 1 USB memory stick :$b colour illustrations ;$c 6 cm, in DVD container
336 __ $a text $2 rdacontent
336 __ $a still image $2 rdacontent
337 __ $a computer $2 rdamedia
338 __ $a computer chip cartridge $2 rdacarrier
500 __ $a Photos © Hugh Nicholson.
500 __ $a USB memory stick is in the shape of a key.
505 0_ $a Species information -- Identifying a plant -- Rainforest information.
520 __ $a This treatment is based on the revised editions of the Red and the Green Books, Rainforest Trees and Shrubs (Harden, McDonald & Williams, 2006) and Rainforest Climbing Plants (Harden, McDonald & Williams, 2007). The interactive key includes 1,139 species of rainforest trees, shrubs and climbing plants, from Rockhampton to southern Victoria. Each species has a fact sheet that describes the diagnostic features of the leaves, flowers and fruit. The distribution and rainforest type is outlined, and as to whether the species is native or introduced and whether it is listed as rare or threatened in any of the states. Each fact sheet includes line drawings and images of general and detailed features used in the identification process. The features and states used in the key are described with attached diagrams and with hotlinks to species that show that particular detail. General sections include how to use the key, hints on identifying rainforest plants, index of scientific and common names (listed separately), references, useful websites and an updated glossary.
538 __ $a System Requirements for Lucid 3.5 : Operating System: Windows XP/2000/Vista/7/8, Mac OSX >10.7.2, Linux and Solaris. System Memory: 256MB RAM or higher is recommended. Browser requirements: It is recommended that you run the key using a modern web browser that supports JavaScript and Java Applets. The following browsers have been tested: Explorer 7 and later, Chrome 30 and later, Firefox 16 and later, Safari 6 and later, Opera 15 and later.
650 _0 $a Rain forests $z Australia.
650 _0 $a Rain forest plants $z Australia.
650 _0 $a Plants, Ornamental $z Australia.
650 _0 $a Ornamental horticulture $z Australia.
700 1_ $a Nicholson, Hugh, $e author, $e photographer.

700 1_ $a McDonald, W. J. F.,$e author.
700 1_ $a Nicholson, Nan,$e author.
700 1_ $a Tame, Terry,$e author.
700 1_ $a Williams, J. B. (John B.),$e author.
700 1_ $i expanded version of (work):$a Harden, Gwen. J. $q (Gwen Jean).$t Rainforest trees and shrubs.
700 1_ $i expanded version of (work):$a Harden, Gwen J. $q (Gwen Jean).$t Rainforest climbing plants.

18. Kit

```
007    co mgu||||||||
008    yymmdds2006    cau    q b        eng d
040 __ $a ABCD $b eng $e rda $c ABCD
050 __ $a G70.212 $b .A75498 2006
245 00 $a ArcView 9.2 :$b media kit.
246 1_ $i At head of title: $a ArcGIS 9
250 __ $a Version 9.2 Single Use.
264 _1 $a Redlands, CA :$b Environmental Systems Research Institute, $c c2006.
300 __ $a 1 DVD ;$c 4 3/4 in. + $e 2 manuals + 1 quick start guide + 1 desktop short cut booklet + 1 memo + ESRI data & maps (5 DVDs).
336 __ $a computer program $a text $a cartographic image $a cartographic dataset $2 rdacontent
337 __ $a computer $a unmediated $2 rdamedia
338 __ $a computer disc $a volume $2 rdacarrier
520 __ $a "ArcView is full-featured GIS software for visualizing, analyzing, creating, and managing data with a geographic component"--ESRI website.
538 __ $a System requirements: PC-Intel; Windows 2000, XP (Home and Professional edition); 512 MB RAM; 1 GHz processor.
650 _0 $a Geographic information systems $v Software.
650 _0 $a Digital mapping $v Software.
710 2_ $a Environmental Systems Research Institute (Redlands, Calif.)
```

19. Book

```
008    yymmdds2013    ilua    b    001 0 eng
020 __ $a 9781450459631
020 __ $a 1450459633
040 __ $a ABCD $b eng $c ABCD $e rda
050 00 $a RC682 $b .G76 2013
082 00 $a 616.1203 $2 23
110 2_ $a American Association of Cardiovascular & Pulmonary Rehabilitation,$e author.
245 10 $a Guidelines for cardiac rehabilitation and secondary prevention programs /$c AACVPR American Association of Cardiovascular and Pulmonary Rehabilitation.
250 __ $a Fifth edition.
264 _1 $a Champaign, Ill. : $b Human Kinetics, $c [2013]
264 _4 $a ©2013
300 __ $a xii, 323 pages :$b illustrations, maps ;$c 28 cm.
336 __ $a text $b txt $2 rdacontent
```

336	__	$a still image $b sti $2 rdacontent
336	__	$a cartographic image $b cri $2 rdacontent
337	__	$a unmediated $b n $2 rdamedia
338	__	$a volume $b nc $2 rdacarrier
504	__	$a Includes bibliographical references and index.
505	0_	$a Cardiac rehabilitation, secondary prevention programs, and the evolution of health care providing optimal care for all patients -- The continuum of care : from inpatient and outpatient cardiac rehabilitation to long-term secondary prevention -- Behavior modification and risk factor reduction : guiding principles and practices -- Nutrition guidelines dietary patterns -- Cardiac rehabilitation in the inpatient and transitional settings -- Medical evaluation and exercise testing -- Outpatient cardiovascular rehabilitation and secondary prevention -- Modifiable cardiovascular disease risk factors -- Special populations -- Program administration -- Outcomes assessment and utilization -- Management of medical problems and emergencies.
650	_0	$a Heart $x Diseases $x Rehabilitation.
650	_0	$a Cardiovascular system $x Diseases $x Prevention.
650	_0	$a Heart $x Diseases $x Patients $x Rehabilitation.
650	_0	$a Heart $x Diseases $x Prevention.

20. Book on CD-Rom

007		co cga||||||||
008		120411s2014 wea bq i eng d
020	__	$a 9781741267020
028	52	$a RIC-10003L $b R.I.C. Publications
040	__	$a ABCD $b eng $e rda $c ABCD
082	04	$a 510.71 $2 23
082	04	$a 372.7044 $2 23
245	00	$a 100 maths interactives. $p Ages 5–7.
246	30	$a One hundred maths interactives. $p Ages 5–7
264	_1	$a Greenwood, W.A. : $b RIC Publications, $c 2014
300	__	$a 1 CD-ROM :$b sound, colour ;$c 12 cm.
336	__	$a computer program $b cop $2 rdacontent
337	__	$a computer $b c $2 rdamedia
338	__	$a computer disc $b cd $2 rdacarrier
500	__	$a For use with electronic whiteboard, computer, projector.
505	0_	$a Calculating -- Handling data -- Using and applying mathematics -- Understanding shape -- Knowing and using number facts -- Measuring -- Counting and understanding number.
521	1_	$a 5–7.
538	__	$a MAC and WIN compatible.
538	__	$a Minimum requirements PC: Operating system Windows XP onwards; 1GB of RAM; Intel Core Duo 2.0 processor or faster.
538	__	$a Minimum requirements MAC: Operating system OSX 10.1 onwards; 1GB of RAM; Power PC G5 processor or better. (For optimum viewing, your screen resolution should be set to 800 x 600 or higher).
650	_0	$a Number concept in children $v Juvenile software.

650 _0 $a Mathematics $v Interactive multimedia.
650 _0 $a Mathematics $v Juvenile software.

21. Website
006 suu woo   0 a0
007 cr cn|---uunuu
008 *yymmdd*c20139999mau   o j   eng d
040 __ $a ABCD $b eng $e rda $c ABCD
245 00 $a dataZoa.
264 _1 $a Boston, MA :$b Leading Market Technologies, Inc., $c [2013?]–
300 __ $a 1 online resource
336 __ $a computer program $b cop $2 rdacontent
336 __ $a computer dataset $b cod $2 rdacontent
337 __ $a computer $b c $2 rdacarrier
338 __ $a online resource $b cr $2 rdacarrier
520 __ $a This is the website for dataZoa, a universal translator for data series on the Web. dataZoa gives you literal drag-and-drop access to over 3 billion data series in Economics, Health, Energy, Demographics, Finance, and more, from the US and the world. dataZoa users graze the Web and gather chosen data into their own personal web-based account, where they have the option of uploading and hosting their own original data as well. From there, dataZoa users view, analyze, share, download, and create vivid website embeddable charts and tabular displays with this data.
588 __ $a Description based on contents viewed on December 16, 2014; title from homepage.
650 _0 $a Business $x Electronic data processing.
650 _0 $a Economics $x Electronic data processing.
650 _0 $a Health $x Electronic data processing.
650 _0 $a Population $x Electronic data processing.
650 _0 $a Statistics $x Electronic data processing.
655 _0 $a Information storage and retrieval systems.
710 2_ $a Leading Market Technologies, Inc.
856 40 $u https://www.datazoa.com/

22. Book
008 *yymmdd*e201410 acaab   b s000 0 eng d
020 __ $a 9781921648427
040 __ $a ABCD $b eng $e rda $c ABCD
043 __ $a u-at-we
082 04 $a 919.4104 $2 23
245 00 $a 20 years of modern recreational trails in Western Australia 1994–2014.
246 3_ $a Twenty years of modern recreational trails in Western Australia 1994–2014
264 _1 $a [Perth, Western Australia] :$b Department of Sport and Recreation, $c October 2014.
300 __ $a viii, 66 pages :$b chiefly colour illustrations, colour maps ;$c 30 cm.
336 __ $a text $2 rdacontent
336 __ $a still image $a cartographic image $2 rdacontent

ANSWERS

337	__	$a unmediated $2 rdamedia
338	__	$a volume $2 rdacarrier
500	__	$a At head of title: ...delivering on the vision.
500	__	$a "A trail is a journey that takes people into unmodified environments".
504	__	$a Includes bibliographical references (page 66)
505	0_	$a Introduction -- Development of the Bibbulum Track -- Development of the Munda Biddi Trail -- The Cape to Cape Track -- Trails - more than just walking -- Management of our long distance trails network -- The value of world-class trails -- Personal journeys from some trails champions -- The role of volunteers in managing our trails -- Passionate trails people in government and the wider community -- The current agenda -- Down the track -- Modern trails timeline -- Appendices.
650	_0	$a Trails $z Western Australia.
650	_0	$a Recreational areas $z Western Australia.
710	1_	$a Western Australia. $b Department of Sport and Recreation,$e issuing body.

23. Music CD

006		g172 vl
007		sd fu|gnn|m|ed
007		vd cvaizk
008		*yymmdd*p20141994xx opnn q n mul d
028	02	$a 825646337378 $b Warner Classics
040	__	$a ABCD $b eng $e rda $c ABCD
041	0_	$d eng $d fre $d ger $d ita $d spa
050	_4	$a M1505 $b .A13 2014
082	04	$a 782.1 $2 23
245	04	$a The 3 tenors in concert 1994.
246	3_	$a Three tenors in concert 1994
250	__	$a 20th anniversary celebration
264	_1	$a [Place of publication not identified] :$b Warner Classics, $c 2014.
264	_4	$c ℗2010 $c©2010
300	__	$a 1 audio disc (73 min.) :$b CD audio, digital ;$c 4 3/4 in. + $e 1 videodisc (172 min. : sound, color ; 4 3/4 in.)
336	__	$a performed music $b prm $2 rdacontent
337	__	$a audio $b s $2 rdamedia
337	__	$a video $b v $2 rdamedia
338	__	$a audio disc $b sd $2 rdacarrier
338	__	$a videodisc $b vd $2 rdacarrier
344	__	$a digital $2 rda
347	__	$a audio file $b CD audio $2 rda
500	__	$a Sung in English, French, German, Italian, and Spanish.
500	__	$a Title from container.
511	0_	$a José Carreras, Plácido Domingo, Luciano Pavarotti, tenors ; Los Angeles Music Center Opera Chorus ; Los Angeles Philharmonic ; Zubin Mehta, conductor.
518	__	$o Recorded live $d 1994 July 16 $p Dodger Stadium, Los Angeles.
650	_0	$a Operas $v Excerpts.
650	_0	$a Songs (High voice) with orchestra.

266 LEARN CATALOGING THE RDA WAY

650 _0 $a Vocal trios with orchestra.
650 _0 $a Popular music $y 1991–2000.
700 1_ $a Pavarotti, Luciano, $d 1935–2007,$e singer.
700 1_ $a Domingo, Plácido, $d 1941–   , $e singer.
700 1_ $a Carreras, José,$e singer.
700 1_ $a Mehta, Zubin,$e conductor.
710 2_ $a Los Angeles Philharmonic Orchestra,$e instrumentalist.
710 2_ $a Los Angeles Music Center Opera. $b Chorus,$e singer.

24. Movie DVD

007 vd cvaizq
008 *yymmdd*s2012   cau141 g   vleng d
024 30 $a 9398521594032
028 41 $a E15940 $b Buena Vista Australia
040 __ $a ABCD $b eng $c ABCD $e rda
082 04 $a 791.43/72 $2 23
245 00 $a War horse / $c Dreamworks Pictures and Reliance Entertainment present an Amblin Entertainment, Kennedy/Marshall Company production ; a Steven Spielberg film directed by Steven Spielberg ; screenplay by Lee Hall and Richard Curtis ; produced by Steven Spielberg, Kathleen Kennedy ; executive producers, Frank Marshall, Revel Guest.
264 _1 $a [Universal City, Calif.] :$b DreamWorks Pictures, $c2012.
264 _2 $a South Yarra, Vic. :$b Distributed by Buena Vista Australia, $c 2012.
264 _4 $c ©2012.
300 __ $a 1 videodisc (141 min.) :$b sound, colour ;$c 12 cm.
336 __ $a two-dimensional moving image $b tdi $2 rdacontent
337 __ $a video $b v $2 rdamedia
338 __ $a videodisc $b vd $2 rdacarrier
344 __ $a digital $b optical $g surround $h 5.1 Dolby Digital $2 rda
347 __ $a video file $b DVD video $e region 4 $2 rda
500 __ $a "Based on the novel by Michael Morpurgo".
508 __ $a Director of photography, Janusz Kaminski ; production designer, Rick Carter ; edited by Michael Kahn ; costume designer, Joanna Johnston ; music by John Williams.
511 1_ $a Emily Watson, David Thewlis, Peter Mullan, Niels Arestrup, Tom Hiddleston, Jeremy Irvine, Benedict Cumberbatch, Toby Kebbell, David Kross, Eddie Marsan, Nicolas Bro, Rainer Bock, Patrick Kennedy, Liam Cunningham.
520 __ $a "Based on the Tony award-winning Broadway play, and set against the sweeping canvas of World War I, this deeply heartfelt story begins with the remarkable friendship between a horse named Joey and his young trainer Albert. When they're forced apart by war, we follow Joey's extraordinary journey as he changes and inspires the lives of everyone he meets"--Container.
521 __ $a Censorship classification: M.
538 __ $a DVD region 4; colour recording system: PAL.
650 _0 $a Horses $v Drama.
650 _0 $a World War, 1914–1918 $v Drama.
650 _0 $a Human-animal relationships $v Drama.

700 1_ $a Morpurgo, Michael.
700 1_ $a Spielberg, Steven, $d 1946–
700 1_ $a Watson, Emily, $d 1967–
700 1_ $a Thewlis, David, $d 1963–
710 2_ $a Dreamworks Pictures
710 2_ $a Buena Vista (Australia)

25. Conference on USB

007 cb cz ||||||||
008 *yymmdd*s2014   xnaa   qab   100   eng d
040 __ $a ABCD $b eng $e rda $c ABCD
043 __ $a u-at---
111 2_ $a Australian Earth Sciences Convention $n (22nd :$d 2014 :$c Newcastle, N.S.W.)
245 10 $a Australian Earth Sciences Convention 2014, 7–10 July, Newcastle City Hall and Civic Theatre, Newcastle, NSW :$b scientific program and abstracts.
246 3_ $a Scientific program and abstracts, Australian Earth Sciences Convention 2014
246 3_ $a AESC 2014 scientific program and abstracts
264 _1 $a Sydney : $b Geological Society of Australia, $c 2014.
300 __ $a 1 USB flash drive :$b colour illustrations ;$c 5 x 9 cm.
336 __ $a text $b txt $2 rdacontent
337 __ $a computer $b c $2 rdamedia
338 __ $a computer chip cartridge $b cb $2 rdacarrier
500 __ $a Conference organised by the Geological Society of Australia.
504 __ $a Includes bibliographical references.
650 _0 $a Geology $z Australia $v Congresses.
650 _0 $a Earth sciences $z Australia $v Congresses.
710 2_ $a Geological Society of Australia

GLOSSARY

AACR2 *See* Anglo-American Cataloguing Rules, second edition

access point Any part of a catalog or database record, or entry in a bibliography, that enables a user to find the item

access point control The control of access points by establishing and using consistent headings. AACR2 called this concept 'authority control'

adaptation A modification of a work, to suit a different group of readers, or in a different literary form or medium

added entry In AACR2, any entry, other than the main entry and subject entries, by which the user can access the catalog. *See also* main entry

alternative title The second part of a title proper consisting of two parts; the parts are joined by the word 'or'—e.g., As You Like It, or, What You Will

analytical description In RDA, a bibliographic description for a part of a larger resource (e.g., a single volume of a three-volume biography, a single map forming part of a map series). *See also* comprehensive description, hierarchical description

Anglo-American Cataloguing Rules, second edition (AACR2). A set of rules for descriptive cataloging adopted by libraries in English-speaking countries. Replaced by RDA (*Resource Description and Access*) in 2010

area of description In an AACR2 catalog record created using the International Standard Bibliographic Description (ISBD), an area of description constitutes a major category within the bibliographic description—e.g., publication details. ISBD nominates nine areas of description. *See also* International Standard Bibliographic Description

attribute A property or identifying characteristic of an entity, used to describe entities in RDA. Attributes can include title, language, medium of performance, intended audience, date, physical format, edition, provenance, condition, etc. for library materials; and titles, gender, occupation, address, field of activity etc. for people, families or corporate bodies

author 1. In RDA, a person, family or corporate body responsible for creating a work that is primarily textual in content, regardless of media type (e.g., printed, electronic or tactile text or spoken word) or of genre (e.g., poems, screenplays, blogs). 2. In AACR2, the person chiefly responsible for the intellectual or artistic content of a work. *See also* creator

authority control *See* Access point control

authority file A collection of authority records containing the preferred forms of headings for names, series and subjects. It can be on cards, microfiche or online. A library can develop one integrated authority file, or separate name authority files and subject authority files

authority record A record of the preferred heading for a person, place, corporate body, series or title, giving information about the preferred heading and non-preferred alternatives, as well as notes about how these were derived

authorized access point In RDA, the preferred title or name to be used as an access point in a descriptive catalog record. *See also* variant access point

authorized access point for related entity The RDA term for the concept known in AACR2 cataloging as a 'see also reference', it provides a direction from one heading to another when both are used in cataloging

bibliographic description Information about a resource that can be derived from the resource itself, including title, statement of responsibility, edition, publication details, physical description, series and ISBN

bibliographic record Data about a resource that describes the intellectual and physical characteristics of the resource and contains sufficient information to identify the resource. It includes a physical description, access points, subject headings, and a classification number

carrier / carrier type The packaging that houses a resource—e.g., audio disc, slide, volume, online resource, etc. *See also* container

catalog A list of library materials contained in a collection, a library or a group of libraries, arranged according to some definite plan

cataloger A person who prepares catalog entries and maintains a catalog so that library materials can be retrieved efficiently

cataloging The preparation of bibliographic information for catalog records. Cataloging consists of descriptive cataloging, subject cataloging and classification

cataloging-in-publication (CIP) Cataloging data produced by the national library or other agency of the country of publication, included in the work when it is published

cataloging source The agency that creates and/or modifies a MARC record

cataloging tools Publications of the international cataloging rules and standards, including *Resource Description and Access (RDA), Library of Congress Subject Headings (LCSH), Library of Congress Classification (LCC), Dewey Decimal Classification (DDC)*

chronological designation Numbering of serials in date order – e.g., January 1991

CIP *See* cataloging-in-publication

classification number The number allocated to a resource to indicate its subject and group it with similar items

cloning, Also close cataloging, close copy cataloging. Creating a new catalog record based on a record for a similar resource—e.g., the spoken word version of a monograph, or a new edition of the monograph—by copying the original record and making appropriate changes. *See also* copy cataloging

code In MARC, a symbol used to designate a particular data element

collaboration A work developed by two or more creators performing the same function (e.g., three co-authors, or joint illustrators in a children's book). This concept was known previously as 'shared responsibility' for the work

compilation 1. A collection of works by one or more creators. 2. A work created by assembling material from other books

compound surname A surname consisting of two or more proper names, sometimes connected by a hyphen or conjunction and/or preposition

comprehensive description A bibliographic description for a resource as a whole (e.g., a map, a periodical, a collection of posters assembled by a library, or a kit consisting of a filmstrip, an audiotape and a teacher's manual). *See also* analytical description, hierarchical description

consortium A group of libraries joined by formal or informal agreement to achieve a specific purpose—e.g., to share the cost and use of a library management system. *See also* network

container The outer casing of an item or group of items, that can be physically separated from the item/s—e.g., the jewel case of a compact disc. *See also* carrier type

content 1. In RDA, the physical characteristics (color, illustrations, scale, sound etc.) of a resource. 2. The bibliographic information contained in a MARC record

content designator In MARC, a tag, indicator or subfield code that designates an element of the content of a record—e.g., $a London

content type The form of communication by which the content of a resource is expressed—e.g., spoken word, still image, text, etc.

control field Also variable control field. A field in a MARC record with a tag 001–009 and no indicators or subfield codes. Control fields contain coded data used in processing the record

copy cataloging The process of copying cataloging details from an existing catalog record, and adding local location and holdings details. *See also* cloning

copyright date The date associated with a claim of protection under copyright, identified in a resource by the symbol ©

core element An attribute that is part of RDA's set of minimum data required for describing either a resource or a person, family or corporate body associated with a resource. Core elements are those attributes that must be included in a record, if they are applicable to the resource being cataloged, to make it RDA–compliant

corporate body An organization or group of people identified by a particular name, and acting as an entity

creator In RDA cataloging, a person, family or corporate body responsible for the intellectual or artistic content of a work—e.g., writer of a book, compiler of a bibliography, composer of a musical work, artist, photographer etc.

data element A single piece of information—e.g., date of publication

data element identifier In MARC, the lower-case letter that identifies a data element in a subfield—e.g., $a 25 pages : $b photographs

data field A field in a machine-readable record used to store data

date of publication The earliest year in which the particular edition of the resource was published—e.g., if a second edition was published in 1991, and reprinted without alteration in 1993, the date of publication of this edition is 1991

delimiter In MARC, a symbol used to introduce a new subfield

descriptive cataloging The part of cataloging that describes a resource in terms of its physical (or electronic equivalent) details, indicates relationships, and identifies and formulates access points

dimensions In RDA, the size measurement of the carrier and/or the container of a resource

distribution Transporting, marketing and selling a resource

distribution statement In RDA, a statement identifying the place of distribution, distributor and date of distribution of a published resource

distributor An agent who has marketing rights for a resource

edition All the copies of a work produced from the same original

edition statement The part of a bibliographic description that indicates the particular edition of the resource—e.g., revised, illustrated, student, abridged

editor Person who prepares another person's work for publication

element A distinct piece of bibliographic information. *See also* core element

entity The FRBR (*Functional Requirements for Bibliographic Records*) term for materials, people or concepts that are the basis for bibliographic or authority descriptions. FRBR identifies three Groups of entities (Group One: works, expressions, manifestations, items; Group Two: persons, families, corporate bodies; Group Three: concepts, objects, events, places)

enumeration Numbering of a serial using numbers – e.g., Volume 1, number 1

expression In RDA, one of the Group One entities described in *Functional Requirements for Bibliographic Records* as a particular intellectual or artistic realization of a work, or, the means by which a work is expressed—e.g., spoken word, language translation, with illustrations, etc. *See also* item, manifestation, work

extent Also extent of resource. In RDA, the number and type of units and/or subunits making up a resource

extent of item 1. In AACR2, the number and specific material designation of the parts of the item being described. 2. In MARC, a subfield of the 'Physical Description' tag that indicates the number and type of the parts of the item—i.e., how many pages in a book, how many slides in a slide set, etc.

family Two or more persons related by birth, marriage, adoption, civil union, or similar legal status, or who otherwise present themselves as a family

family name The hereditary surname of a family

field A unit of information in a MARC record. Different fields contain either coded information or text

filing indicator In MARC, the indicator that tells the computer how many characters to ignore when filing

FISO The acronym used to describe FRBR's 'user tasks' for a catalog: to help Find, Identify, Select and Obtain material for the user

fixed length field A MARC field that has its length determined in advance. The coded data control fields 001–009 are fixed length fields

forename The name that precedes the family name or surname; a first name

Group One entities In FRBR and RDA, the products of intellectual or artistic endeavor that are named or described in bibliographic records. These Group One entities are: work, expression, manifestation and item (WEMI)

Group Three entities In FRBR and RDA, entities that serve as the subjects of intellectual and artistic endeavors. These Group Three entitles are: concepts, objects, events, places, and Group One and Group Two entities as subjects

Group Two entities In FRBR and RDA, entities responsible for the intellectual and artistic content, the physical production and dissemination, or the ownership or custodianship of Group 1 entities. These Group Two entities are: persons, families and corporate bodies

heading Used in AACR2, a name, word or phrase at the top of a catalog entry to provide an access point. RDA uses the term 'authorized access point'

hierarchical description In RDA, a bibliographic description that combines a comprehensive description of the whole resource with analytical descriptions of one or more of its parts. *See also* comprehensive description, analytical description

holdings Stock of a library or information center; the items owned by a library and listed in the library's catalog and in union catalogs

identifier A standard number or character set that is widely recognized as a means of uniquely identifying a resource, e.g., ISBN or LC control number. In RDA, identifiers are core elements for every Group One and Two entity

imprint Publication details—place, publisher, date of publication

indicator In a MARC record, a character that gives additional information about a field—e.g., the first indicator 1 added to the tag 245 shows that a title added entry is to be made

initial article The word that introduces a noun at the beginning of a title–e.g., the, a, an, le, la, les, los

integrating resource A resource that is added to or changed by means of updates that do not remain discrete but are integrated into the whole. One of RDA's four modes of issuance. An integrating resource may be tangible (e.g., a loose-leaf manual that is updated by means of replacement pages) or intangible (e.g., a website that is updated either continuously or on a cyclical basis). *See also* mode of issuance

International Standard Bibliographic Description (ISBD). Standard set of bibliographic elements in standard order and with standard punctuation, developed to facilitate global exchange of cataloging data. Published by IFLA, the International Federation of Library Associations and Institutions

International Standard Book Number (ISBN). A number intended to be unique, assigned by an agency in each country to book, kits, software and other resources published. The ISBN identifies the publisher, language and title. Adopted internationally in 1969

International Standard Music Number (ISMN). An internationally recognized number assigned to printed music by the International Standard Music Number Agency in Berlin or one of its associated national agencies

International Standard Serial Number (ISSN). An internationally recognized number assigned to each serial publication by the International Serials Data System (ISDS), a network of national centers sponsored by Unesco

ISBD *See* International Standard Bibliographic Description

ISBN *See* International Standard Book Number

ISMN *See* International Standard Music Number

ISSN *See* International Standard Serial Number

item In RDA, a single object with particular characteristics that differentiate it from the rest of the collection in that manifestation—e.g., the specific copy of a publication held by a library, with the library barcode 12345. *See also* expression, manifestation, work

journal A periodical issued by an institution, corporation or learned society containing current information and reports of activities or works in a particular field

kit An item containing more than one kind of material, none of which is predominant—e.g., a set of slides and an audiocassette

leader Top line of a MARC record, that gives information about the record to the computer program that processes it

legacy data Existing catalog records that were created using former cataloging conventions like AACR2. These are the library's 'legacy' of information

library consortium *See* consortium

library network *See* network

machine-readable cataloging *See* MARC

main entry In AACR2, the principal entry in a catalog, that contains the complete record of a resource. Still used in MARC coding, but RDA does not use this terminology, or have an equivalent concept. Main and added entries are all considered authorized access points in RDA and have equal weighting. *See also* added entry, authorized access point

manifestation One of the RDA Group One entities described in *Functional Requirements for Bibliographic Records* as the physical embodiment of the expression of a work. *See also* expression, item, work

manufacture statement In RDA, a statement identifying: the place or places of manufacture; manufacturer or manufacturers; and date or dates of manufacture of a resource in a published form

manuscript A hand-written or typescript document

MARC An acronym for MAchine Readable Cataloging. A format developed by the Library of Congress in 1966 so that libraries can share machine-readable bibliographic data. The MARC data elements are the foundation of many library catalogs

MARC 21 The current MARC format, used extensively in North America and Australasia, and in many parts of Europe. It is increasingly the international standard for representing and communicating bibliographic and related information in machine-readable form. MARC 21 is maintained by the Library of Congress in consultation with various user communities

media type The type of device needed to view, play or run a resource—e.g., audio, video, computer, unmediated (for print material) etc.

mixed responsibility The AACR2 term for the concept RDA calls 'multiple statement of responsibility'

mode of issuance A categorization reflecting whether a resource is issued in one or more parts, the way it is updated, and its intended termination. RDA recognizes four modes of issuance: single unit, multipart monograph, serial, and integrating resource

monograph A publication either complete in one part or in a finite number of separate parts

monograph in series A resource with its own title proper, that is part of a series with a common series title

multipart monograph A resource issued in two or more parts (either simultaneously or successively) that is complete or intended to be completed within a finite number of parts (e.g., a dictionary in two volumes, three audiocassettes issued as a set). One of RDA's four modes of issuance

multiple statements of responsibility Different persons or bodies make different kinds of contributions to a work—e.g., author and illustrator. *See also* statement of responsibility

name-title added entry In AACR2 cataloging, an added entry under the combined name of a person, family or corporate body and the title of a resource—e.g., Dickens, Charles, 1812–1870. *A Christmas carol*

network Two or more libraries that share resources or exchange information. *See also* consortium

notes Descriptive information that cannot be fitted into other areas of the bibliographic description

numeric designation *See* enumeration

OCLC Online Computer Library Center. A bibliographic network that provides cataloging, resource sharing and reference services worldwide

original cataloging Cataloging done for the first time, using cataloging tools to create the record. *See also* copy cataloging

other title information Title information on a resource other than the title proper or parallel or series title. Other title information includes subtitles and any phrases appearing in conjunction with the title proper

pagination The number of pages or leaves (or both) of a book identified in its bibliographic description; part of the 'extent' attribute of a manifestation

parallel title Title proper in another language and/or script

periodical A serial with a distinctive title intended to appear in successive parts at stated and regular intervals. Often used as a synonym for serial

person An individual or an identity established by an individual (either alone or in collaboration with one or more other individuals).

physical description 1. A general term used when discussing the physical characteristics of a resource that are included in a catalog record. 2. In AACR2, information about the physical form of an item—e.g., pagination, type of recording, dimensions. RDA cataloging uses the terms 'extent', 'content', 'dimensions' and 'carrier type' for this concept

preferred name The form of name chosen to identify a person, family or corporate body. It is the basis for the authorized access point representing that entity

preferred sources of information The places where information that can be used to create a bibliographic description are found. These include the resources themselves and in some cases reference tools or catalogs about the resources

preferred title for the work The title chosen to identify a resource at the work level. This is used as the basis for the authorized access point representing that work. It is similar, but not totally equivalent, to the AACR2 concept 'uniform title'

production statement A statement identifying the place of production, the producer, and date of production of an unpublished resource

pseudonym A fictitious name used by an author

publisher A person or body issuing copies of a resource to the public

publication statement A statement identifying the place of publication, the publisher, and date of publication of a resource

qualifier An addition to a name etc. enclosed in parentheses

record (n) The data relating to a document—e.g., in a catalog or database. (v) In RDA cataloging, to use the information found on a resource, or in another source, to create a bibliographic record. One can adjust the information slightly if required for readability or presentation purposes. *See also* transcribe

record structure The organization of the MARC record into the leader, the directory and the variable fields

relationship In RDA cataloging, the link between and among entities, often recorded using access points controlled by authority records. Relationships give users pathways to other relevant material

relationship designator In RDA, a term that indicates the nature of the relationship to or between entities. Relationship designators are listed in vocabularies that enable catalogers to describe relationships consistently

repeatable Able to be used more than once within a record—e.g., some MARC fields and subfields are repeatable in a bibliographic or authority record

revision A new edition of a work containing alterations and/or additions

scale The ratio of distances on a map to the corresponding values on the earth

see also reference A direction from one heading to another when both are used. RDA uses the term 'authorized access point for related entity'

see reference A direction from one heading (that is not used) to another heading (that is used). RDA uses the term 'variant access point'

serial A resource issued in successive parts, usually bearing numbering, that has no predetermined conclusion—e.g., a journal, a magazine, a newspaper. Includes reproductions of serials, and also resources that exhibit characteristics of serials but whose duration is limited—e.g., newsletters for specific events. One of RDA's four modes of issuance

series A group of separate resources related to each other by the fact that they have a collective title applying to the group as a whole, as well as each resource having its own title proper. Individual resources in a series may or may not be numbered. *See also* monograph in series

series title The collective title of a group of monographs or other resources, each of which also has an individual title

series title page An added title page in each monograph in a series, bearing the series title and sometimes a list of all the works in the series

shared responsibility *See* collaboration

specific material designation In AACR2, a term indicating the specific class of material—e.g., poster—to which an item belongs. In RDA, this concept is covered by RDA carrier types

standard number An ISBN, ISSN or other internationally agreed upon standard number that identifies the resource uniquely. RDA uses standard numbers as identifiers for manifestations

statement of responsibility A statement that identifies the person/s, family/families or corporate body or bodies responsible for the intellectual or artistic content of a resource

subfield Part of the MARC record that contains an element of description or other small piece of information

subfield code The two-character code that precedes a data element in a MARC record—e.g., $a

subfield delimiter The character used to introduce a subfield in a MARC record—e.g., $

subject cataloging Describing the topics or subject content of a resource using subject headings and a classification number

subject heading A type of authorized access point that describes a topic and provides subject access to a catalog

subordinate body A corporate body that is part of a larger corporate body. It is often identified by referring to the parent body

subtitle *See* other title information

tag A label that identifies each field of a MARC record—e.g., 245 identifies the 'Title and Statement of Responsibility' field

terms of availability Terms on which the item is available, including price

title A word or phrase that names a resource

title page The page in a printed resource that provides the most complete information about the author and title, and is used as a primary source of cataloging data

title page verso The reverse side of the title page in a book, that often contains publication and copyright details

title proper The main name of a resource, including alternative title/s but excluding parallel titles and other title information

transcribe In RDA cataloging, copying exactly the details that are seen on a resource (including any errors) into a bibliographic record. *See also* record

Uniform Resource Locator *See* URL

Uniform Resource Name *See* URN

uniform title An AACR2 cataloging concept, with different definitions for monographs and serials. RDA uses 'preferred title of a work' as a similar, but not exactly equivalent concept. 1. In AACR2 cataloging, a title chosen to identify a monograph appearing under varying titles—e.g., Bible. 2. In AACR2 cataloging, a title used to distinguish the heading for one serial or series from the heading for another serial or series—e.g., Bulletin (UNESCO)

union catalog Catalog of the holdings of more than one library

unmediated One of RDA's 'media types', used to indicate the types of resources (texts, objects, etc.) that do not require equipment to view

URL (Uniform Resource Locator). The address of a site on the World Wide Web

URN (Uniform Resource Name). A unique, stable, location-independent identifier for an object or service, for example ISBN, ISSN. Generally contains the naming authority and the string—e.g., ISBN/082478431X

user tasks The key functions that users expect a catalog to help them with. FRBR and RDA identify the user tasks for bibliographic records as to find, identify, select and obtain (FISO), and for authority records as to find, identify, justify or clarify and contextualize or understand (FIJC, FICU)

variable control field *See* Control field

variable field A field in a MARC record containing either control or bibliographic data

variant access point In RDA cataloging, a non-preferred variation of a title or name. Known as a 'see reference' in AACR2, a variant access point directs the reader from an access point that is not used to an authorized access point that is used. *See also* authorized access point

variant title / variant access point for a title A different form of the title—e.g., other than the preferred title of a work or the title proper of a manifestation—by which a resource is also known

verso of title page *See* title page verso

volume 1. One or more sheets bound or fastened together to form a single unit. 2. What is contained in one binding of a monograph. 3. A number of issues of a serial, usually those published in one twelve-month period. 4. In RDA, one of the unmediated carrier types, used to indicate a printed resource

WEMI The acronym used to describe RDA's Group One entities: Work, Expression, Manifestation, Item

Work In RDA, one of the Group One entities described in *Functional Requirements for Bibliographic Records* as representing the initial intellectual or artistic creation—e.g., the concept that becomes Shakespeare's *Hamlet. See also* expression, item, manifestation

BIBLIOGRAPHY

International Federation of Library Associations Study Group on the Functional Requirements for Bibliographic Records. *Functional requirements for bibliographic records*. Munich, K.G. Saur Verlag, 1998. (IFLA Series on Bibliographic Control 19). http://www.ifla.org/en/publications/functional-requirements-for-bibliographic-records.

Joint Steering Committee for Development of RDA website.
http://www.rda-jsc.org/index.html

Joint Steering Committee for Development of RDA website, *RDA page*.
http://www.rda-jsc.org/rda.html

Library of Congress. *RDA: resource description & access training materials*.
http://www.loc.gov/catworkshop/RDA%20training%20materials/

Maxwell, Robert L. *Maxwell's handbook for RDA, resource description & access: explaining and illustrating RDA: resource description and access using MARC21*. London, Facet Publishing, 2014.

Oliver, Chris. *Introducing RDA: a guide to the basics*. London, Facet Publishing, 2010.

RDA Toolkit. Chicago, American Library Association; Ottawa, Canadian Library Association; London, Chartered Institute of Library and Information Professionals (CILIP), 2010– .
http://www.rdatoolkit.org.

Rowe, Helen and Trina Grover. *Learn basic library skills*. International edition. Friendswood, Texas, TotalRecall Publications, Inc., 2015.

Teaching RDA: train-the-trainer course RDA: resource description and access presented by the National Library of Australia in 2012 and made available under a Creative Commons Attribution 3.0 Australia License.

Tillett, Barbara. *What Is FRBR?: a conceptual model for the bibliographic universe*. [Washington, D.C.], Library of Congress, Cataloging Distribution Service, [2004?].
http://www.loc.gov/cds/downloads/FRBR.PDF

INDEX

AACR2, 16-17, 30, 107, 115-116, 175, 176
abbreviations, 16-17, 54, 77, 91, 100, 115, 116, 128, 138, 170, 176, 177, 178
access points, 7, 10, 12, 38, Chapter 12, 114-115, 149, 169, 178
   see also authorized access points
attributes, 24-25, 27, 55, 63, Chapters 9-11, Chapters 13-14
authority data, 113-114, 115
authority record, 9, 11-13, 109, 113-116, 123, 127, 143, 156
authorized access points, 109
   for conferences, 134
   for corporate bodies, 132
   for expressions, 112
   for families, 123, 124
   for persons, 120
   for works, 109-110
   punctuation for, 33, 115
bibliographic record, 2, 9-10, 19, 120, 143, 151
capitalization, 54, 68, 71, 100, 170
carrier type, 88, 90, 178
catalog, objectives of, 1
catalog record, 2-3, 9, 69-70
cataloging, Chapter 1
   see also descriptive cataloging
cataloging networks, 5
cataloging standards, 3
classification, 2-3, 7
cloning, 175
collaborations, 110, 176
compilations, 110, 176
concepts, objects, events, Chapter 14, 157
conferences, 127, 134
content, 104
content designators, 45
content type, 101-102, 178
contributors to Expressions, 150
copy cataloging, Chapter 19
   checklist, 176-178
   editing of, 169-170
copyright date, 80

core elements, 25, 57-58, 69
   for authority data, 114
   for conferences, 134
   for corporate bodies, 127
   for expressions, 101-102
   for families, 122-124
   for items, 94
   for manifestations, 71-72, 77-80, 84
   for primary relationships, 152
   for works, 100-101
'core if necessary' elements, 101, 104, 114, 123
corporate bodies, 127-132
   as creators, 148
   subordinate bodies 129-130
creators of Works, 148
dates, 54, 78-79, 80, 114
   for conferences, 127, 134
   for corporate bodies, 127, 132
   for families, 123
   for persons, 115, 120
   in authority records, 114-115
   publication date, 78-79, 177
descriptive cataloging, 2, Chapter 2, 53
   process of, 8
dimensions, 44, 91
edition statement, 77, 169, 175, 177
expressions, 20-21, 101-104, 112, 152-153
extent, 44, 90-91
families, attributes of, 122-124
FRBR, Chapter 4
geographical names *see* names of places
Group One entities, 20-21, 147-148, 151-154
Group Three entities, 24, 137-138, 157
Group Two entities, 23, 147-148, 150, 156
identifiers, 84, 101, 104, 114, 123, 134, 153
initial articles, 54, 100, 128
integrating resource, 65, 71, 79, 170, 177
ISBD, Chapter 5
   punctuation, 32-33
ISBN, ISSN, ISMN *see* identifiers

items, 20-21, 94, 153
manifestations, 20-21, Chapters 9-10, 100, 152, 153
mappings, 59, 113-114
MARC, Chapter 6
    coding, 45-46, 51, 110, 143, 156
    fields, 45, 48-50, 120, 169
    formats, 37, 41-42
    indicators, 46, 78-80, 177, 178
    records, 39-40, 43-44, 69
    tags, 38, 39, 41, 44, 45, 110, 169
    terminology, 38
MARC and RDA, 51
media type, 87-88
mode of issuance, 65
multipart monograph, 65, 79, 177
multiple statements of responsibility, 72
names, forms of names, 54, 115, 117, 120
    for corporate bodies, 127-130
    for families, 123
    for government bodies, 130
    for persons, 117-118
    of places, 138
notes, 93
occupations, 120
OCLC, 5
persons, attributes of, 117-118, 120
place of publication, 46, 78, 177
places, 138
preferred source of information, 8, 67
preferred title for a Work, 100, 109, 110
production, publication, distribution, manufacture statements, 78-79

pseudonyms, 117
publication statement, 78-79
RDA, Chapter 3, Chapters 9-17
    terminology, 17
RDA and MARC, 51
RDA Instruction Set, 53-58, Chapter 8
RDA Toolkit, Chapter 7
    appendices, 54, 142-143, 147, 153-154
relationship designators, 142-143, 152-154, 157, 176, 178
relationships, 19-20, 23, 24, 54-55, Chapters 15-17, 150, 157
    primary relationships, 151-152
    structural relationships, 153-154
resolving conflicts, 114, 127, 138
'see' reference *see* variant access points
serials, 50, 65, 71, 78, 79, 151, 170
series statement, 84, 178
single unit, 65, 66, 79
standard numbers *see* identifiers
statement of responsibility, 23, 43, 72, 176
subject cataloging, 2, 137
title proper, 71-72, 100
transcribing vs recording, 68
type of description, 65-66
uniform title, 100, 110
variant access points, 12, 109, 118, 124, 130, 132, 138
variant title, 72, 100, 177
works, 20, 100-101, 109-110, 148, 152-153

LEARN LIBRARY SKILLS SERIES

This series of paperback workbooks introduces skills needed by library science students and library technicians, as well as librarians seeking refresher materials or study guides for in-service training classes. Each book teaches essential professional skills in a step-by-step process, accompanied by numerous practical examples, exercises and quizzes to reinforce learning, and an appropriate glossary.

Learn About Information
International Edition ©2015
Helen Rowe
ISBN: 9781590954331 Paperback

Learn Basic Library Skills
International Edition ©2015
Helen Rowe and Trina Grover
ISBN: 9781590954348 Paperback

Learn Cataloging the RDA Way
International Edition ©2015
Lynn Farkas and Helen Rowe
ISBN: 9781590954355 Paperback

Learn Dewey Decimal Classification (Edition 23)
International Edition ©2015
Lynn Farkas
ISBN: 9781590954362 Paperback

Learn Management Skills for Libraries and Information Agencies
International Edition ©2015
Jacinta Ganendran
ISBN: 9781590954379 Paperback

Learn Library of Congress Classification
International Edition ©2015
ISBN: 9781590954386 Paperback

Learn Library of Congress Subject Access
International Edition ©2015
Lynn Farkas
ISBN 9781590954393 Paperback

Learn Reference Work
International Edition ©2015
ISBN: 9781590954416 Paperback

LIBRARY SCIENCE TITLES

LibrarySpeak:
A Glossary of Terms in Librarianship and Information Technology,
International Edition ©2015
Lynn Farkas
ISBN: 9781590954423 Paperback

My Mentoring Diary:
A Resource for the Library and Information Professions
Revised Edition ©2015
Ann Ritchie and Paul Genoni
ISBN: 9781590954430 Paperback

Quality in Library Service:
A Competency-Based Staff Training Program
International Edition ©2015
Jennifer Burrell and Brad McGrath
ISBN: 9781590954447 Paperback

TOTALRECALL PUBLICATIONS, INC.
1103 Middlecreek,
Friendswood, TX 77546-5448

Phone: (281) 992-3131
email: Sales@TotalRecallPress.com
Online: www.totalrecallpress.com

www.ingramcontent.com/pod-product-compliance
Lightning Source LLC
Chambersburg PA
CBHW081102070526
44584CB00021B/3171